THE BLACK PRINCE

LE PRINCE NOIR

POÈME DU HÉRAUT D'ARMES

CHANDOS

TEXTE CRITIQUE SUIVI DE NOTES

PAR

FRANCISQUE-MICHEL

Correspondant de l'Institut de France, etc., etc.

THE LIFE & FEATS OF ARMS

OF

EDWARD THE BLACK PRINCE

BY CHANDOS HERALD

A METRICAL CHRONICLE

WITH AN ENGLISH TRANSLATION AND NOTES

BY FRANCISQUE-MICHEL

F. A. S. Lond., Scot. and Normandy, etc., etc.

LONDON & PARIS

J. G. FOTHERINGHAM

M.DCCC.LXXXIII.

PREFACE

It will not be necessary in the present instance to enter into any preliminary dissertation to prove to the reader that the contents of the following poem are of an interesting character. If the brilliant achievements of his ancestors are dear to him and he has a spark of chivalric feeling within his breast, it will be enough to announce that the subject of it is the Black Prince, and the writer, not only a contemporary, but one who had been with his hero in the field, and witnessed probably some of those glorious exploits which he has described. It is only remarkable that the contents of the manuscript have not been long since made public, and that they should have escaped the researches of Barnes and Collins.

The first printed notice of the volume occurs in Warton's *History of English Poetry* [1], where it is described as written in the short verse of romance by « the Prince's herald, who attended close by his person in all his battles, according to the established mode of those times; » and it is added: « This was John Chandois-Herald, frequently mentioned in Froissart [2]. » The

---

[1] London, 1824, 8vo., vol. ii, p. 166.

[2] A further error is committed in the note at the foot of the page respecting our poet. The reader is directed to a curious description in Froissart of an interview between the Chandos Herald above mentioned, and a marshal of France, where they are said to enter into a dispute concerning the « devices d'amour » borne by each army. The dispute in question arose on the day preceding the battle of Poitiers from the meeting of Sir John Chandos with the Marshal of Clermont, who bore the same armour with himself, upon which some angry words passed between them.

christian name is an addition by Warton; Froissart does occasionally mention him, as we shall presently see, but always simply as Chandos the Herald. It is indeed from this historian that the little we know concerning the author of the poem has been gathered, if we except one or two entries in records mentioned in the following account drawn up by indefatigable John Anstis, Garter King at Arms. It has been taken from Anstis's papers deposited in the Herald's College.

«Chandos was the herald of the famous Sir John Chandos, constable of Aquitaine, who was frequently employed by him, and in the service of the public. Froissart informs us that Sir Robert Knolles and Sir John Chandos besieged Domme, and from thence sent a message to the Prince of Wales by Chandos le Heraut, who brought them the commands of the Prince [1]. Sir John Chandos intimated his desire to the earl of Pembroke that he would be pleased to join with him in order to give battle to the Marshal of France, which message was sent by Chandos le Heraut, who at his return found his master and his sons at Châtellerault. In our records there is an entry of a protection granted to this herald in Nov. 41 Ed. III.; and what is memorable, he retained this

---

[1] Froissart thus describes the interview of Chandos with the Prince at Angoulême: «When the herald Chandos was arrived in the presence of the Prince, he dropped on his knees, and recommended to him his masters who had sent him, and whom he had left at the siege of Domme. He then related their situation most wisely, as he had been ordered to do, and gave the credential letters which he had brought to the Prince. The Prince listened attentively to all that was told him, and said he would consider this subject. He kept the herald with him five days, and, on the sixth, he had letters delivered to him under the Prince's seal, who said to him on his departure: « Chandos, salute from me all our companions. » He replied: « Most willingly, my lord. » — When the herald set out, he took the road through Quercy.

title after the death of his founder or master, which happened in battle 44 Ed. III., for he was soon afterwards by the title of *Chandos* sent by the Earls of Cambridge and Pembroke [1] to offer battle to the Duke of Bourbon, and in 1380 was sent with Aquitaine Herald [2] to defy the Duke of Burgundy by the Earl of Buckingham, in whose coat armour they were both invested; and two years afterwards we find mention of an herald, Ireland King of Arms and Chandos by name, which was above mentioned as a supposed instance of the retaining the titles of heraldship as a surname after their promotions. But whether that was the case here, may be somewhat doubted in regard that Chandos Herald, without the addition of Ireland King of Arms, is soon afterwards in 7 Ric. II. entered as receiving a reward for going to Calais with letters of credence to the Duke of Lancaster and others, though this service, notwithstanding the time of payment, might have been performed by him before he was made Ireland [3]. »

[1] He was then the bearer of the challenge following : « My masters and lords send me to you, and inform you by my mouth that they are quite astonished you have allowed them to remain fifteen days here, and you have not sallied out of your fort to give them battle. They therefore tell you that if you will come forth to meet them, they will permit you to choose any plot of ground for the field of battle, and let God give the event of it to whom so ever pleases. »
Upon the duke's refusing to accept the challenge, he was again sent with this message : « Noblemen, my masters and lords inform you through me that since you are not willing to accept the offer they have made you, three days hence, between nine and twelve o'clock in the morning, you, my lord Duke of Bourbon, will see your lady mother placed on horseback and carried away. Consider this, and rescue her, if you can. »
[2] Where they are called two kings at arms.
[3] References to all the passages in Froissart's Chronicles wherein Chandos Herald is mentioned, are pointed out in the *Table analy-*

In the poem he speaks of himself only twice by name, in both which passages he styles himself *Chandos le Herault*; and of anything further concerning his personal history, we are left in entire ignorance.

The reader however has a right to know on what grounds our poet is entitled to his credit; and with this view we must consider the nature of the office he filled in the scenes which he describes. From his title it is evident that he was the domestic [1] herald of Sir John Chandos, appointed probably to the post, after that knight had been raised to the rank of banneret at the battle of Nájera. In this capacity it would have been a part of his duty to attend his master to the field of battle, and in such a situation he must have had ample means, both from personal observation and opportunities of enquiry, for, what he himself calls, « writing a good history » of passing events. Indeed we find that it was another part of a herald's duty to keep a register of what he saw and

---

tique des noms, in the recent edition of Froissart published by the Baron Kervyn de Lettenhove, t. xxi, p. 540. — In the last paragraph of his note on the herald « qui racontait les exploits des Anglais en vers élégants », the learned editor risks the supposition that the rhymer was not an Englishman, on the authority of a charter printed by Jules Delpit (*Collection générale des documents français qui se trouvent en Angleterre*, t. i, Paris, 1849, 4to., p. 132), and which does not in the least refer to Chandos Herald.

[1] Before the foundation of the Herald's College by Richard the Third, it was no unusual thing for noblemen to have their pursuivants and heralds, appointed by themselves and giving their name for them. (Anstis, *The Register of the most noble Order of the Garter*, London, 1724, fol., vol. i, p. 287.) Thus Mowbray, duke of Norfolk, had Mowbray herald, the earl of Pembroke, Pembroke herald, Viscount Lisle, Lisle herald, and so others. (Randle Holmes, *The Academy of Armory*, etc. Chester, 1688, fol., p. 3. Compare Anstis, vol. i, p. 288, note, and *Glossarium mediæ et infimæ Latinitatis*, t. iii, p. 646-649.)

heard. Warton, from Menestrier [1], observes that there are several proofs which indicate that many romances of the fourteenth century, if not in verse, at least those written in prose, were the work of heralds [2]; and if at that period the same discrimination was exercised in the persons selected to the office, as we afterwards find to have been the case, we could not wish the compilation of a chronicle to be entrusted to better hands; for, according to Upton [3], to make an accomplished herald, a knowledge of all arts, sciences and faculties, divine and profane, noble and ignoble, were essentially necessary [4]. It was probably for the reason above-named that Froissart, in his preface, tells us that amongst other sources he gathered the material for his history from heralds, and since he has recorded the very words of our

[1] *De la Chevalerie ancienne et moderne*, etc. Paris, 1683, 12mo., ch. v. p. 225. Cf. *De l'Office des Roys d'armes, des herauds*, etc., par Marc de Vulson Sr de la Colombiere. Paris, 1645, 4to.

[2] Price has a very interesting note upon a collection of German poems compiled from heraldic registers by Peter Suchinwirt (who lived at the close of the XIVth century), in which accounts are given of the battles of Crécy and Poitiers by Germans who were present. (*The History of English Poetry*, edit. 1824, vol. ii, p. 167, note n.)

[3] *Nicholai Uptoni de Studio militari Libri quatuor*, etc., Lond., 1654, fol., lib. i, cap. xii.

[4] « Hiraux appellati videntur, qui fortium virorum facta laudesque verbis suis prædicabant. » — « En celuy saint disner soit bien gardé que hiraux et bordeurs ne fassent leur offices ; mais à collation du roy (soir ?), et en presence des vaillans chevaliers, se pourront bien reciter, au lieu d'instrumens bas, aucunes ditiés à la louenge de Dieu », etc. (*Statuta ordinis Coronæ spinarum*, cap. xxii ; ap. du Cange's *Gloss. med. et inf. Lat.*, t. iii, p. 671, col. i, v° *Hiraudus*.

. . . . Un hiriaus,

Un jouglerres, un menestraus, etc., Vitæ Patrum. (*Ibid.*)

There is a stroke against heralds and minstrels in the *Miroir de Mariage*. (Poésies morales et historiques d'Eustache Deschamps, Crapelet's edition, p. 216, 217.)

poet in his interview with the Black Prince, and elsewhere, it is not unlikely that he had held personal communication with him.

We will proceed to examine how in his duties as a historian Chandos has acquitted himself. As a poet, we have not so much sympathy with him, and it is perhaps fortunate that he was gifted with so little imagination as he appears to have possessed, for we are thus probably saved from the flights of fancy and heightened colourings of the poets of his time, which would have detracted much from his credit in his more important capacity. He is, indeed, a most matter of fact writer, at the same time that his style is vigorous and often elegant; but we have little talk of " ladye loves," nor any dwelling upon the gaieties of the times of peace, of the feats of the tournament, or the revelries of the hall. As a historian, he has higher claims to our attention. His object appears to have been, according to his own declaration in his poem, and we give him credit for it, to record things as he saw or gathered them, that truth might not be lost. In imitation of Froissart [1], he expressly disclaims having any

---

[1] " Pluseurs jougliours et enchantours en place ont chantet et rimet les guerres de Bretaigne, et corromput par les chançons et rimes controuvées la juste et vraie histoire : dont trop en desplait à monsseigneur Jehan le Bel, qui la commencha à mettre en prose et en cronique, et à moy, sire Jehan Froissart, qui loyaument et justement l'ay poursuivy à mon poolr ; car leurs rimes et les canchons controuvées n'ataindent en riens la vraie matere, " etc. (Manuscript of Amiens, 1st redaction of the Prologue.) — " Je ne sçay pas dire toutes les aventures qui leur sourvindrent ; car je n'y fus pas, et ceulx qui m'en ont raconté m'en ont dit en tant de manieres, que je ne m'en sçay à quoy tenir de la verité. J'ay trouvé en ung livre rimé, qué ung jougleur a fait, tant de bourdes et de menteries, que je ne les oseroie dire. " (*Les vrayes Chroniques de messire Jehan le Bel.* Bruxelles, 1863, tom. II, p. 11, A. D. 1342.) — " Je ne m'ose plus avant entremettre de couter comment ces deux

motive in common with the jongleurs and jogeleurs, and laments that the age in which he lived should encourage them. He is too an original writer, and no copyist. Of a great part of the events which he relates, he himself appears to have been an eye-witness, and the remainder he has collected apparently from persons who were present. Corroborating the accounts which Froissart has also recorded, he differs frequently in points of detail sufficiently to shew that he could not have had his material from him [1]. Thus on the first landing of Edward and

grandes assemblées se departirent, ne quelles aventures il y eut, car je n'y fus mye; et jasoit que je trouve en ces romans rimés, dont j'ay parlé ci-dessus, biacop de choses, neantmoins, pour ce qu'elles sont plus plaines de mensonge que de verité, je ne les ose dire. » (*Ibid.*, p. 18.)

There is no doubt that by those « rimes and livres rimés » the reverend chroniclers meant chiefly some *chansons de geste* like that known under the name of Cuvelier; but what is become of them, and what must we believe of another of Froissart's statements?

Giving an account of the battle of Poitiers, Froissart says : « Si ay tousjours à mon povoir justement enquis et demandé du fait des guerres et des aventures qui en sont avenues, et par especial depuis la grosse bataille de Poitiers, où le noble roy Jehan de France fut prins, car devant j'estoie encores jeune de sens et d'aage. Et ce non obstant si emprins-je assez hardiement, moy yssu de l'escolle, à dittier et à rimer les guerres dessusdites, » etc.

Baldwin, earl of Hainault, found at Sens in Burgundy the life of Charlemagne, and at his death gave it to his sister, Yoland, countess of Saint Paul, who begged him to write it in the vulgar dialect in prose, « because people delight in the roman, or vulgar dialect, who do not care about Latin; and in the former it will be more perused. Many people have heard it related and sung, but what the story-tellers and jesters say and sing of it are only lies. No rhymed tale is true, all that is said therein is untrue. » (Warton's *History of English Poetry,* ed. 1824, sect. liii, vol. i, p. 139, note *h*. Cf. Sir Fred. Madden, *William and the Werwolf,* Introd., p. ix.)

[1] Although it may be that Chandos and Froissart had held communication with each other abroad, yet, as Froissart tells us that, in

his army at la Hogue, Chandos in his account is altogether at variance with Froissart, as he also is with that given by Michael de Northbury, as left us by Robert d'Avesbury. He states distinctly that Bertrand, marshal of France, was there to oppose Edward's landing:

> Là fut li mareschaux Bertrans,
> Qui moult fut hardy et vaillantz;
> Et lors quida trop les defendre
> A prendre terre, au voir entendre;
> Mais la puissance d'Engleterre
> Pristrent là par force la terre. — L. 155.

In the accounts of Froissart and the rest, the French marshal's name is not to be found.

Again, in the treacherous dealings of Aimery, or Amerigo, of Pavia, respecting the surrender of Calais to Geoffroy de Chargny, our author's story stands alone; he introduces a third person into the business, and mixes up in the affair a sire de Beaujeu, wholly unnoticed by any other authority.

We may here also remark that in the repulse of Chargny, on the night of 31st of December, the King is stated distinctly by our poet to have owed his life to the personal exertions of the Black Prince, in rescuing him from the hands of superior numbers.

The next case we have to adduce in proof of the originality of our writer, is in the minuteness with which he details the exertions of the Cardinal Talleyrand de Périgord, in his endeavours to avoid the necessity of a battle at Poitiers: here he records the words of the legate and the French King, as also those of the Prince

---

1395, it had been twenty-seven years since he had seen England, and Chandos, as we shall find, that he wrote his poem before 1385, it is not likely that he is indebted to that chronicler for any of his facts, although it is possible that he may have seen the first part of Froissart's chronicles, presented to Queen Philippa before 1360.

of Wales, in his respective interviews with them, and we have no reason to believe that he has drawn upon his imagination for what he relates. To mention only one instance, further, we are indebted to Chandos for an anecdote connected with the same battle, which we do not find elsewhere. It is the proposal of Geoffroy de Chargny to the English barons, who had been appointed to confer with the King of France previously to the battle, that they should decide the quarrel by combat, a hundred men being selected from either army.

Other points of difference might also with ease be mentioned; but as these points occur after the time when it is obvious that he was a personal observer of what he writes, they will make nothing for our present purpose.

For instance, to the list of knights given by Froissart, as made by the Duke of Lancaster prior to the battle of Nájera, Chandos adds the names of Prior, Elton and Curzon, not otherwise, that I am aware of, noticed. In the passage also of the army over the Pyrenees, he mentions the names of several persons as forming part of the army, which do not occur in Froissart.

A few words will suffice to shew the plan upon which our herald has proceed with respect to the composition of his history. His general object has been to record the three great expeditions of the Black Prince, or perhaps we should be speaking more correctly to say, the most briliant individual actions of his hero — but principally the expedition into Spain, as he expressly states in the introduction to that portion of his poem, when, after noticing,

> Or n'est pas raison que je faigne
> D'un noble voiage d'Espaigne;
> Mais bien est raisons que hom l'emprise :
> Car ce fut la plus noble emprise
> Que onques cristiens emprist, — L. 1638.

he goes on :
> Ore est bien temps de comencer
> Ma matiere, et moy addresser
> Au purpos où je voil venir
> A ce que je vys avenir ; » — L. 1648.

during the progress of which, at it is implied in the lines quoted, we may believe him to have been actually present.

The poem therefore may be resolved into these two divisions : a summary namely of the wars in which the Black Prince was engaged previous to the time of his espousing the quarrel of Don Pedro, and the history of his life subsequent to that period. The account of the war in Spain, it will be found, occupies more than one third of the whole poem. In the first part of his work, he merely just notices the youth of Edward, his object being to bring him forward as quickly as possible into active life. The landing at la Hogue, the conquest of Cotentin, and the progress of the army is passed over quickly, until the meeting with the French forces at Crécy. His account of the battle is also very short, and evidently not the report of an eye-witness ; nor have we any more minute particulars, until he comes to the description of the battle of Poitiers. Here, as has been before observed, he details the exertions of the Cardinal to procure peace, the challenge of Chargny, with the answer of the Earl of Warwick ; and the battle itself is given at considerable length, probably as he received it from some one who had been present at that great victory [1]. Of the events of the ten following years he notices

---

[1] One anecdote connected with this victory recorded by Chandos, deserves notice : he states that Isabella, the queen-mother, was allowed to be present to witness the entry of her grand-son into London with the King of France as his prisoner.

There is a letter in old French from Queen Philippa and her

scarcely more than the marriage of the Black Prince with the Countess of Kent, and his proceeding with his bride to Bordeaux, to enter upon the duties of his new appointment as governor of Aquitaine. But at this point the work assumes a different character : he arrives at the chief object of his history, he comes to what he had himself seen and heard, (« à ce que je vys avenir » are his words,) and he gives us a spirited narrative of the civil war in Spain, that part of it at least in which the Prince of Wales was concerned, at considerable length. The application of Don Pedro to the Prince, the conduct of the Free Companies, and Don Enrique, the correspondence with the King of Navarre, the passage of the Pyrenees, with other details respecting the march of the army, the remonstrance of the Bastard with the Prince's

daughter Isabella to the priour of Saint Swithin's at Winchester,.. to admit Agnes Pateshill into an elemosinary sisterhood belonging to his convent. » Registr. Priorat. S. Swithini Winton., quatern. xix, fol. 4. Apr. 25 (1350 ?)

In the same register, there is a letter in the same language from the Queen-Dowager Isabella to the priour and convent of Winchester, to show that it was at her request that King Edward the third had granted a church in Winchester diocese to the monastery of Leeds in Yorkshire, for their better support ; « à trouver sis chagnoignes chantans tous les jours en la chapele du chastel de Ledes pour l'aime Madame Alianore, reyne d'Engleterre, » etc. A. D. 1341, quatern vi.

In one of our notes, p. 345, l. 159, we have spoken of the treatment of Queen Isabella by her son Edward III.; an interesting charter will more completely illustrate the subject : « Rex senescallo suo Vasconiæ... cum... dederimus... Isabellæ, reginæ Angliæ, matri nostræ carissimæ, totam terram que fuit olim vicecomitis de Castellione, ac pedagium de Petrafrice, et quicquid habuimus... apud locum de Langon... et alia bona que in castro et vicecomitatu de Benauges et villa d'Eylaz, salino in Burdegala, » etc. (*Rot. Vasc.* 18 Edw. III. membr. 8. — Rymer, vol. iii, p. 15. A. D. 1344. Cf. p. 18-20, 146.)

reply, are all recorded, whilst the circumstances connected with the battle of Nájera, and the battle itself, are especially dwelt upon, as are also the lamentable results consequent upon it. The distress of the army from sickness and want, the illness of the Prince, the unsuccessful applications to Don Pedro, and the retreat to Bordeaux, are told in a simplicity of style, at the same time with a depth of feeling that does honour to the narrator of this sad story; but from this period again our Herald resumes the brief mode of treating his subjects, which has distinguished the early portion of his work. He appears anxious to close « this sad eventful history » as quickly as may be. He passes over actions, where we may believe from Froissart that he was actually present, because his hero was not there, and mentions only in the most casual manner, after the summons of the French King to the Prince to appear before his concil at Paris, the retaking of Limoges, the fall of la Rochelle and the unsuccessful attempt of the Prince and his father to relieve Thouars.

The poem closes with a very affecting account of the last illness and death of the Black Prince, to which is added the epitaph upon his tomb in Canterbury cathedral, with a list of the different officers who served under him in his government of Aquitaine. The precise time at which our Herald composed his work appears to be determined with tolerable accuracy by the passage following, in which he is speaking of the affairs of Don Pedro previously to his asking the Black Prince for assistance :

> Coment depuis ce jour avint,
> Ne passa mye des ans vint; — L. 1814.

the time he is speaking of being 1366, would give the date of the poem 1386, or perhaps a year or two before.

To the foregoing notice of the Poem and its author, it seems only necessary to say a few words on the volume itself, and its history. It is an oblong octavo, on vellum, containing sixty-one leaves, and fifty-two lines on a page, remarkably well written, ornamented with illuminated capital letters at the beginning of each chapter and with rubricated titles. It was formerly in the collection of Sir William Le Neve, Mowbray, and afterwards Clarencieux, herald [1], whose collections, at his death, came into the possession of Sir Edward Walker, knight of the Garter, and Sir John Clopton, who had married his daughter. Of the present volume we know nothing further, until it fell into the hands of Dr George Clarke, fellow of All Souls College, and one of the members for the University of Oxford, by whom, with the bulk of his very valuable library, it was bequeathed to Worcester College, its present owners. Affixed to the volume is the following letter upon its contents from Anstis, the well known author of the History of the Garter, whose notice of Chandos Herald we have before seen : « Many thanks for the loan of your MS. of the life and valiant actions of the Black Prince wrote by Chandos Herald. It is very valuable in many respects, not only as being wrote by a contemporary author, who (though he mentions nothing himself of it in this poem) was an eye witness, and employed in some of those actions as far as related to his function, but likewise on many other accounts, as that this Chandos Herald (for I suppose there was never more than one officer by that title, who was the herald of the famous Sir John Chandos)

---

[1] A sketch of his life is given by Mark Noble in his *History of the College of Arms*, etc. London, 1804, 4to., p. 278. John Weever has an anecdote of his being shipwrecked on the coast of Kent, near Dover, on his return from France in 1629. (*Ancient funeral Monuments within Great Britain*, etc., p. 678.)

is frequently mentioned in Froissart (when I go to the Herald's office, I can send you reference to the pages); and though his master was killed in 44 Edw. III., he, according to the doctrine of that age, that the character of an herald was indelible, retained always the title of *Chandos*, and was afterwards promoted to be Ireland king of arms. The copy is also very fairly written, the names of the Englishmen right spelled, the chronology exact, and the epitaph on the Black Prince, at the end, is the very same that Prince ordered in his will, [1] » etc.

The greater part of the foregoing has already been given in the preface to a previous reproduction of this manuscript made by the late Rev^d. H. O. Coxe, the librarian of the Bodleian Library, for the Roxburghe Club. It must be stated that the copy of the manuscript in Worcester College, Oxford, has been the work of a person ignorant of the language that he has copied. Numerous words are therein found repeated or omitted; two words are often written as one, or one word divided into two. Syllables also are found repeated or omitted. M^r. Coxe has reproduced the manuscript in this form, without even having attempted to punctuate, or in any way to elucidate it. He has however gone a step farther, and with a great deal of labour tried to translate into English what was unintelligible in French and of course untranslatable. What he has frequently given are not French words of any period of the language, but merely conglomerations of detached syllables, the attempt to translate which into any other language could only end in failure.

---

[1] It may be interesting to the admirers of Anstis to learn that there is another letter from him on Father Lelong's *Bibliothèque historique de la France*, in the *Mélanges de Clairambault*, Bibl. Nat. of Paris, vol. 495, fol. 761.

I have gone over the manuscript line by line, scanning every syllable; and from my long familiarity, and I think I may say without boasting, my intimate acquaintance with the language of this period, I have reconstituted a critical text which I maintain to be exact in form to the original. In this I have not found any great difficulty, nor have I had any hesitation as to doubtful readings. Some errors of omission there may be, and for these I ask the reader's indulgence.

Acting as I have, am I sure to obtain a bill of indemnity ? To plead not guilty, I shall call for help from a recent critic.

In the Preface to *Macaire*, the late Francis Guessard defines exactly how far one ought to have confidence in even the most judiciously executed critical restitutions : « It results from what precedes, he says, that my attempt may appear excusable, provided that I have established the text of *Macaire*, if not at least absolutely what it was, at least what it might have been, that is to say, provided that for an inadmissible word or expression I have substituted a word, or a locution, current at the time when, in my opinion, the original of which I have tried to give an idea, was written. » He does not boast of guessing, which would be, he says, almost impossible, but also almost useless. In a word, he defines very well what may be expected from this new method of which he has made, in France, the first, necessarily a little hazardous, experiment [1].

In the English rendering I have striven to be literal and to employ the corresponding English word, when possible, as an equivalent. Chandos Herald avails himself often of a poet's licence in padding out his lines to the requisite length by a few set expressions affirming for

---

[1] *Macaire*, etc. Paris, 1866, 12mo., p. cxxv, cxxvi. — *Bibliothèque de l'Ecole des Chartes*, t. xliii, 1882, p. 572, 576, 577.

the most part his veracity. The frequent repetition of these becomes somewhat banal and give a bald look to the prose translation; yet I have judged it right to render them all literally into English without any greater variety of expression than the original presents. Any attempt at elegance of expression would have been out of place and only misleading for the English reader, for whom of course the translation is intended, to aid in reading the original.

One word more, and this preface, commenced by the Rev. H. O. Coxe, will be brought to a close.

The last chapter of the Poem of Chandos, containing a list of the names of the great officers of the Black Prince, offers a remarkable particularity: the lines which compose it, only conceal under an imperfect disguise a pretence of being verses. Is this a signe of fatigue on the part of the author? or, is it the lucubration of an ill-advised continuator?

In presence of obstacles much greater than those offered by the text of the chronicle itself, we have been obliged, if not to halt, at least to advance with measured steps and prudence.

VIE ET GESTES

DU

PRINCE NOIR

Cy comence une partie de la vie et des faits d'armes d'un très-noble Prince de Gales et d'Aquitaine, qu'avoit à noun Edward, eigné. filtz au roi Edward tierce, queux Dieux assoile.

ORE veit-hom au temps jadys
Que ceux qui faisoient beaux dyts
Estoient tenu pur aucteur
Ou pur ascun amenteveur
De monstrer les bons conissance 5
Pur prendre en lour coers remembrance
De bien et de honour recevoir;
Mais hom dit, et si est-ce voir,

Here beginneth a part of the life and deeds of arms of a right noble Prince of Wales and Aquitaine, Edward by name, eldest son of King Edward the Third, whom God absolve.

Now it was seen in days gone by that those who wrote fine poems were accounted as authors, or as a sort of recorders, whose office was to exhibit to the virtuous a knowledge which might enable them to take to heart, how to receive wealth and honour; but man declares, and it is evident enough, that there is nothing that fadeth not

Qu'il n'est chose qui ne desseche
Ne qu'il n'est arbres qui ne seche   10
Qu'un soul : c'est luy arbres de vie ;
Mais cils arbres en ceste vie
Florist et botonne en toutz temps.
Ci ne serai plus arestans ;
Car combien que hom n'en face compte   15
Et que hom tiendroit plus grant acompte
D'un janglour ou d'un faux menteur,
D'un jogelour ou d'un bourdeur,
Qui voudroit faire une grimache,
Ou contreferoit le lymache,   20
Dount hom purroit faire risée,
Que hom ne feroit sans demorée
D'un autre qui sauroit bien dire ;
Car cils ne sount, saunz contredire,
Mie bien venuz à la court   25
En le monde qui ore court.

---

away, neither any tree that dieth not, save one alone, the tree of life. But that tree in this world flowers and fades in all times. Here I will not longer stop; for although it would not be accounted of by men, who would rather regard a boaster or a false liar, a jester, or a buffoon, who would deal in grimace, imitate the slug at which they might laugh, which they would do without delay at another who might know how to speak well; for these, it must be confessed, are not welcomed at court nor in the world as it now is. But although men do not

Mais coment que hom ne tiegne rien
De ceux qui demonstrent le bien,
Si ne se doit-hom pas tenir
De beaux ditz faire et retenir 30
Cils que s'en scevent entremettre,
Ains les doivent en livre mettre,
Par quoy après ce qu'ils sont mort
Soit fait d'eux un juste recort.
Car c'est almoigne et charité 35
De bien dire et de verité ;
Car bien ne fut unques perduz
Qu'en ascun temps ne feust renduz.
Pur ce voil-je mettre m'entente,
Car volentés à ce me tempte, 40
De faire et recorder beaux ditz
Et de novel et de jadys.

---

prize those who demonstrate what is good, so neither must those refrain, from composing good histories, who have the capacity, rather ought they to write them in a book, by which (means) a just record may be made of them after they are dead, for it is alms and charity to speak well and truly, because good is never lost, but is ever sometime repaid. Therefore I will put my intent, being tempted by my impulse, to make and record fine poems both new and of times past.

Or cy comence la matiere.

ORE est bien temps de comencer
    Ma matiere et moy adresser   45
Au purpose où je voil venir.
Ore me laisse Dieux avenir,
Car je voil mettre m'estudie
A faire et recorder la vie
Du plus vaillant prince du mounde,   50
Si come il tourne à le reounde,
Ne qui fut puis les temps Claruz,
Jule Cesaire ne Artuz,
Ensi comme vous oïr purrez,
Mais que de bon coer l'escoutez !   55
C'est d'un franc Prince d'Aquitaine,
Qui fut, c'est bien chose certayne,
Filtz au noble roi Edward,
Qui n'avoit pas le coer coward,

Now here commences the matter.

IT is now good time to commence my subject and address myself to the purpose whereat I would arrive. For if God give me time, I will give my mind to observe and record the life of the most valiant Prince, such as has not been, if you seek the world round, since the days of Clarus, of Julius Cæsar or of Arthur, as you may also hear but if you listen with a good will : it is of a noble Prince of Aquitaine, who was, as is well known, son of the noble King Edward, who had no coward heart, and

Et filtz Philippe la roïgne,   60
Qui fut la perfite racine
De tout honour et nobleté,
De sens, valour et largité.

Des nobles condiciouns du Prince avant-nommé.

CIL franc Prince dount je vous dy,
Depuis le jour qu'il fut nasquy   65
Ne pensa fors que loiauté,
Franchise, valour et bounté,
Et si fut garniz de proesce.
Tant fut cil Prince de hautesce
Qu'il volt toutz les jours de sa vie   70
Mettre toute son estudie
En tenir justice et droiture,
Et là prist-il sa noriture.
Très dont que il fut en enfance,
De sa volunté noble et france   75

---

of Queen Philippa, who was the very root of all honour and nobleness, of feeling, of valour and of bounty.

Of the noble qualities of the Prince above named.

THIS frank Prince of whom I tell you, from the day that he was born thought only of loyalty, of free courage and of gentleness, and endowed was he with prowess. So much was this Prince of such lofty mind that he wished all the days of his life to give all his mind to upholding justice and integrity, and therein was he nurtured. From the time of his infancy, of his own noble

Prist la doctrine de largesce ;
Car jolieté et noblesce
Fut en son coer parfitement
Très le primer commencement
De sa vie et de sa joefnesse. 80
Ore est bon temps que je m'adresse
A bouter avant ma matiere,
Coment il fut, c'est chose clere,
Si prus, si hardi, si vaillant
Et si curtois et si sachant ; 85
Et si bien amot seinte Esglise
De bon coer, et sur toute guyse
La très-hauteine Trinité ;
La feste et la solempnité
En comencea à sustenir 90
Très le primer de son venir,
Et le sustint toute sa vie
De bon coer, saunz penser envie.

---

and free will he learned liberality ; for goodness and nobleness were in his heart perfectly from the first commencement of his life and of his youth. Now it is good time that I address myself to the commencement of my subject, how he was, it is well known, so preux, so hardy and so valiant, so courteous and so wise, and loved so well Holy Church with all his heart, and, above all, the most Holy Trinity; the festival and holy day he began to uphold from his earliest days, and upheld them all his life heartily, without thinking of any harm.

De la passage du roy et du Prince, son filtz, en Normandie oue moult noble baronie.

Ore ay-je voulu recorder
    De sa joefnesse, au voir counter,   95
Ore est raison que je vous counte
De ce dount hom doit faire accompte :
C'est du fait de chivalerie
(En sa personne fut norie),
En laquele il regna xxx. ans.   100
Noblement il usa ses temps ;
Car j'oiseroie dire ensy
Que puis le temps que Dieux nasquy
Ne fut plus vaillant de son corps,
Sicome orrez en mes records,   105
Si voillez oïr et entendre
A matiere à qui je voil tendre.

Of the passage of the King and Prince, his son, into Normandy with many noble lords.

Having now wished to record what is true of his youth, it is reasonable that I tell you of that which should interest all men : that is, of the deeds of chivalry, that in him were nurtured, in which he reigned thirty years. Nobly did he use his time, for I will venture to say thus, that since the birth of Jesus Christ there was none more stalworth, as you shall hear in my record, if you will listen and give attention to the matter I wish to offer.

Bien savez que lui noble roi,
Son piere, à très-graunt arroi,
Par sa haute et noble puissance 110
Fist guerre au roialme de France,
En disant qu'il devoit avoir
La corone, sachez pur voir;
Dount en sustenant la querelle
Il maintint guerre moult cruelle, 115
Laquele dura si longtemps.
Ore avint que droit à ce temps
Passa la mer en Normandie
Ovesque noble baronie,
Barons, banerers et countes. 120
Il arriva en Constantyn.
Là ot main bon chivaler fyn,
De Warrewyk luy noble counte,
De quoy hom devoit faire counte,
Et luy counte de Northamtone, 125
Qui moult estoit noble persone,

Know then assuredly that the noble King, his father, with a mighty host, in his high and noble power, made war against the realm of France, saying that the crown, you know in truth, was his by right; then in sustaining the quarrel he maintained a bloody war, that lasted so long. Now it was just at this time that he crossed the sea into Normandy with many noble lords, barons, and bannerers and counts. He arrived in Cotentin. There was many a good knight, the noble Earl of Warwick, who was to be held in high esteem, and the Earl of Northampton,

Cils de Suffolk et de Stafford,
Qui ont le coer hardi et fort,
Et le counte de Sarsburi,
Et cil d'Oxenford auxi, 130
Et si fut de Beauchamp Jehans,
Raouls de Cobham luy vaillans,
Monsieur Bartholmeus de Burghès,
Qui moult fut hardi en ses faits;
Et de Brian le bon Guyon; 135
Richard de la Vache le bon;
Et le bon Richard Talebot,
En qui moult graünt proesce ot ;
Si fut Chaundos et Audelée,
Qui bien feroient de l'espée ; 140
Et le bon Thomas de Holand,
Qui en luy eut proesce grand ;
Et des autres moult grant foisons,
Dount je ne say dire les nouns.

---

who was a right noble person, the Earls of Suffolk and of Stafford, who had hearts hardy and brave ; the Earl of Salisbury, and him also of Oxford, so also was there John Beauchamp, the valiant Ralph de Cobham, Sir Bartholomew de Burghees, who was very bold in his doings; and the good Guyon de Brian, Richard de la Vache the good ; and the good Richard Talbot, in whom much prowess was ; so were Chaundos and Audeley, who struck well with the sword ; and the good Thomas de Holland, a man of much prowess ; and a very great number of others, whose names I cannot tell.

Comment le poair d'Engleterre arriva en Constantin, et le Prince et altres seigniours furent faitz chivalers, et le roy de France en eut novelle.

<blockquote>

ARIVEZ fut le poair d'Engleterre ;   145
Et quant il devoit prendre terre,
Là fist luy Prince chivalier
Luy roy, qui tant fut à priser,
Le comte de la Marche auxi,
Et le counte de Sarsburi,   150
Johan de Mountagu, son frere,
Et des autres, c'est chose clere,
Plus que ne vous sauroie dire ;
Et bien sachez, sauns contredire,
Là fut li mareschaux Bertrans,   155
Qui moult fut hardy et vaillantz ;
Et lors quida trop les defendre
A prendre terre, au voir entendre,

</blockquote>

How the English power arrived in Cotentin, and the Prince and the other nobles were made knights, and the king of France had tidings of the same.

THE English host arrived; and when they had come to land, there the King, who was of so high esteem, made the Prince a knight, as also the Earl of March and the Earl of Salisbury, John de Montagu, his brother, with others, as is well known, more than I know how to tell you ; but know you will without contradiction, there was the Marshal Bertrans, who was right hardy and valiant; and who then thought to prevent them from landing, the truth

Mais la puissance d'Engleterre
Pristrent là par force la terre. 160
Là y eut-il fait d'armes tant
Que en eust comparé Rolant,
Et Olyver et le Danoys,
Ou Guy, qui tant par fut curtoys.
Là pooyt-hom veoir des preus, 165
Des hardis et des outrageus;
Là fut le Prince noble et gent,
Qui moult ot bel comencement.
Par tout Constantyn chivacha
Et tout ardi et exila, 170
Le Hogge, Barflew, Carenten,
Seint-Lou, Bayeus, jesques à Ken,
Là où ils conquirent le pont,
Et là combatirent-ils moult.
Par force ils pristrent celle ville, 175
Et le counte de Tankarville

---

to understand; but the power of England landed there by force. There were done such feats of arms as might compare with Roland and Oliver and the Dane, or Guy, who was so courteous. There might one see the preux, the hardy and the rash; there was the noble and gentle Prince, who made a right good beginning. He rode victorious throughout all Cotentin and burnt and ravaged, La Hogue, Barfleur and Carentan, Saint-Lo, Bayeux, all up to Caen, where they gained the bridge, and there they much fought. They took the town by storm, and the Count de Tankarville, and the

Et le counte d'Eu y fut pris.
Là ot luy noble Prince pris,
Car de bien faire fut engrans,
Et si n'ot que dis-oept ans.   180
Et luy mareschaux chivacha,
Jeskes à Paris n'aresta;
Au roy ad counté les noveles,
Queux ne lui feurent mie beles.
Tiel mervaille ot, c'est chose voire,   185
Que à paines le pooit croire;
Car pas ne quidoit que tiel gent
Éussent tant de hardiment.
Lors fist assembler son poair
Parmy France, sachez pur voer;   190
N'y demora duc ne counte
De quoy hom pooit faire counte,
Baron, baneret ne bacheler
Que toutz il ne fist assembler.

Count d'Eu also were there taken. There the noble Prince had the prize, for he was eager to do well, though only eighteen years of age. And the Marshal rode away, nor stopped till he arrived at Paris, and told the news to the King, nor were they to him good tidings. Such marvel he heard, it was true, that scarce could he credit it; for he could not believe that such a people would have had such hardihood. Then the King assembled his power throughout France, know for truth; there kept not back duke nor count among them of any fame, baron, banneret nor bachelor, who did not there assemble.

Coment le roy de France manda au roy de Beaume pur luy aider, et le roy de Beaume vint, et les Englois passerent le pont de Poissy et chivacherent parmy Caux.

Au roy de Beaume manda, 195
Que de bon coer auxi ama,
Qu'amenast en sa compaignie
Son filtz, qui fut roy d'Almanye,
Et le bon Johan de Baiumont
De Haynau, qu'homme prisoit moult. 200
A quoy faire vous counteroye
La matiere et alongeroye ?
Bien quidoit sa terre defendre
Au roy Englois, à voir entendre,
Et assetz petit le prisoit 205
Et moult forment le maneçoit ;

How the King of France sent to the king of Bohemia to assist him, and the King of Bohemia came; and how the English passed the bridge of Poissy and marched through Caux.

To the King of Bohemia, whom also he loved heartily, he sent, to ask him to bring in his company his son, who was King of Germany, and the good John de Beaumont of Hainau, whom men much prized. Why should I relate to you the matter at length? He thought well to defend his land against the King of England, to hear the truth, and held him of small account, and threatened him

Mais après, ensi qu'il me semble,
Luy roy oue luy Prince ensemble
Par Normandie chivacherent
Et tout le païs exillerent.   210
Mainte graunt escarmuche firent,
Et maint bon home toutz deux prirent
Et vindrent au pount de Poissi;
Mais la matiere dit ensi
Que le pount lors estoit rumpuz.   215
Mais tant firent que de grauntz fuz
Par force refirent le pount,
Dount François esmerveillez sount;
Et passerent par un matyn.
Parmy Caux pristrent lour chemyn,   220
Ardantz, gastantz et exillantz,
Dount moult furent François dolantz,
Et crierent à haute vois :
« Où est Philippes, notre roys ? »

---

very boldly; but after that, as it seems to me, the King with the Prince together rode throughout Normandy, and ravaged all the country. Many great skirmishes they made, and both took many a good man, and came to the bridge of Poissy; but my subject says also that the bridge was there broken down. But they wrought so that with much wood they rebuilt the bridge, at which the French marvelled much; and they passed the river in the morning. They then took their way through Caux, burning, spoiling, and ravaging, to the great grief of the inhabitants, who cried with a loud voice : « Where is Philip, our king. »

Coment le roy de France fist assembler à Paris son grant poair encoutre le roy d'Engleterre et son host, et coment le roy d'Engleterre oue son poair passa l'eawe de Somme.

A Parys fut, à voir juger ; 225
En ce temps fist apparailler
Son graunt poair et amasser,
Et là fist ses gents assembler,
Et dist que poi se priseroit
Si grant vengeance n'en prendoit ; 230
Car bien quidoit avoir enclos
Les Englois, solonc mon purpos,
Droit entre la Sayne et la Somme ;
Et là endroit, ce est la somme,
Les quidoit-il trop bien combatre. 235
Mès les Englois, pur eux esbatre,

How the King of France made assemble at Paris his great power against the King of England and his host, and how the King of England with his forces passed the river Somme.

HE was at Paris, as one may judge ; at this time he ordered all his great force to get ready and come together, and there made his people assemble ; and said that he should little value himself, if he did not take great vengeance ; for he thought easily to have shut in the English, according to my meaning, right between the Seine and the Somme ; and there was the place in short, he thought it best to engage them. But the English, to amuse themselves, gave

Mistrent tout en feu et à flame.
Là firent mainte veufe dame
Et maint povre enfant orphanyn.
Tant chivacherent soir et main   240
Qu'ils vindrent al eawe de Somme.
De l'autre part avoit maint homme;
Car là feurent, n'en doutez mye,
Les communes de Pikardye,
Et si estoit, sachez de fit,   245
Monsieur Godemard de Faït.
Moult parfut large la riviere
De flum de la mer radde et fiere,
Dount Englois moult se merveilloient
Coment par delà passeroient;   250
Mais lui Prince oue le corps gent
Fist eslire chivalers cent
Des meillours de son avant-garde,
Et les fist aler prendre garde

---

the whole (country) to fire and flame. There made they many a widowed dame and many a poor child an orphan. So they rode night and day till they came to the river Somme; on the other side they found many assembled, for there, ye need not doubt, were the commons of Picardy, and there, as you may know for certain, was messire Godemar dú Faÿ. The river was very wide from the strong and rapid tide, so that the English much marvelled how they could effect a passage; but the Prince with noble bearing made them choose an hundred knights from the best of

Coment ils purroient passer. 255
Et cils, qui furent à loer,
Chivachoient tout environ
Taunt qu'ount trouvé un compaignon
Qui lour ad enseigné le pas
De Somme, je ne vous ment pas. 260
Et toutz les cent à une fie
En l'eawe la launce baissie
Se sont feru sur lour coursers.
Moult furent vaillantz chivalers;
Et lui Prince venoit après, 265
Qui adès les sevoit de près.
Graunt escarmuche ot sur le pas
De Somme, je ne vous ment pas;
Fort combatoient chivaler
Et là de traire et de launcier 270
Se tenoient d'ambedeux parts;
Mais assetz tost furent espars

---

his van-guard, and made them go to ascertain how they might cross. And these, who were praiseworthy, rode all round about, until they had found some one who shewed them the ford of the Somme, I do not lie to you. And all the hundred threw themselves at once upon their chargers with lowered lances into the water; very valiant knights were they. And afterwards came the Prince, who always followed them closely. There was a great skirmish in the crossing of the Somme, I do not lie to you; and the knights fought well, and there shooting and throwing of lances continued on both sides; but very soon were the Picards

Et mys à fuyte lui Picard
Ovesque monsieur Godemard ;
Mais oue l'aÿde de Dieu   275
Tout passa en temps et en lieu.

Coment le roy de France vint oue trois roys et son grant poair vers Crescy pur combatre les Englois.

Quant luy roy Philip l'oÿ dire,
Moult avoit à coer dol et ire,
Et dist : « Par seint Poul le baron,
Je me doute de traïson ; »   280
Mais nepurquant moult soi hasta,
Parmy Abeville passa.
Moult parfut riche ses arois.
Là fut lui quartime des rois :
Cils de Maiole et de Baueme,   285
Et si fut lui rois d'Alemeyne.

---

broken and put to flight, with messire Godemar; but by the help of God all passed over in good time and place.

How the King of France came with three Kings and his great force towards Crécy to engage the English.

When King Philip heard this, his heart was filled with grief and wrath, and he said : « By St. Paul the baron, I doubt there has been treachery. » But nevertheless he made great haste and passed through Abbeville. Very rich was his array. There were with him four Kings : those of Majorca and Bohemia, with the King

Assetz y avoit ducz et countes,
Tant que ce estoit un graunt acountes.
Tant chivacherent saunz nul sy,
Que droit assetz près de Cressy   290
En Pontieu là fut herbergez.
Là fut le roy Edward logez
Et luy Prince, si Dieu me garde,
Qui cel jour avoit l'avant-garde.
Là n'orent gaires demouré
Que de deux partz hom ad counté,   295
Que si près furent ambedoy
Que chescun purra voir le roy
De l'un l'autre et l'ordenement.
Lors se leva le cri forment
Et comencent à ordeigner   300
Lour batailles et devyser.

---

also of Germany. Enough were there of dukes and counts, so that it was a great list. So they rode without halting until very near Crécy in Ponthieu where they took up their quarters. There was also King Edward quartered and the Prince who, so God help me, had on this day the vanguard. They did not remain there long, for on both sides, it was said that both parties were so near each other, that each could see the King and ranks of his adversary. Then they raised loudly the cry (of arms), and began to order and devise the battle.

De la bataille de Crescy, et coment le roy de Beaume et le duc de Loraine, viij. countes et plusours altres seignours, furent occis à mesme la bataille, et trois roys et plusours altres s'en departirent desconfitz.

A quoy faire vous counteroye
La matiere et alongeroye ?
Celuy jour ot une bataille
Si orrible que, tout sanz faille, 305
Unques ne fut corps si hardis
Que n'en pooit estre esbahis.
Qui véist venir la puissance
Et le poair du roy de France,
Graunt mervaille seroit à dire, 310
Espris de mautalant et de ire
Devant ensemble entre-acountier
En faisant d'armes le mestier

Of the battle of Crécy, and how the King of Bohemia and the Duke of Lorraine, eight Counts and many other lords, were slain at the said battle, and three Kings and many others left the field defeated.

WHY should I relate to you the matter at length ? On this day was the battle fought, and so dreadful was it, that truly never was there man so hardy, who would not have been astounded. To see the mighty hosts advance and the forces of the French King, marvellous would it be to tell, how seized by hatred and anger, before together encountering and using their arms, so

Si très-chivalerousement
Que unques puis l'Avenement 315
Ne vist hom bataille plus fiere.
Là veoit-hom maynte baniere
Pointe de fyn or, et de soye;
Et là, si le vray Dieux m'avoye,
Englois estoient tout à pez 320
Com cils qui furent afaitez
De combatre et entalentez.
Là fut lui Prince de bountez,
Qui en l'avant-garde restoit.
Si vaillamment soi gouvernoit 325
Que merveille fut à véir.
A paine lessoit envaïr
Nul hom, tant fut hardyz ne fortz.
Quei vous feroie-je long recortz ?
Tant combatirent celuy jour, 330
Que Englois avoyent le meillour.

---

chivalrously they fought, that never since the Advent, did man behold a fiercer struggle. There was to be seen many a banner painted of fine work of gold, and of silk; and there, so help me the God of truth, were the English all on foot, as those who were ready and right eager to fight. There was the good Prince, who in the vanguard remained. So valiantly did he acquit himself, that it was marvellous to see; scarce for a moment did he cease to attack, there was none so hardy nor so bold. Why should I make a long record ? So did they fight on this day, that

Et là fut mort luy noble roys
De Beaume, qui fut curtoys;
Et le bon duc de Loherayne,
Qui moult fut noble capitayne; 335
Et de Flaundres le noble counte,
Dount hom fesoit un grant acounte;
Et le bon counte d'Alencion,
Qui fut frere au roy Philippon,
Cils de Joii et de Harcourt. 340
Que vous diroye à brief mot court?
Un roy et un duc et oept countes,
Et ensi com dit luy acountes,
Plus que lx. banerès
Furent illoec mortz tout frès, 345
Et trois roys qui s'en departirent,
Et plusours aultres s'enfuyrent,
Dount je ne say mie le noumbre,
Ne n'est pas droit que je le noumbre;

---

the English had the best of it. And there fell the noble King of Bohemia, who was courteous; and the good Duke of Lorraine, a right noble captain, with the noble Count of Flanders, whom people highly esteemed; and the good Count d'Alençon, who was brother of King Philip, Counts de Jouy and d'Harcourt. What should I say in short? One King, one Duke, eight Counts, and also, as the account says, more than sixty bannerets were there all slain. And there were three Kings who retreated, and many others who fled, whose number I neither know nor should I do

Mais je sai bien que celuy jour 350
Luy noble Prince de valour,
Si c'ome doit bien prendre garde,
De la bataille ot l'avant-garde,
Car par luy et par ses vertus
Fut luy champ gaignez et vaincus. 355

Coment après le bataille de Crescy le roy de France s'en ala vers Paris, et le roy de Engleterre oue son host s'en departist vers Caleys.

Luy roy Philippes à Parys
S'en ala, qui moult fut marys.
En son corage regretoit
Ses hommes que perduz avoit.
Et luy noble roy d'Engleterre, 360
Qui fut dignes de tenir terre,

---

right to enumerate. But I know well that on that day the noble and valorous Prince, as one whose duty it was to take great care, had the vanguard of the battle; therefore by him and his courage was the field gained and conquered.

How after the battle of Crécy the King of France retreated towards Paris, and the King of England with his forces moved upon Calais.

The King Philip then retreated towards Paris, much vexed. In his heart he was grieved for the men he had lost; and the noble King of England, who was worthy to hold land, rested upon the field on that night;

En chaump cele noet soy logea,
Qui moult grant honour conquesta.
Les mortz fist aler visiter
Pur conoistre et pur aviser,   365
Et trova le roy de Beaigne,
Qui gisoit mort sur la champaigne ;
Carker le fist en une bere
Et mettre sur une litere
A covert d'un riche drap d'ore ;   370
Arere le tramist, et lore
De la place se deslogea,
Par devers Caleis chivacha.
Pour ce què jeo ne mente mye,
Celle très-noble chivachie,   375
Dount je fai mencion ycy,
Ce fut en l'an que Dieux nasqui
Mille trois centz quarant et sis,
Et ensy com dist luy escris,

---

where he had gained such great honour. He caused the dead to be examined, to discover who they were and to order for the best, and he found the King of Bohemia, who lay dead upon the field; he caused him to be put into a coffin and placed on a litter covered with a rich cloth of gold, and sent him to the rear; and then moving from that place, he rode towards Calais. That I may speak truly, this very noble achievement, which I mention here, was in the year from the birth of Christ one thousand three hundred and forty six, and according to the written

La viegle de Seint-Bartholomeu, 380
Que, ovesque la grace de Dieu,
Le roy ceste bataille fist,
Où tant de noblesse il acquist.

Coment le roy d'Engleterre oue son grant poair assegea la ville de Caleys par xviij. moys, et le roy de France n'oesa lever l'assege : par quoy ladite ville se rendi au roy d'Engleterre.

APRÈS vindrent devant Caleys,
Là ont-ils fait moult de beaux faits ; 385
Là tint siege le noble roy,
Qui fut oue tout son arroy
Dis-oept moys en un tenant.
Illoeques demuroient tant
Que la ville fut afamée 390
Et que là vint sanz demorée

---

account, the vigil of Saint Bartholomew, that by the grace of God, the King fought this battle, where he acquired such honour.

How the King of England with his great host besieged the town of Calais for eighteen months, and the King of France dared not raise the siege : wherefore the said town surrendered to the King of England.

AFTER that they came before Calais, there they did many a feat of arms; and the noble King, who with all his host was there, kept siege for eighteen months continually. There they staid so long, that the town was reduced to famine, and then came there in haste the King

Luy roy Philippe pur lever
L'assege, sicom j'ay oï counter;
Mais ensi fut lui host logie
Et la ville si assegie 395
Que le roy Philippe n'oesa
Lever l'assege, ainz retourna.
Et luy noble roy d'Engleterre
Tint illoec piece de terre.
Mainte escarmuche et maint assaut 400
Y faisoient et bas et haut
Tant que la ville se rendy,
Priantz au roy pur Dieu mercy
Qu'à mercy il les vousist prendre.
Et ensement, à voir entendre, 405
Fut Caleis par force conquise
Par la puissance et par l'emprise
Du noble roy et de son filtz,
Le Prince, qui tant fut hardiz.

Philip to raise the siege, as I have heard it said; but the (English) forces were so disposed and the town so beleaguered, that King Philip dared not raise the siege, but returned. The noble King of England held there a piece of ground. Many skirmishes and attacks were made on every side, so that the town surrendered, praying the King for God's mercy that he would treat them mercifully. And thus, to understand the truth, was Calais reduced by the power and high emprize of the noble King and his son, the Prince, who was so valiant.

Coment le roy d'Engleterre oue son poair retourna en Engleterre, et par traïson la ville de Caleis deust avoir esté vendu as Franceis ; et le roy d'Engleterre oue son poair là-contre restoia, en tant qu'il eust esté pris s'il n'eust esté rescouz par le Prince, son filtz.

Après ceo ne demura guere   410
Qu'ils revindrent en Engleterre,
Luy roy et luy Prince auxi
Et tout li chivalers hardy,
Par une triewe qu'ils avoient.
En lour païs se demuroient   415
Tanque il avint que par traitié,
Par traïsoun et par pecchié,
Devoit estre Caleis venduz,
Au seigniour de Biaugeu renduz,
A monsieur Geffrey de Charny,   420
Par un Lumbard, qui Amery

How the King of England with his army returned to England, and the town of Calais was to have been treacherously sold to the French ; and how the King of England with his forces remained there so long, that he would have been taken had he not been rescued by the Prince, his son.

After this there was no delay before they returned to England, the King and the Prince also with all their hardy knights, under a truce they had made ; and remained at home, until they had tidings that by treaty, by treason and by perfidy, Calais was to be sold and given up to a Sire de Beaujeu, to messire Geoffroy de Chargny, by a Lombard of Pavia, who Aimery was called, and there

Estoit appellez, de Pavye.
Et là furent de Pikardye
Et de Fraunce tout ly baron,
Au meins la pluis grant fuÿson ;   425
Mais là fut, à voir acountier,
Luy noble roys à deliverer.
Et luy noble Prince, son filtz,
Qui moult fut vaillant et hardyz,
Là combati si vaillamment,   430
Qu'il rescout veritablement
Par force son piere, le roy.
Là furent mis en desarroy
Fraunçois et Pikards celle nuyt,
Dount plusours Engloys grand deduyt   435
Faisoient contre lour retour ;
Car là furent tout luy meillour
Du noble païs d'Engleterre,
Qui pur graunt los et pris conquere

---

were of Picardy and France all the nobles, at least the greater number ; but there were, to tell the truth, the noble King to save. And the noble Prince, his son, who was right valiant and hardy, there fought valiantly, so that he rescued in good truth by his might the King, his father. There were put to the rout that night Frenchmen and those of Picardy, in preventing whose return many English took great delight ; for there were all the best of the noble land of England, who to obtain honour and credit were

S'i furent vaillamment prové. 440
Là furent pris pur verité
Les plus nobles barons de France,
Et deceu de volenté france;
Que unques mais le roy d'Engleterre
N'eut en une heure tant à fere 445
Come il eut en celle heure adont,
Car plusours gentz recordez ont
Que le roy éust esté pris
N'eut esté le Prince, son filtz.
Mais sa puissance et sa hautesse 450
Et sa très-parfite proesse
Rescout illoec le roy, son piere :
Si ne doit pas ceste matiere
Estre en nulle estorie oblie.
Ore est bien droit que j'el vous die. 455

---

most stoutly bent. There were taken in good truth the most noble barons of France; and of his own free will never had the King of England so busy an hour, as he had on this same day. For many have said that the King would have been taken, had it not been for the Prince, his son. But his strength and his bearing and all perfect prowess, rescued there the King, his father : so ought not this event in any history to be forgotten. Then it is well fit that I tell it to you.

Coment après le rescous de Caleys le roy d'Engleterre oue son poair y retourna. Après ceo avint la bataille sur la mer, et là furent les Espainardes occiz et descoumfitz.

E<small>N</small> Engleterre retournerent
Et moult grant joie demenerent,
Grant joie firent lour amy,
Et toutes les dames auxi.
La roÿgne les festoia,   460
Qui son seignour de coer ama.
Donc dist le roy à sa mulier :
« Dame, car veulliez festoier
Votre filtz; car jeo fusse pris
Si n'eust esté par son grant pris.   465
Mais par lui fui-jeo socurruz. »
— « Sire, fait-ele, bienvenuz

How after the recovery of Calais the King of England with his forces returned home. Afterwards they had an engagement at sea with the Spaniards, who were slain and put to flight.

To England the army returned, where very great joy awaited them ; right glad were all their friends, and all the ladies also. The Queen, who loved her lord from her heart, celebrated their return with festivities. Then said the King to his wife : « Lady dear, be pleased to entertain your son; for I should have been taken had it not been for his great emprise ; but by him was I rescued. » — « Sire, said

Soit-il, et vous auxi à moy ;
Si m'est avis que dire doy,
A bone héure fut-il nez. » 470
Là furent conjoÿ assetz
Luy chivaler et luy baron.
Daunser et festoier veist-hom
Et faire festes et reveaux.
Moult parfut bon le temps entre eaux, 475
Et là fut amours et noblesse
Et jolieté et proesse.
Ensi demorerent longtemps
Tant qu'il avint à ceo temps
Que à Lescluse assemblez estoient 480
Niefs d'Espaigne, queux se vantoient
De passer en despit du roy,
Maugré luy et tout son arroy ;
Dount le roy, par son vasselage,
Fist assembler son graunt barnage, 485

---

she, welcome are you both to me; it is my mind, and I ought to say it, in a good hour was he born. » There were very kindly entertained knights and barons. Dancing and feasting might there be seen and entertainment and revels. Much happy time was there passed : there were deeds of love and nobleness, of pleasantry and of prowess. Thus they remained a long time, until it befell that at Sluys was assembled a Spanish fleet, that boasted to cross the sea in defiance of the King, and in spite of him and his array; upon which the King, by his bravery, assembled his great

Et fist sur la mer une armée,
Qui moult fut de grant renomée.
Là estoit luy Prince, son filtz,
Et maint bon chivaler de pris,
Tout li counte et tout li baron   490
Et tout li chivaler de noun.
Là ot bataille fiere et dure.
Là lui dona Dieux aventure,
Car par lui et par sa puissance
Et par sa très-haute vaillance   495
Furent toutz mortz et disconfitz
Les Espaniardes, sachez de fit.
Et là fut chivaler Johans,
Son frere, qui moult fut vaillantz,
Qui de Lancastre fut puis ducz ;   500
Moult grantz parfurent ses vertuz.
Là se proverent vaillantment
Li noble baron ensement.

---

baronage, and fitted for sea an armament, that was of much renown. There was the Prince, his son, and many knights of fame, all the earls and barons and all the knights of name. Then was there a fierce engagement; but God was with the attempt, for by him and his power and by his all high valour all the Spaniards, know ye surely, were slain or beaten off; and there was John made knight, the Prince's brother, who did valiantly; who afterwards was Duke of Lancaster, and whose virtues were very great. There also acquitted themselves valiantly the noble barons;

Là ot-il mainte nief gaignée,
Mainte prise et maint percée, 505
Et là ot maint bon home mort,
Sicom j'oÿ en mon recort,
Et sachez que ceste journée
Si fut devant Wynchelesee.

Coment après la bataille sur la mer la roïgne d'Engleterre enfaunta un filtz qu'avoit à noun Thomas; et après ceo vint le captal de Gascoigne en Engleterre pur avoir le Prince lour chiften en Gascoigne; et sur ceo fut ordeigné par parlement que le Prince s'en passeroit en Gascoigne oue plusours countes et altres seignours.

Après ceste noble bataille, 510
Qui moult fut horrible sanz faille,
A terre furent retournez.
Là graunt avoir ont amesnez

---

there were also many ships won, many taken and many broken; there too perished many good men, as I have heard it reported. Know too that this action was fought off Winchelsea.

How that after this sea fight the Queen of England gave birth to a son, who was called Thomas, and how after that came the Captal of Gascony to England to make the Prince their chief in Gascony, and how that upon this it was ordered by parliament that the Prince should pass over into that country with many earls and other noblemen:

After this noble battle, which doubtless was most horrible, they had returned home. They had brought

Qu'ils eurent gaignez et conquis,
Dount chescun de eux fut resjoïs.   515
Après ce ne demora guere
Que la roÿne d'Engleterre
Enfanta un filtz de darrein,
Qu'elle porta, c'est bien certein,
Et cil filtz ot Thomas à noun.   520
Grant joie et grant feste fist-hom,
Grantz justes et feste criée
Adonques parmy la contrée.
Et à ce temps vint de Gascoigne
Le Captal, n'est pas mençoigne,
Qui moult estoit vaillant et preus,   525
Moult hardis et moult corageus
Et moult amez de toute gent.
Festoiez fut moult noblement.
Graunt joie fist de sa venue
Lui Prince, qui se resvertue.   530

---

with them the great property they had gained and conquered, at which each of them rejoiced. Scarcely did there any time elapse, before the Queen of England gave birth to her last child that she bore, as is well known, and this son was named Thomas. Great rejoicings were there then, jousts and festivities proclaimed throughout the whole land. There came at this time from Gascony the Captal, this is no untruth, who was right valiant and preux, of great daring and courage, and much loved of all people. Very nobly was he entertained. The Prince rejoiced much at his

Un jour il dist au roy, son piere,
Et à la roïgne, sa miere :
« Sire, fait-il, pur Dieu mercy
Vous savez bien qu'il est ensy
Qu'en Gascoigne vous ayment tant   535
Luy noble chivaler vaillant
Qu'ils ont graunt payne pur la guerre
Et pur le votre honour conquere ;
Et si n'ount point de chieftayne
De votre sang, c'est de certaine.   540
Et pur ce, si bon le trovez
En votre conseill que faissiez
Envoier là un de vos filtz,
Ils en seroient plus hardys. »
Et chescun dit qu'il disoit voir.   545
Lors fist lui roy, sachez pur voir,
Assembler son grant parlement.
Toutz furent d'accord ensement

---

coming, and took courage and exerted himself. One day said he to the King, his father, and to the Queen, his mother : « Sire, said he, by God's grace you know well that in Gascony the noble valiant knights love you so much that they take great trouble in your wars, and thereby enhance your honour ; but they have no chieftain of your blood, as you know : wherefore if you like it, and by the aid of your counsel determine to send there one of your sons, they will be the more strong. » And every one said that he spoke for the best. Then the King called, know for truth, a meeting of his great parliament. They were all

Du Prince en Gascoigne envoier,
Pur ce que tant fut à priser ; 550
Et ordeignerent là endroit
Ensi que ovesque lui iroit
De Warrewyk luy noble counte,
De quoy hom fesoit grand accounte,
Et lui counte de Sarsbury, 555
Qui moult estoit vaillant auxi,
Cil de Suffolk, qui fut prudhom
(Ufford ensi estoit son noun),
Et le bon counte d'Oxenford,
Et le bon counte de Stafford, 560
Monsieur Bertreme de Burghès,
Qui moult fut hardi en ses fès,
Monsieur Johan de Montagu,
Qui coer avoit fier et agu,
Et le sire le Despenser ; 565
Basset, qui moult fut à priser,

---

unanimous to send the Prince into Gascony, because of the high esteem in which he was held ; and they ordered straightway, that there should also go with him the noble Earl of Warwick, whom men highly esteemed, and the Earl of Salisbury, who was also right valiant, the Earl of Suffolk, who was a worthy man (Ufford was his name), also the good Earl of Oxford and the good Earl of Stafford, Sir Bartholomew de Burghersh, who was very doughty in his deeds, Sir John de Montagu, who had a fierce and keen heart, and the Lord le Despenser ; Basset, who was much esteem-

Et si fut le sire de Maunle ;
Et auxi, ensi qu'il me semble,
Le sire de Cobham, Renaut,
Qui eut esté à maint assaut. 570
Si furent Chaundos et Audlée ;
Cils deux eurent graunt renomée,
Et furent ordeignez ou frayne
Du Prince, sachez de certaine.

De l'ordinance pur le passage du Prince à Plummuth vers Gascoigne, et coment il prist congé du roy, son piere, et de la roÿgne, sa miere.

Q UANT la chose fut devisée, 575
Et tout l'ordinance acomplée,
A Plummuth fist-homme mander,
Pur toutes lour niefs assembler,

---

ed, and so was the Lord of Meinel ; and also, as it seems to me, the Lord Raynald of Cobham, who had been in many an assault. There were also Chandos and Audley ; those two had great renown, and were told off to be at the bridle-rein of the Prince, know for certain.

Of the ordinance at Plymouth for the Prince's passage into Gascony, and how he took leave of the King, his father, and the Queen, his mother.

W HEN the matter was determined, and every ordinance complete, at Plymouth they were summoned, all to assemble their ships, men at arms and archers also,

Gentz d'armes et archiers auxi,
Et lour vitailles sanz nul si. 580
Moult parfut riches luy arrois.
Après le terme de deux mois
Il prist congié du roy, son piere,
Et de la roygne, sa miere,
De toutz ses freres et ses soers. 585
Moult grant dolour font en lour coers
Quant se vint à son departir;
Car là véissez sanz mentir
Dame et damoiselle plorer
Et en compleintes dolouser. 590
L'une pur son amy ploroit,
L'autre son amy regretoit.

---

and their victuals without any demur. Very rich indeed was the array. After the lapse of two months the Prince took leave of the King, his father, and the Queen, his mother, and all his brothers and sisters. Very great sorrow they had in their hearts when the time of his departure came; for there might you see indeed wives and damsels in tears, and loud in their complainings; the one weeping for her lover, the other grieving for her friend.

Coment le Prince est venuz à Plummuth oue son grant poer, et illoeques ad demoré tanque il fust tut prest pur passer avaunt, et est arrivez à Burdeaux ; et coment les nobles seigniours et barons de Gascoigne luy ont receu oue grant joie et honour ; et coment après ceo le Prince prist les champs oue vj. mille combatauntz, et prist et xeilla par force plusours chastels et villes en Gascoigne.

Ensi prist le Prince congié,
Qui le coer avoit haut et lié;   595
Vers Plummuthe prist son chemin.
Tant chivacha soir et matyn
Qu'en Plummuthe fut arrivez ;
Et illoeques est tant demorez
Que toutz son graunt arrois fut près.   600
Et s'avint auxitost après

How the Prince arrived at Plymouth with his great force, and there tarried until he was ready to pass over; and how he arrived at Bordeaux, and the noble lords and barons of Gascony received him with great joy and respect; and how afterwards the Prince took the field with six thousand fighting men, and took and ransacked many castles and towns in Gascony.

THUS the Prince took leave with a high and glad heart; he took his way towards Plymouth. He rode night and day until he arrived there, where he remained until all his great armament was ready. And soon afterwards it

Qu'il fist carker toutz ses vessealx,
Toutz de vitailles et joialx,
Hauberks, helmes, launces, escutz,
Arcs, saectes; et encor plus,   605
Fist toutz ses chivalx eskipper,
Et assetz tost se mist à mer
Et tout lui nobles chivaler.
Là poïst-hom, à voir juger,
Veoir la flour de chivalerie,   610
Et très-noble bachelerie,
Qui furent en grant volunté
De bien faire et entalenté.
Lors comencerent à sigler.
Tant siglerent parmy la mer   615
Qu'ils arriverent à Burdeaux,
Dount moult fesoient grantz reveaux
Lui noble baron du païs.
Là véissez grantz et petitz

---

happened that he loaded all his ships with all, victuals and jewels; hauberks, helms, lances, shields, bows, arrows; and still more, he got on board his cavalry, and soon after put to sea with all his noble knights. There might a man, to judge the truth, see the flower of chivalry and a right noble bachelry, all anxious and well able to achieve honorable deeds. Then they began to sail. They navigated so far across the sea that they arrived at Bordeaux, where the noble lords of the country received them with great rejoicings. There might you see the great and small coming straight

Venir vers le Prince tout droit, 620
Qui doucement les festoioit.
Devers lui vint tout entreset
Lui noble Prince de la Bret,
Et lui sire de Montferrant,
Qui ot le coer preu et vaillant, 625
Mussinden, Roson et Courtoun
Et de Faussard Amenion,
Et le grant sire de Pomiers,
Et meintz des nobles chivalers,
Et le droit sire de Lesparre. 630
Quei vous feroy-je longe barre
Pur alongier plus la matiere ?
Là viendroient, c'est chose clere,
De Gascoigne tout lui baron ;
Et le Prince de très-grant noun 635
Les savoit trop bien conjoïr.
Quei vous dirai-je sanz mentir ?

---

to the Prince, who received them with all kindness. There came meanwhile the noble Prince d'Albret, and the Sire de Montferrand, a man of fine and high courage, Mucidan, Rauzan and Courton, and Amenion de Faussard, the great Sire de Pomiers, with many noble knights, and the rightful Sire de Lesparre. Why should I make a long speech to lengthen out my story ? There came there, the matter is clear, all the barons of Gascony ; and the Prince of very high renown knew well how to share their joy. What

A Burdeaux sojourna un poy
Tant qu'il ot fait tout son arroy
Et bien ses chivalx reposer.   640
Bientost après fist apprester
Et mist ensemble sur les champs
Plus que vj. mille combatantz.
Devers Tholouse chivacha.
Unques ville n'y demora   645
Qu'il ne faisist tout exillier;
Et prist Carkason et Vesier
Et Narbone, et tout le païs
Fut par luy gastez et malmis,
Et plusours villes et chasteaux,   650
Dount pas ne firent grantz reveaux
En Gascoigne lui enemy.
Plus que quatre mois et demy
Demora ès champs ceste fois,
Adonques il fist moult desrois.   655

---

shall I in truth tell you? At Bordeaux he sojourned a while, until he had got together all his forces, and given his cavalry rest. Soon afterwards he made ready more than six thousand fighting men. He rode towards Toulouse; nor did he pass by any town, that he did not entirely ransack; and took Carcassonne, Beziers and Narbonne, and all the country was overrun and laid waste, as also many towns and castles; for which in Gascony the enemy had no reason to rejoice. He remained at this time in the field, for more than four months and a half, and there caused great disorder.

Coment le Prince se retourna vers Burdeaux, et illoeques demora en grant deduit et grant joie tanque l'ivere fut passé, et lors il mist ses gentz par ordinance en ses chastels tout entour.

Puis devers Burdeaux retourna
Lui Prince, et là il demora
Tanque y fut passé tout l'yver.
Il et si noble chivaler
En grant deduit et en grant joie   660
Estoient là, si Dieux m'avoie.
Là fut jolité et noblesce,
Franchise, bounté et largesce ;
Et, à ce que j'ay de semblance,
Il mist ses gentz par ordinance   665
En ses chastelx trestout entour,
Là où ils firent lour sejour.

How the Prince returned towards Bordeaux, and there remained in relaxation and joy until the winter was passed, and then he sent his forces into his strongholds in that part.

AFTERWARDS the Prince returned, and remained at Bordeaux till the winter was over. He and all his knights in great joy and festivities were there, so God lead me. There was jollity and nobleness, sincerity, bounty and liberality; and then, as I have heard, he ordered his forces to the different fortresses round about, where they took up their quarters. Warwick was at La Réole, and also,

Warrewik fut à La Réole,
Et auxi, à courte parole,
Salsbury fut à Seinte-Foy ; 670
Et si fut, ensi com je croy,
Suffolk droit à Seint-Million ;
A Leybourne et tout environ
Furent ses hommes herbergiez.
Quant ensi feurent hostagiez, 675
Luy bon Chaundos et Audlé,
Qui moult estoient renommé,
Ovesque le noble Captal,
Qui le coer ot preu et loial,
S'alerent logier sur les champs, 680
Là où demurerent longtemps.
Maint bele escarmuche firent
Et mainte fois se combatirent
Pur conquestre lour logement.
Dusque à Caours et vers Agent 685

---

to be brief, Salisbury was at Sainte-Foy ; and also, as I believe, Suffolk was at Saint-Emilion ; at Libourne and all around were his men quartered ; as also were lodged the good Chandos and Audley, those men of high renown, with the noble Captal, who had a right loyal heart, and took up their station in the fields. There they sojourned a long time, and often had skirmishes and oftentimes fought, to obtain their position. They undertook an expedition, as far as Cahors and towards Agen, and took Port-Sainte-Marie;

Entreprisent lour chivachie,
Et pristrent Port-Seinte-Marie,
Puis s'en retournerent arere
Tout encontremont la ryvere ;
S'alerent prendre Pieregos,   690
Une cité que ot grant los.
Illoec s'alerent herbergier
Tut une grant part de l'yver.
Moult parfut noble le seigniour,
Car maint assaut et maint estour   695
Fesoient contre le chastel,
Car n'avoit que petit praiel
Entre le chastel et la ville.
Là estoit lui counte de Lylle
Et lui counte de Pieregos.   700
Quei vous diray-je plus des motz ?

---

they then returned back, keeping up the river, and made an attack upon Périgueux, a city of much note. There they were quartered a great part of the winter. Most noble was the lord, for many a sally and many an attack they made against the castle ; for there was only a small meadow between it and the town. There was the Count de Lylle and the Count de Périgord, why should I say more ?

*Coment le Prince reassembla son poair et fist sa chiva-
chie en Seintonge et en altres diverses parties de
Gascoigne; et prist certeins fortresses et seigniours
devant la bataille de Paitiers, et les novels en vindrent au roy de Fraunce.*

Ensi le Prince sojourna
En Gascoigne et si demora
L'espace de viij. mois ou plus.
Moult parfurent grant ses vertus. 705
Quant ce vint encontre l'esté,
Lors ad son poair assemblé ;
Puis refit une chivachie
En Seintonge, je vous affie,
En Pieregos et en Kersin, 710
Et vint jusques Roumorentyn.
Là prist-il la tour par assaut,
Là prist messire Buscikaut

---

*How the Prince reassembled his forces and marched upon
Saintonge and other parts of Gascony, and took certain forts
and lords before the battle of Poitiers, and how the news had
reached the King of France.*

The Prince then took up his quarters in Gascony, and remained there for the space of eight months or more. Very great were his virtues. When the summer came, he reassembled his forces, and made a march upon Saintonge, Périgord and Quercy, and came, I assure you, as far as Romorantin. There he took the tower by assault, and made prisoner messire Boucicault and the great Lord

Et le grant sire de Craon
Et des autres moult grant fuyson.　　　715
Plus de cc. en y ot pris,
Toutes gentz d'armes de grant pris,
Quinze jours devant la bataille
De Paitiers, sachez tout sanz faille.
Après chivacha en Berri　　　720
Et parmy la Gascoigne auxi
Et jesques à Tours en Tourayne.
Adonques, c'est chose certeyne,
Les noveles au roy Johan
Vindrent, dont moult fist grant ahan,　　　725
Et dist que poy se priseroit
Si grant vengeance n'en prendoit.

---

of Craon, and very many others; more than two hundred were there taken, all fighting men of great valour, five days before the battle of Poitiers, rest assured. I speak truly. Afterwards he rode into Berry, and also through Gascony, as far as Tours in Touraine. Then it is very certain that the news reached King John, who was greatly moved, and said that he should lightly esteem himself, if he took not great vengeance.

Coment le roy de Fraunce fist assembler sa grant puissance à Chartres encontre le Prince et son poair, et luy Prince ad pris son chemyn vers Paitiers, et coment il prist deux countes, et plusours autres furent pris et mortz

Lors fist assembler sa puissance
De tout le royalme de France ;
N'y demora ne duc ne counte 730
Ne baron dont hom fesist counte,
Que tout ne fesoit amasser.
Ensi com j'ay oï counter,
Fut fait à Chartres l'assemblée.
Noble gent avoit amassée ; 735
Car, ensi que homme count le stille,
Il en avoit plus de x. mille.
De Chartres se sont departy,
Et chivacherent sans nul si

How the King of France assembled his great power at Chartres against the Prince and his forces, and how the Prince had taken his route towards Poitiers, and how he took prisoners two counts, and many others were taken and slain.

Then the French King gathered his forces from all the realm of France; there demurred not duke nor count, nor baron of any note, whom he did not bring together. And so, as I have heard, the gathering was made at Chartres. A noble assemblage was there; for, according to the numbering, there were more than ten thousand. They departed from Chartres and rode without any hesitation straight

Tout ensi com par devers Tours. 740
Moult parfut noble lour atours.
Lui Prince en ot oï noveles,
Queux lui semblent bones et beles;
Devers Paitiers prist son chemin;
Moult oue lui menoit grant train, 745
Car moult eurent fait de damage
En France par lour grant barnage.
Et sachez que le samedy
Le noble counte de Joygny,
Ovesque le counte d'Auçoire, 750
Prist le Prince, c'est chose voire;
Et combatirent vaillamment
Les François à lour logement;
Mais ils furent toutz mortz ou pris;
Ensement le dit lui escriptz: 755
Dount Englois fesoient grant joye
Parmy lour host, si Dieux m'avoie.

---

towards Tours. Very noble was their array. The news then reached the Prince, and good tidings did they seem to him; towards Poitiers he took his way, and a great train with him; much damage had they done in France by their great valour, and know for truth that on the Saturday the Prince took (prisoner) the noble Count de Joigny with the Count d'Auxerre; and the French fought valiantly at their camp, but they were all taken or slain; at which, as the report is, the English host made great rejoicings, so

Et lui roy Johan chivacha
Tant que le Prince adevantcea,
Et que l'un host l'autre choisi.   760
Et, à ce que je entendi,
L'un devant l'autre se logerent
Et si très-près se herbergerent
Qu'ils abuvroient, par seint Piere,
Lour chivax à une riviere.   765

Comment le cardinal de Pieregos vint, à briefs mos, oue grant clergie au roy de Fraunce pur faire accord par entre luy et le Prince; et sur ceo oïe et entendue la volunté et avis du roy de France, s'en chivacha le cardinal devers le Prince pur meisme la cause.

Mais là endroit vint, à briefs mos,
Lui cardinal de Pieregos,
Qui amena ovesque lui
Maint clerc et maint legat aussi.

God lead me. The King John rode until he got before the Prince, and one army distinguished the other. And, as I have heard, the one camped before the other, and pitched their tents so near that, by Saint Peter, they watered their horses at the same river.

How, in a few words, the Cardinal of Périgord with many of the clergy came to the King of France to make peace between him and the Prince, and when he had heard the wishes of the King of France, the Cardinal rode to the Prince upon the same errand.

But there then came, in short, the Cardinal of Périgord, who brought with him many of the clergy and

Dount doucement au roy de France 770
Ad dit de humble volunté france :
« Sire, fait-il, pur l'amour Dieu,
Bone parole tient bon lieu.
Car il vous plese à moy lesser
Que je puisse aler chivacher 775
Devers le Prince pur parler
Si hom vous purroit accorder ;
Car certes ceste grant bataille
Tant sera horrible, sanz faille,
Que pité sera et damages 780
Et orgoilles et grantz outrages
Que tant beale creature
Faudra morir de grief mort seure ;
Et si ne poit hom destourner
Morir, defaille à l'assembler : 785
Dount certes countrere en faudra
Cely qui le tort en aura,

---

followers. He spoke pleasantly to the King of France with all humble frankness : « Sire, said he, for the love of God, a good word holds a good place. Then may it please you to suffer me to ride to the Prince to see if it be possible to make peace ; for certes this great battle will doubtless be so horrible, that it will be very pitiful and hurtful, presomptuous and wicked, that so many noble creatures should suffer grievous and certain death ; and if no one can avert death, let him avoid the meeting : then surely against him must be the wrong who

Par devant Dieu au jugement,
Si le Escripture ne ment. »
Dont respondi luy roy Johans : 790
« Cardinal, moult estez sachantz.
Bien voillons que vous y alez ;
Mais sachez et bien entendez
Pais ne ferons en notre vie
Si ne reavons en no baillie 795
Les chastelx et toute la terre
Que puis qu'il vint hors d'Engleterre
Nous ad gasté et exillez
A malveis droit et à peciez,
Et auxi quite la querelle 800
Dont la guerre se renouvelle. »
— « Sire, ce dist lui cardinaus,
Tant ferai que bien serez saus
Et à suffit de votre droit. »
Lors se parti de là endroit. 805

---

shall have done it, before God at the judgment, if the Scriptures lie not. » Upon which King John answered : « Cardinal, you are very wise. We are willing that you should go ; but know and understand thoroughly that we will come to no terms, if we have not restored to us the castles and all the land, that since his arrival from England he has wasted and ravaged in bad faith and sinfully, and also let him abandon the quarrel for which he has renewed the war. » — « Sire, answered the Cardinal, all shall be done for your safety and to the full of your rights. » Then he straightway took his leave.

Coment le Cardinal chivacha du roy de Fraunce vers l'ost du Prince pur entraiter de l'accord avant-dit.

VERS l'ost du Prince chivacha ;
　　Sitost que vers lui arriva,
Moult doucement l'ad salué
Et en plorant par graunt pité :
« Sire, fait-il, pur Dieu merci, 810
Car prendrez ce jour-de-hui merci
De si mainte noble persone
Que au jour-de-hui, c'est la some,
Purroient ci perdre la vie
En yceste graunt estormye. 815
Fetez tant que n'aiez pas tort.
Si hom vous poit mettre d'accort,
Dieux et la Seinte Trinité
Vous en purroit savoir bon gré.

How the Cardinal rode from the King of France to the Prince's camp to treat on the above named matter.

TOWARDS the Prince's army he rode, and as soon as he arrived there, he saluted him kindly, and weeping with great pity, « Sire, said he, for God's mercy, take pity to-day upon so many noble men, that this day, so it is, may lose their lives in this great battle. Believe that you will suffer no wrong. If one might make you agree, God and the Holy Trinity would take it in good part of you.

Coment le Prince respondi au Cardinal sur le traité dudit accord.

Luy Prince dist à coer entieu : 820
« Certes, beaux douce piere en Dieu,
Bien savons que ce que vous dites
Est voirs : ce sont raisons escriptes ;
Mais nous volons bien sustenir
Que notre querel, sanz mentir, 825
Est juste, vraye et veritable.
Bien savez que ce n'est pas fable
Que mon piere, luy roy Edwardz,
Certes estoit le plus droitz hoirs
Pur tenir et pur posseder 830
France, que chescuns doit amer,
Au temps que fut coronez roys
Lui roy Phelippes de Valois ;

How the Prince answered the Cardinal upon the subject of the said treaty.

THE Prince answered with all sincerity : « Certainly, good and holy father, we know well what you say is truth, as Scripture reasoning ; but we will uphold stoutly, that our quarrel without doubt is just, true, and veritable. You know well that this is no invention, that my father King Edward was doubtless the most lawful heir to hold and to possess France, that each should love, from the time when Philip of Valois was crowned King ; but never-

Mais nient contresteant pas ne voil
Que hom die que par mon orgoil   835
Moerge tant bele juvente;
Mais ce n'est mye mon entente
Qu'onques je face le contraire
De la paix, s'hom le pooit faire;
Ainz en feray tout mon pooir.   840
Mais sachez que, tout pur le voir,
Je ne puis pas ceste matiere
Acomplir sanz le roy, mon piere;
Mais respit puis-je bien doner
De mes hommes et accorder   845
Pur partraitier plus de la paix.
S'accorder ne voillent cest faitz,
Je su ci tut prest pur attendre
La grace Dieu, au voir entendre;
Car notre querelle est si vraye   850
Que de combatre ne m'esmaye;

---

theless would I not wish men to say, that through my pride so much good youth was slain; neither is it my intention ever to act contrary to peace, if one can effect it; rather will I use my power to do so. Only know, to speak the truth, that I cannot settle this matter without the King, my father; but I might very well grant a respite to my men, and meet to treat further of peace. If they cannot settle that matter, I am all ready to abide by the will of God, to understand the truth, for our quarrel is so just that I do not fear to

Mais pur destourner le damage
De la mort et le grant outrage,
Le ferai à votre plaisir
Ou gré de mon piere assentir. » 855

Coment lui Cardinal tout en plorant s'en departi du Prince, et retourna par devers le roy de France, et lui fist relacion de la traitié ; et coment sur ceo le roy de France assigna pur sa part evesques et autres seigniours pur en traitier et excuser la bataille.

Luy Cardinal tout en plorant
Se parti de lui maintenant
Et chivacha sanz detriance
Devers le roy Johan de France,
Et ad counté de son attrait ; 860
Et le roy pur alongier le fait
Et pur la bataille excuser,
Fist toutz les barons assembler

---

fight; but to prevent the loss by death and the great outrage, I leave to your pleasure or to the will of my father. »

How the Cardinal all in tears departed from the Prince and returned towards the French King, and related to him the conditions; and how then the King of France appointed, on his part, bishops and other noblemen to treat and avoid the action.

THE Cardinal all in tears now took his departure, and rode without hindrance towards King John of France, and told him of his endeavour ; and the King, to gain more time and to avoid the necessity of a battle, called a

Et mettre ensamble de deux partz.
De parler ne fut pas escars. 865
Là vint le count de Tankerville,
Et, ensi come dit le stille,
Fut luy arcevesque de Sens,
Cils de Thalrus, qui ot grant sens;
Chargny, Buscicaut et Clermont, 870
Toutz ceux illoeques venuz sont.

*Coment autres seigniours englois feurent de par le Prince
ordeignez pur entraitier oue les François dudit accorde.*

Par le conseil du roy de France,
D'autre part par volenté france
Y fut de Warrewick lui counte;
Et, ensi com dit lui acounte, 875
Lui counte de Suffolk y fu,
Qui ot le poil gris et kenu.

---

council of all his barons to consider both sides of the question. He was not sparing of speech. There came the Count de Tancarville, and also, as the list tells us, there was the Archbishop of Sens, him of Talaru, a man of great learning; Chargny, Boucicault, and Clermont, all those were come thither.

How other English lords were appointed by the Prince to treat with the French upon the said truce.

To the council of the French King, on the Prince's part, there came willingly the Earl of Warwick; and also, as the story is, the Earl of Suffolk was there, who had grey

Si fut Bertrem cil de Burghès,
Qui du Prince fut le plus près ;
Si furent Audlée et Chaundos, 880
Qui en ce temps avoient grant los.
Illoeques firent parlement,
Et là chescun dist son talent ;
Mais de lour conseil ne vous say ;
Mais je say bien tout pur verray 885
Qu'ils ne pooient estre d'accort,
Com j'ay oï en mon recort.
Dont chescun de eux s'en departy.
Adonc dist Geffroy de Chargny :
« Seigniour, fait-il, puisqu'ensi est 890
Que cest traitié plus ne vous plest,
J'offre que nous nous combatoms
Cent pur cent, et nous choisiroms
Chescun par devers son costé.
Et bien sachez pur verité 895

---

and hoar hair, Bartholomew de Burghersh was one, who was very dear to the Prince; as were Audeley and Chandos, who at this time acquired great praise. There they made their parliament, and every one spoke his view; but of their counsel I know not, but this I know for truth that they could not agree together, as I have heard in my record. When each of them departed, then said Geoffroy de Chargny : « Lords, said he, since it is so that this treaty pleases you not, I propose that we have a combat, that each on his side select a hundred men ; and let it be

Lequel cent qui sont disconfit,
Tut lui autre, sachez de fit,
De cest champ se departiront
Et la querelle lesseront.
Je croy que le meillour sera 900
Et que Dieux gré nous en saura
Que la journée se deporte
Où tant persone seroit morte.

De la final responce donée à les François par les seigniours englois de la traité, et coment les seigniours du traité, si bien de l'un costé come de l'autre, sount retournez chescun devers son seigniour sanz accorde entre eux fait, et le Cardinal s'en chivacha tout en plorant devers Paitiers.

Et adonques lui respondi
Lui counte de Warwick ensi : 905
« Seigniour, fait-il, quei voillez-vous
Prendre par ce encontre nous ?

---

abided by, that whichever hundred be defeated, their side consider themselves vanquished, and quit the field and thus end the quarrel. I think that so it will be better, and that God will take kindly to us that the days work should so end, than that so many men should fall.

Of the final answer given to the Frenchmen by the English Lords upon the treaty, and how the Lords appointed to treat on either side returned towards their chief without agreeing, and the Cardinal rode all in tears towards Poitiers.

Then answered to him the Earl of Warwick : « Sire, said he, what will you gain by this encounter? You

Bien savez que vous estez plus
Des gentz d'armez et fervestuz
Quatre foitz que nous ne soions, 910
Et votre terre chivachons.
Vez-ci la champaigne et la place.
Chescun qui poet, son meillour face.
Nule autre part je ne seray,
Ne autre jeo n'accorderay. 915
Dieux voille conforter le droit
Où il semble que meillour soit. »
Lors se partent sanz plus parler,
Vers lour host prirent à tourner.
Chescun disoit en son parti : 920
« Cil Cardinal nous ad traï. »
E las ! pur Dieu, mais noun avoit,
Car tout plorant s'en departoit
Et chivachoit devers Paitiers.
Cela lui estoit bien mestiers, 925

---

know well that you have more men at arms and steel clad, by four times than we are, and we are on your territory ; here is the field and the place, let each side do its best. Nowhere else will I be, nor agree to any other conditions. May God defend the right, as it shall seem best to him. » Then they parted without further parley, each returning to his camp ; and on both sides it was said : « This Cardinal has betrayed us. » But alas ! for God it was not so, for he departed all in tears and rode towards Poitiers. This was as he might have expected, for truly there was neither

Car certes il n'avoit bon gré
N'onques grace de nul costé.
Lors ont lour bataille ordeignée
Chescun sanz point de demorée.

Coment le roy de Fraunce assigna le mareschal de Cleremount et plusours autres seigniours, oue iij. mille combatauntz, deux mille servauntz et bien deux mille arblastiers, pur estre en l'avant-garde de son host.

PRIMEREMENT le roy de Fraunce　　　　　930
　　Ad mis sez gents en ordinance
Et dist : « Beau seigniour, par ma foy,
Tant me detrirez, ceo croy,
Que lui Prince m'eschapera.
Cil Cardinal bien traÿ m'a,　　　　　　　935
Qui ci m'ad fait tant demorer. »
Donques commence à apeller

---

good will nor any mercy on either side. Then each without delay set his army in battle array.

How the King of France assigned to the Marshal of Clermont and many other Lords, the advanced guard of his army, with three thousand fighting men, two thousand soldiers and full two thousand cross bowmen.

FIRST the King of France set his men in array, and said : « Good lords, by my faith, the thought vexes me much that the Prince will escape me, this Cardinal who has so stayed our movements has betrayed us. Then began

Le bon mareschaux de Clermont
Et cely d'Audenham, qui mont
Fut en toutz temps à priser,   940
Car en lui ot bon chivaler;
Oue le noble duc d'Ataine,
Qui moult fut noble chieftaine :
« Seigniour, ce dist lui riche rois,
Faitez aprester vos arrois,   945
Car vous serés en l'avant-garde.
C'est votre droit, si Dieux me garde.
Ovesque vous aurez sanz doute
Trois mille hommes de votre route,
Et si aurez ij. mil servauntz   950
A glaives et à dartz trenchantz,
Et bien deux mille arbalastiers,
Qui vous aideront voluntiers.

---

he to summon the good Marshal of Clermont, and he of Audenham, who was much esteemed at all times, for in him he had a good knight; with the noble Duke of Athens who was a right noble chieftain : « My Lord, said the rich King, make ready your array, for you shall be in the van-guard. This is your right, God preserve me! Doubtless you shall have with you three thousand men to your company, and also two thousand soldiers, with swords and cutting darts, and full two thousand cross-bowmen who shall lend you willing aid. Take care if you find the

Gardez si vous Englois trovez,
Ovesque eux vous vous combatez, 955
Et si n'aiés point de deport
Que toutz ne les mettez à mort. »

Coment le roy de Fraunce ordeigna le duc de Normandie, son filz, le duc de Burboyne, et plusours autres seigniours, oue quatre mille combatantz, pur estre en la seconde bataille de son host.

LORS appella à ceste fie
son filtz le duc de Normandie,
Et lui ad dit : « Beau filtz, par foy, 960
Roy de France serés après moy,
Et pur ce auretz-vous sanz faille
La votre seconde bataille ;
Et le noble duc de Burbone
Aurez à votre compaignone, 965

English, that you bring them to action, and show no favour but slay them utterly.

How the King of France appointed the Duke of Normandy, his son, the Duke of Bourbon, with many other Lords and four thousand fighting men, to be the second division of his army.

THEN he at this time summoned his son the Duke of Normandy, and said to him : « Good son, by my faith, you will be King of France after me wherefore doubtless you shall have command of the second division, and the noble Duke of Bourbon you shall have as your companion,

Et le seigniour de Saint-Venant,
Qui ad le coer preu et vaillant.
Le bon Tristan de Magnelers,
Qui moult est noble bachilers,
Il portera votre baniere,   970
Qui est de soie riche et chiere.
N'esparniez jà, pur Jesus-Cris,
Englois, tout soit grantz ne petitz,
Que tout à mort ne les mettez ;
Car je ne voil que si osez   975
Ils soient jammès pur passer
Un soul pé par decea la mer
Pur moy grever ne guerroier,
Ensy les vorray-je arraier. »
Dist lui Dauffyns : « Piere, par foy,   980
Tant ferons, ensi com je croy,
Que votre bon gré en aurons. »
Adonc banieres et peignons

---

with the Lord of Saint-Venant, who has a preux and a valiant heart. The good Tristan de Magnelais, who is a right noble bachelor, shall carry your banner, of rich and precious silk ; spare not, for Jesus Christ, the English, great or small, but slay them utterly ; for I would wish that they may never dare to cross over the sea a single foot to harass and make war upon me : thus then would I see them disposed of. « Father, answered the Dauphin, by my faith, we will so act, that I think we shall have your approval. » Then might you see banners and pennons

Véissez desploier au vent,
Où fin or et aseur resplent, 985
Pourpres et goules et hermynes.
Trompes, taburs, chors et bussynes,
Oïssez parmy l'ost bondir.
Tout faisoit la terre tentir
La grant bataille du Dauffyn. 990
Là ot maint bon chivaler fyn ;
Et ensy, come dist le nombre,
Quatre mille furent en nombre.
D'un des costés sa place prist,
Et moult grant espace comprist. 995
Ensi ad lui le roy devisée
Ceste bataille et ordeignée.

---

unfurled to the wind ; bright shining in gold and azure, purple, gules and ermine. Trumpets, tabors, horns and bassoons, might be heard sounded through the host; the great division of the Dauphin made all the earth ring. There was many a good knight; and also, they were, it is said, four thousand in number; which took their post on one side, occupying a great space. And as the King had appointed, so was this division arranged.

Coment le roy de France ordeigna le riche duc d'Orliens, son frere, oue trois mille combatauntz pur amener l'arere-garde de son host.

Adonc appela, ce est chose clerc,
Le riche duc d'Orliens, son frere :
« Frere, fait-il, si Dieu me garde,   1000
Vous menrez notre arere-garde
Oue trois mille combatantz
De gentz d'armes preus et vaillantz ;
Et gardés bien, pur Dieu mercy,
Que n'aiés jà d'Englois mercy,   1005
Mais les mettez trestoutz à mort :
Car ils nous ont moult fait de tort
Et ars et destruit notre terre
Puis qu'ils partirent d'Engleterre.

How the King of France appointed the rich Duke of Orleans, his brother, with three thousand fighting men, to bring up the rear guard of his army.

Then, as is well known, he called the rich Duke of Orleans, his brother : « Brother, he said, so God keep me, you shall bring up our rear guard with three thousand fighting men, and men at arms preux and valiant ; and take good care, by God's mercy, that you have no pity on the English, but put them all to the sword ; for much wrong have they done us in burning and wasting our land, since they left England. Mind, if you take

Gardez, si le Prince preignez,   1010
Que par devers moy l'amenez. »
— « Sire, ce dist lui riche ducs,
Volentiers et encore plus. »

Coment le roy de Fraunce meismes, ovesque trois de ses filz et plusours countes et autres seigniours au nombre de xxiij. banieres, iiij^c. chivals armez et iiij^c. chivalers desus, armez, furent en la quart bataille illoeques.

ENSEMENT ad lui noble rois
Johan ordeigné ses conrois.   1015
En la quarte bataille fu,
Moult parfut riche sa vertu ;
Ovesque lui trois de ses filtz,
Qui moult furent de très-grant pris.
Le duc d'Anjou, cil de Barry,   1020
Estoit auxi ovesque luy ;

---

the Prince, that you bring him before me. » — « Sire, said the noble Duke, willingly and much more. »

How the King of France himself, with three of his sons and many counts and other noblemen, to the number of twenty-three banners, four hundred armed horses, and four hundred armed knights upon them, made the fourth division of the army.

THUS had the noble King John disposed his army. He himself of right noble valour was in the fourth division with three of his sons, who were of very great courage. The Dukes d'Anjou and de Berry were there also with him;

Et si fut Philip ly Hardys,
Qui moult fu joefnes et petitz,
Là estoit Jaques de Burbon,
Lui count d'Eu, qui ot bon noun,   1025
Et lui counte de Longueville.
Cils deux si estoient, sanz guille,
Filtz à monsieur Robert d'Artois;
Et si estoit à ceste foitz
Lui noble counte de Sansoire   1030
Ovesque lui, ce est chose voire.
Et estoit le count Daunmartyn.
Que vous ferroy-je lonje fyn?
Tant parfut riche ses arroiz,
Car banieres eut vint et trois.   1035
Puis ordeigna à l'autre lez
Bien cccc. chivalx armez
Et cccc. chivalers desus
De trestoutz ses meillours escus.

---

so was Philip the Bold, who was then young and little; there was Jacques de Bourbon, the Count d'Eu of good name, and the Count de Longueville. These were two, without guile, sons of messire Robert d'Artois; and there was with him, at this time, the noble Count de Sancerre as is well known, and so was the Count de Dammartin. But why should I make a long story? so noble was his array, that he had twenty and three banners. Then he drew up on the other side a body of four hundred armed horses, with four hundred knights upon them, all of the noblest

Guychard d'Angle les conduisoit, 1040
Qui noble chivaler estoit,
Et le bon sieur d'Augebugny,
Qui ot le coer preu et hardy;
Et Eustace de Ribemont,
En qui le roy se fioit mont. 1045
Et lour pria sanz alentir
Qu'ils pensassent de bien ferir,
Et qu'ils ne s'esparnassent mie
D'avoir la bataille partie,
Et chescun les sieweroit après, 1050
Qui de bien faire seroit près.
Et chescun lui ad acordé
De bien faire sa volenté.
Là avoit-il tiele noblesse,
Si Dieux me poet doner leesse, 1055

---

escutcheon. Guichard d'Angle was their leader, a noble knight, and the good Lord d'Aubigny, who had a preux and a valiant heart; with Eustache de Ribemont, on whom the King greatly relied. And he prayed them to be nothing slack in dealing out their blows, and to spare no pains to engage the battle, and each one ready to do well would follow. All then assented to do the King's will. There had he such a noble host, so God give me joy, that it was in truth a great marvel : never had men seen

Que ce fut une grant merveille :
Onc hom ne vist tiel appareille
De noblesse ne d'ordinance
Com furent de la part de France.

Coment le Prince mist ses gentz en ordinance pur combatre, et assigna le counte de Warrewik pur l'avant-garde, et le counte de Salesbury pur amener l'arere-garde de son host, et comaunda sire Eustace d'Abrichecourt et le seigniour de Courton à courir pur l'ost françois descouverir; lesquex coururent si avant qu'ils furent pris par les François, et les François en fesoient grant joie.

DE l'autre part, n'en doutez mye,   1060
Fut l'oost des Engloys logie,
Et ensement en celui jour
Lui noble Prince de valour

---

such an array of valour, nor such an ordinance as were there on the side of France.

How the Prince disposed his forces for action, and assigned the vanguard to the Earl of Warwick, and the rear guard to the Earl of Salisbury, and issued orders to Sir Eustace d'Abrichecourt and the Lord Courton to sally out and reconnoitre the French army, who advanced so far, that they were taken by the French, who much rejoiced.

ON the other side do not doubt, the English army was encamped, and also on this day the noble

Mettoit ses gentz en ordinance;
Et voluntiers, à ma semblance,   1065
Vousist la bataille excuser,
Si le pooit avoïder,
Mais bien voit que lui covient faire.
Adonc appela sanz retraire
De Warrewyk le noble counte,   1070
Et très-parfitement lui counte :
« Sire, fait-il, il nous covient
Combatre; et puisqu'ensi avient,
Je vous prie en ceste journée
Aiez l'avant-garde menée.   1075
Lui noble sire de Pomiers,
Qui moult est noble chivalers,
Sera en votre compaignie ;
Et si aurez, je vous affie,
Toutz ses freres ovesque luy,   1080
Qui sont preuz, vaillantz et hardy.

Prince of valour drew it up in battle array; and willingly, as I think, would have been spared the action, could he have avoided it; but he knew well how to act. Then without reserve he summoned the noble Earl of Warwick, and very clearly told him : « Sir, said he, it behoves us to fight; and since it is so, I pray you on this day take command of the vanguard. The noble Lord of Pomiers, who is a right noble knight, shall be in your company ; and you shall have, I assure you, all his brothers with him, who are preux, valiant, and hardy. At first you will cross

Primers passerez le passage
Et garderez le cariage.
Je chevacherai après vous
Ovesque mes chivalers toutz.   1085
En cas qu'à meschief aviendrez,
De nous serez reconfortez;
Et le count de Salesbury
Chivachera après auxi,
Qui menra notre arere-garde;   1090
Et sera chescun sur sa garde,
En cas que ils vous curront sus.
Que chescun à pé descenduz
Soit le plus tost que il purra. »
Et chescun dist qu'il le fera.   1095
Quei vous auroy-je detriée
La matiere et plus destourbée ?
Ensi deviserent la nuyt.
Là n'avoit pas trop grant deduit,

---

the pass and protect our carriages; I shall ride after you with all my knights, so that, if you meet with mischance, you may be reinforced by us; and the Earl of Salisbury shall also ride after me, bringing up our rear guard; and let each be upon his guard, in case they fall upon us. Each may dismount and engage as quickly as he possibly can. » And each said that he would do so. Why should I confuse, or delay further this matter? Thus talking they passed the night. There they had not too much comfort, for each lay in

Car chescun y fesoit enbusche.   1100
Là avoit-il mainte escarmuche ;
Et quant s'en vint à grant matyn,
Lui noble Prince oue coer fyn
En appela à brief mot court
Daun Eustace d'Abrichecourt   1105
Oue le seigniour de Courton,
Qui ot le coer fier com lion,
Et lour comanda à courir
Pur l'ost de François descovrir.
Et chescun prist à chivachier   1110
Mountez sor son noble courser;
Mais, ensi com dist le romant,
Cils deux coururent si avant
Qu'ils furent retenuz et pris :
Dont fut le Prince moult marris,   1115
Et François en fesoient grant joie
Pur lour hoost, si Dieux m'avoie ;

---

ambush, and there was much skirmishing ; and when the morning came, the noble and highly courageous Prince summoned hastily to him Sir Eustace d'Abrichecourt with the Lord Courton, who had a lion's heart ; and commanded them to run and reconnoitre the French army. And each rode off, mounted upon his noble courser ; but, as it is related in the tale, they both advanced so far, that they were taken prisoners, to the great grief of the Prince, and the French host throughout exulted greatly, so God

Et disoient par motz exprès :
« Toutz les autres viendront après. »

Coment la grant huée est comencée, et lui Prince se deslogea et chivacha, et ne quidoit mye cel jour avoir la bataille. Et les François crioient à lour roy à haute vois que les Englois fuyoient ; mais noun fut ensi, et le savoient les François bientost après.

<pre>
A   DONC comença la huée   1120
    Et moult grant noise s'est levée ;
Et lui Prince se deslogea,
A chivacher s'achimina ;
Car celui jour ne quidoit pas
Combatre, je ne vous ment pas ;   1125
Mais il quidoit trestout sans faille
Toutz jours excuser la bataille.
</pre>

---

help me, and said, in so many words : « All the others will come after. »

How the great uproar commenced, and the Prince left his quarters riding, not thinking that on this day the action would take place. And the French cried to their king with a loud voice, that the English fled ; but it was not so, as the French learned soon afterwards.

THEN commenced the uproar, and a mighty noise was stirred up; and the Prince left his quarters, and took a ride; for on this day he did not think to fight, I speak the truth, but thought altogether without fail to be able to avoid the engagement. But on the other side the

Mais de l'autre part les François
S'escrioient à haute vois
Au roy que les Englois fuyoient 1130
Et que par temps les perderoient.
Lors comencent à chivachier
Toutz les François sanz atargier.
Et dist lui mareschaux d'Audenham :
« Certes poi prise votre aham. 1135
Tost aurons les Englois perduz,
Si ne les alons courir sus. »
Dist lui mareschaux de Clermont :
« Bieu frere, vous vous hastez mont.
Ne soiez mie si engrantz, 1140
Car nous y viendrons bien à temps ;
Car Englois ne s'enfuyent pas,
Ainz veignent plus tost que le pas. »
Dist d'Audenham : « Votre demoere
Les nous fera perdre en cele hoere. » 1145

French cried with a loud voice to the king that the English fled, and, if allowed time, might escape. Then began the French to follow them without delay. The Marshal d'Audenham cried : « Certes I little prize your bustle. We shall soon lose the English, if we do not go and fall upon them. » The Marshal de Clermont answered him : « Fair brother, you make too much haste. Be not so excited, we shall be there in good time ; for the English fly not, rather will they presently be here. » — « Your delay at this moment, said d'Audenham, will make us lose them. » Then

Dount dist Clermont : « Par saint Denys,
Mareschaux, moult estez hardys. »
Et puis lui dist par mautalent :
« Jà n'aurez tant de hardement
Qu'aujourd'huy puissez faire tant   1150
Que jà vous soiez si avant
Que la pointe de votre lance
Au cul de mon chival avance. »
Ensi de mautalent espris,
Ont vers Englois lour chemyn pris.   1155

Coment la huée et la noise est levée, et les deux hosts approcherent, et le counte de Salesbury, qui menoit l'arere-garde, assembla tut primerement ; car lui mareschaux vindrent sur lui et lui combatoient moult fortement.

ADONC comença la heuée,
Lui cris et la noise est levée,
Et les hosts prirent approcher.
Adonc de traire et de lancer

---

answered Clermont : « By Saint Denis, Marshal, you are too headstrong; » and then added in ill humour : « But you will never have such hardihood, as to-day to enable you, to be so far in advance, that the point of your lance may reach my horse's croup. » Then with no friendly spirit they took their route towards the foe.

How the uproar and the noise was raised, and the two armies drew near, and the Earl of Salisbury, who brought up the rear guard, first engaged, for the marshals came upon him and fought him very hotly.

THEN began the uproar, the cry and the noise is raised, and the armies begin to draw near. Then began both

Comencerent d'ambedeux partz ; 1160
Nul de eux ne se tenoit escars.
Seiniour, à ce que j'entendi,
Lui francs counte de Salesbury
Du Prince avoit l'arere-garde ;
Mais celui jour, si Dieux me garde, 1165
Assembla tout primerement,
Car plain de ire et de mautalent
Vindrent sur lui li mareschal,
Sachez, à pé et à chival,
Et lui coururent sus par force. 1170
Quant lui countes voit ceste force,
Sa bataille vers eux tourna
Et à haute vois s'escria :
« Avant, seigniour, pur Dieu mercy !
Puis qu'il plest à seint George ensy 1175
Que nous estoiasmes derere,
Et nous seirons tout li primere,

---

sides to draw the bow and throw the lance, nor were either sparing in doing so. Sirs, I have understood, the noble Earl of Salisbury commanded the Prince's rear guard; but on this day, so God save me, he was the first engaged; for the Marshals, full of anger, came down upon him both with horse and foot, and attacked him violently. When the earl saw this force, he turned his division upon them, and cried with a loud voice : « Advance, Sirs, in God's name ! Since it hath pleased Saint George that we who were the rear, should now be the front, let us take care

Façons tant que honour y aions. »
Adonc véissez les barons
De combatre bien esprouver. 1180
Grantz deduitz fut à regarder
Cely que rien n'y conteroit ;
Mais certes grant piece seroit
Et merveillouse chose et dure.
Là avoit meinte creature 1185
Qui celui jour fut mis à fin,
Là combatoient de coer fin,
Archiers traoient à la volée
Plus drut que plume n'est volée,
Qui furent sur les deux costés 1190
Par devers les chivalx armés.
Atant veissez venir poignant
Un chivaler preu et vaillant
Qui appelez fut *Guychard d'Angle*.
Cil ne se boutoit pas en l'angle, 1195

---

to do honourably. » Then might you see the barons acquit themselves well in the combat. Great delight was it to witness, what no words can relate; but surely it was a great pity, a marvellous thing and a desperate. Many a man was there, who on that day met his death. There they fought right nobly. The archers drew their arrows in volleys thicker than ever feather flew before; they were on either side (of the road) by the side of the armed horses. Then might you see coming spurring on a preux and valiant knight Guichard d'Angle by name, who did not put

Ains feroit parmy le meslée,
Sachez, de lance et de espée ;
Et lui mareschal de Clermont
Et Eustace de Ribemont
Et le droit sire d'Aubegny, 1200
Chescun bien luy fesoit auxi.

Coment le counte de Salesbury, oue l'arere-garde, desconfist les mareschaux, et trestouz les armés chivalx devant que l'avant-garde pust estre retournée; et aprés ceo reassemblerent tout ensemble, et approcherent à la bataille du Daufyn au pas d'une hayetie, et là fust desconfitz le Daufyn oue la bataille de Normandie; et les François s'enfuyoient, et plusours de eux furent pris et occis, et lors approcha le roy

---

himself in a corner but struck with lance and sword, know you, amidst the melée. There too was the Marshal de Clermont, and Eustace de Ribemont, and the rightful Sire d'Aubigny, all there acquitted themselves well.

How the Earl of Salisbury with the rear-guard defeated the Marshals and all the armed horses, before the van-guard had returned ; and afterwards the forces joined together, and approached the division of the Dauphin by the side of a hedge, and there was the Dauphin defeated with the army of Normandy; and the French fled, and many of them were taken and slain; and how then advanced the French King

françois oue sa très-graund puissance devers le honurable Prince et son graund host.

<blockquote>

Mais à quoy faire conteroye
La matiere et alongeroye ?
Le roman dist et lui acountes
Que de Salesbury lui countes   1205
Entre lui et ses compaignons,
Qui furent plus fiers que lions,
Desconfirent les mareschalx
Et trestouz les armez chivalx
Devant que poist estre tournée   1210
L'avant-garde et repassée,
Car jà fut outre la riviere ;
Mais au voilloer Dieu et son Piere
Se reassemblerent tout ensemble
Et vindrent, ensi qu'il me semble,   1215
Come gent de noble compaigne
Tut contremont une montaigne

</blockquote>

---

with his immense power towards the noble Prince and his main body.

But why should I relate the matter and lenghten ? The account reports that the Earl of Salisbury by himself and his companions, who were braver than lions, defeated the Marshals with all their armed horses, before the vanguard could repass and return to them, for they were beyond the river; but by the will of God and his Father, they assembled themselves together and came there, as it seems to me, like a noble host up the side of a hill, until

Tant que ils mirent lour trahin
A la bataille du Dauffyn,
Qui fut à pas d'une hayette ; 1220
Et là de volunté entette
Si vont ensemble rencontrer
En fesant d'armes le mestier
Si très-chivalerousement
Que, sachez veritablement, 1225
Grant merveille fut à véir.
Là gaignerent à l'envaïr
Par force le pas de la haye,
Dount maint François à coer s'esmaye,
Et comencerent à tourner 1230
Le dos et à chival mounter.
Là crioit homme à haute gorge
En maint lieu : *Guyane ! Saint George !*
Que voillez-vous que je vous die ?
La bataille de Normandie 1235

---

they brought their course upon the Dauphin's division, which was by the passage of a hedge ; and there with right good will so rushed to the contest, following up so chivalrously their profession of arms, that, know you truly, it was marvellous to behold. There at the first onset they won by assault the hedge pass, whereat the French were sore dismayed and began to turn their back and mount their horses. There men cried with a loud voice in many places : *Guienne ! Saint George !* What would you that I tell you ? The division of Normandy was that morning defeated, and

Fut desconfit à cel matyn,
Et s'en departi le Dauffyn.
Là en éust maint mort et pris,
Et lui noble Prince de pris
Se combatoit moult vaillamment, 1240
Et en reconfortant sa gent
Disoit : « Seigniour, pur Dieu mercy
Pensez du ferir; vetz-me-cy. »
Donc approcha le roy de France,
Qui amenoit sa graund puissance; 1245
Car vers lui se voilloit retraire
Cils qui vouloir out de bien faire.

Coment le Prince voet venir le roy de Fraunce oue son très-grant poer, et plusours Englois furent departiz du Prince pur chacier les François à lour fuitiez pur ceo qu'ils quidoient ce temps qu'ils eussent tut

---

the Dauphin left (the field). On that field were many slain and taken, and the noble and high Prince fought most valiantly, and in encouraging his men said : « Sirs, for God's mercy think of striking; here I am. » Then drew near the French King, who brought up his great forces, for he wished to rally around himself those who were minded to do well.

How the Prince saw the King of France come with his great force, and how many English had left the Prince to follow the French in their flight, because they thought then that all

fait; et lui Prince fist ses prieres à Dieu tout-puissant, et dist : « Avant, baniere ! » Et après ceo comença la mellée, dount Audelée fut ly primer à l'assemblée; et adonc combatoient très-fortement les seigniours englois et les nobles barons de Gascoigne encontre les François; et le Prince en avoit, par la grace de Dieu, la victoire et le roy françois et Philippes, son fiz, oue plusours autres countes et altres seigniours de Fraunce, furent pris par les Englois; et le duc de Burboine et plusours altres seigniours et chivalers et esquiers de Fraunce, à le noumbre de trois mille, furent mortz à cele graunt bataille.

Q<small>UANT</small> lui Prince le vist venir,
Un poi se prist à esbahir
Et regarda environ lui, 1250
Et vist que plusours sont party,

---

was over; and the Prince made his prayers to God Almighty and said : « Advance, banners ! » And after that began the action, at which Audley was the first to engage; and how then there fought stoutly the English lords and the noble barons of Gascony against the French; and how the Prince, by the grace of God, obtained the victory and the King of France and Philip, his son, with many other counts and noblemen of France, were taken by the English; and how the Duke of Bourbon and many other lords and knights and esquires of France, to the number of three thousand, fell at this great battle.

W<small>HEN</small> the Prince saw the French approach, he was a little astonished, and looking about him, saw

Qui furent alez purchasier ;
Car bien quidoient, à voir jugier,
Que ce temps éussent tout fait ;
Mais ore lour accreut le fait : 1255
Car le roy françois s'en venoit,
Qui si grant poair amenoit
Que merveilles fut à veer.
Quant luy Prince vist ce pur voir,
Encontre le cel regarda, 1260
A Jhesus-Crist mercy cria
Et dist ensi : « Piere puissantz,
Ensi come je sui croyantz
Que vous estes roi sur toutz roys
Et que pur nous toutz en la croys 1265
Vousistes la mort endurer
Pur nous hors d'enfer rechatier ;
Piere, qu'ies vrai dieu et vrai homme,
Voillez par votre saintism nomme

---

that many had left him, who had gone off in pursuit ; for they thought, with good reason, that then all was over ; but now fresh work was at hand : for the French King came on bringing with him all his force, which was marvellous to see. When the Prince saw it, in truth, he looked towards heaven, and to Jesus Christ cried for mercy, and said also : « Father Almighty, as I have ever believed that you are King over all kings, and that for us upon the cross you were content to suffer death, to save us from the pains of hell ; Father, who art very God and very man, be pleased

Moi et ma gent garder de mal, 1270
Ensi, vrai Dieux celestial,
Que vous savez que j'ai bon droit. »
Adonc le Prince en là endroit,
Quant il avoit fait sa priere,
A dit : « Avant, avant baniere ! 1275
Chescun pense de son honour. »
Deux chivalers plains de valour
La tenoient de deux costés ;
Moult estoient plains de bontés :
Ceo fut Chaundos et Audlée. 1280
Adonc comença la mellée,
Et Audlée moult doucement
Pria au Prince humblement :
« Sire, fait-il, jà ay voé
A Dieu, et promis et juré, 1285

---

for thy holy name, me and my people to guard from ill; even as, O true heavenly Father, you know that I have a good cause. » Then the Prince straightway, when he had made his prayer, cried : « Advance, advance, banners ! Let each look to his honour. » Two knights full of valour were on each side of him, right full of goodness were they ; they were Chandos and Audley. Then began the melée, and Audley very gently and humbly prayed the Prince : « Sire, said he, I have vowed, promised and sworn to God, that where I shall see in great force

Là où je veray en puissance
La baniere du roy de France,
Que je assembleray le primer,
Si que pur Dieu vous voil prier
Que congié me voillez doner ; 1290
Car il est bien temps d'assembler. »
Adoncques dist lui Prince : « Voir,
James, faites votre vouloir. »
Adonc James se departi
Du Prince, que pluis n'attendi. 1295
Par devant les autres s'avance
Pluis que de longur d'une lance,
Et si fiert sur les enemys
Comme hom corageus et hardys.
Mais gaires ne poet endurer 1300
Qu'à terre lui covient verser:
Là véissez à l'encontrer
Ces grosses launces abaisser

---

the banner of the French King, that I will be the first to engage; so that I would beseech you to give me leave, for it is now time for action. » Then replied the Prince : « Truly, James, have your will. » Upon which James departed from the Prince without farther delay. He went on in advance of the rest of his men more than a lance's length, and so fell upon the enemy like a bold and courageous man. But scarcely could he endure, for to the ground he was overthrown. There might be seen at the encounter the stout lances lowered and thrust on

Et bouter de chescune part.
Chescun en prendoit bien sa part.   1305
Là véissez ferir Chaundos,
Qui ce jour y acquist grant los,
Warrewik et le Despenser,
Montagu qui fut à priser,
Cils de Mawne et cils de Basset,   1310
Qui bien combatoient souvent,
Et monsieur Raoul de Cobehem,
Qui François causa grant ahen ;
Le bon Bartrem de Burgheès,
Qui moult fut hardi en ses fès.   1315
D'autre part combatoient fort
Salesbury et Oxenfort,
Et auxi, ce n'est pas mençoigne,
Lui noble barons de Gascoigne :
Le Captal et cils de Pomiers,   1320
Qui moult fut vaillantz et entiers,

---

either side. Each wanted well to take his part. There might you see Chandos fight, who this day gained great praise, Warwick and le Despenser, Montagu, who was to be praised, the Lords of Mohun and of Basset, who fought well and constantly ; and Sir Ralph de Cobham, who did the French great harm ; the good Bartholomew de Burghersh, a knight of doughty deeds. On the other wing both Salisbury and Oxford fought valiantly, and also, it is not a lie, the noble barons of Gascony : the Captal, with him of Pomiers, who was very valiant and upright; d'Albret,

Labret, Lesparre et Lagoulam,
Fossard et Couchon et Rosain,
Mussiden et cils de Caupayne,
Montferantz, qui sur toutz se payne   1325
Atout son poair de bien faire.
Ces bachilers de noble affaire
Véissez là ferir à tas
Et doner si grantz hatiplas
Que ce fut une grant mervaille.   1330
Là avoit moult grande bataille.
Là véissez maint homme mort.
Longuement dura cest effort
Tant qu'il n'i avoit si hardy
Qu'il n'éust le coer esbahy ;   1335
Mais lui Prince à haute vois
S'est escriez par mainte fois :
« Avant, seigniour, fait-il, pur Dieu !
Gaignons ceste place et cest lieu,

Lesparre and Langoiran, Fossard and Couchon and Rauzan ; Mucidan and him of Caupene ; Montferrant, who above all strove with all his might to acquit himself well. These bachelers of noble lineage might you see there striking right and left, and giving such great blows that it was marvellous to see. This indeed was a great battle, and there died many a man. Long did that struggle last, so that there was none so hardy whose heart was not dismayed; but the Prince with a loud voice many a time cried out: « Sirs, said he, advance for God's sake, let us win this

S'avons counte de notre honour. »　　　　1340
Tant fist le Prince de valour,
Qui tant avoit sens et memoire,
Que vers lui tourna la victoire
Et que ses enemis fuyrent,
Et plusours qui s'en departirent :　　　　1345
Dont luy roy Johan s'escrioit,
Qui vaillamment se combatoit,
Oue lui maint bon chivaler,
Qui bien lui quidoient aider.
Mais la force poi lui vailli ;　　　　1350
Car le Prince tant l'assailli
Que illoeques fut à force pris,
Oue Phelippe auxi, son fitz,
Et monsieur Jakes de Burbon
Et des autres moult graunt fuyson :　　　　1355
Lui counte d'Eu et cil d'Artois
Charles, qui moult estoit curtois ;

---

field, if we regard our honour. » And so wrought the Prince of valour, who had such good sense and memory, that victory turned towards him, and his enemies fled away; many were they who left the field, at which King John who stoutly fought with many good knights around him, who nobly thought to assist him cried aloud ; but his force availed him little, for the Prince so hotly attacked him, that he was there taken prisoner, with Philip also, his son, and messire Jacques de Bourbon, and a great many others ; the Count d'Eu, and him of Artois, Charles, who

Et le bon counte Daunmartyn,
Qui ot le coer loial et fin,
Et le bon counte de Jogny, 1360
Celui de Tankarville auxi,
Et le counte de Salesburce,
Qui pas derere ne se muce,
Et le bon counte de Sansoire,
Ventadour, ce fut chose voire, 1365
Toutz ceux furent pris en cel jour
Et maint haut baneret de honour
Dount je ne puis les nouns nomer.
Mais à ceo que j'oy conter,
Bien en y eut sessante pris, 1370
Countes et baneretz hardis,
Et des autres pluis de trois mille
Dount je ne say dire le stille,
Et, à ce que je entendy,
Morurent là, je vous affy : 1375

---

was right courteous, with the good Count de Dammartin, who had a loyal and fine heart; the good Count de Joigny, with him of Tancarville, and the Earl of Saltsburg who did not hide himself behind, and the good Count of Sancerre, Ventadour, all of whom it is clear were this day taken prisoners, with many a high baneret of honour, whose names I cannot tell. But, as far as I have heard tell, there were over sixty taken, counts and brave banerets, and of others more than three thousand of whom I know not the list : and besides, as I understand, there died on that

De Burbon li noble ducs,
Cils d'Atainnes, qui ot vertus,
Et le mareschal de Clermont,
Matas, Landas et Ribemont,
Oue monsieur Renaud de Pontz, 1380
Et des autres de quoy les nouns
Je ne vous voil mye nomer;
Mais à ce que j'oÿ conter
Et à ce que j'oÿ retraire
Et la matiere sanz retraire, 1385
Bien en y eut iij. mille mortz :
Dieux ait les almes ! car les corps
Furent demorez sur les champs.
Là veoit hom Englois joyantz,
Et crioient à haute gorge 1390
En maint lieu : *Guyane ! Saint George !*
Là véissez François espars
A gaignage de toutes parts,

---

day, I assure you, the noble Duke de Bourbon, the virtuous Duke of Athens, and the Marshal of Clermont, Matas, Landas and Ribemont, with messire Renard de Pons, and others whose names I will not record; but as I have heard it said, and from all I can learn without going further into the matter, there fell more than three thousand men : God have mercy on their souls! for their bodies lay upon the field. There might be seen the English rejoicing and shouting with a loud voice in many places : *Guienne ! Saint George !* There might be seen the French scattered over the field

Véissez courir maint archier,
Maint chivaler, maint esquier,   1395
De toutes parts prisoners prendre.
Ensi furent, à voir entendre,
François celi jour pris et mort,
Sicom j'oÿ en mon recort.

Des mois et jour quant ceste graunt bataille fut faite.

SEIGNOUR, cel temps que je vous dy   1400
Ce fut après que Dieux nasquy
Mille ans trois centz cinquant et sis,
Et auxi, solonc mon avys,
Dis et noef jours droit en Septembre,
Le mois qui est devant Octobre,   1405
Avint ceste grande bataille,
Qui moult fut horrible sanz faille.
Pardonez si j'ay dit briefment,
Car jeo l'ay passé legierment.

---

in all directions; and many archers, knights and esquires, on all sides running taking prisoners. Thus on this day were the French made prisoners and slain, as I have heard recorded.

Of the month and day on which this great battle was fought.

SIRS, the time I speak of was, from the birth of Christ, one thousand three hundred and fifty six years; and, as I am advised, the nineteenth day of September, the month preceeding October, on which was fought this great battle, that was doubtless right terrible. Pardon me if I have told it briefly, for I have passed it over lightly.

*Coment le roy Johan de Fraunce fut amenez devant le
Prince, et le Prince lui fist aider et desarmer; et
doulcement parloient ensemble, et se logerent cel nuit
sur le zabulon entre les mortz, et lendemain au
matin le Prince se deslogea et s'achimina vers
Burdeaux et toute la clergie de Burdeaux vindrent à
procession vers eux; et demorerent à Burdeaux en
très-grant joie tant que l'yver fut passé; et adoncques
le Prince envoia au roy, son piere, et à la roïgne, sa
miere, les novels de son fait et pur avoir vesseaux
pur amener le roy Johan en Engleterre.*

 Mays pur ceo que je voil retraire   1410
 De ce Prince de noble affaire,
Qui moult fut vaillantz et hardis,
Preud'homme et en faitz et en ditz,

---

*How King John of France was brought before the Prince, and
the Prince helped him in taking off his armour; and they
talked kindly together, and lodged there that night upon the
plain amongst the dead; and how the next morning the Prince
removed and marched towards Bordeaux, and all the clergy
of Bordeaux came in procession to meet them; and how they
remained at Bordeaux with much joy until the winter was
passed; and then the Prince sent to the King, his father, and
the Queen, his mother, news of his doings, and (asked) for
ships to convey King John to England.*

But that I may renew my account of this Prince of
noble deed, a Prince so valiant and hardy, good
and wise both in deed and word. Then was there brought

Là fut devant luy amenez
Lui roy Johan, c'est veritez. 1415
Lui Prince moult le festoia,
Qui Dampne-Dieu en gracia ;
Et pur le roy plus honourer
Lui voet aider à desarmer ;
Mais luy roy Johan lui ad dit : 1420
« Beaux dous cosyns, pur Dieu mercit
Laissez : il n'appartient à moy ;
Car par la foy que jeo vous doi,
Plus avez ce jour de huy honour
Qu'onques n'éust prince à un jour. » 1425
Dont dist li Prince : « Sire douls,
Dieux l'ad fait, et non mye nous :
Si l'en devons remercier,
Et de bon coer vers lui prier
Qu'il nous voille ottroier sa gloire 1430
Et pardoner ceste victoire. »

---

before him King John, as is well known, and the Prince entertained him well, and gave thanks to God ; and to do the King more honour, wished to aid in pulling off his armour; but King John said to him : « Good kind cousin, for God's sake, desist, for I have no claim to this; for, by the faith I owe you, you have to-day gained more honour, than ever Prince had in one day. » To which the Prince replied : « Kind Sire, it is the work of God, and not mine : so ought we to thank him, and to pray with all our heart, that he will give us his grace, and pardon this victory. »

Ensi ambedeux devisoient,
Doucement ensemble parloient.
Englois fesoient grant deduit.
Lui Prince logea celle nuit   1435
Entre les mortz, sur le zablon,
Dedeinz un petit pavillon,
Et ses hommes tut entour luy.
Icele noit moult poy dormy,
Le matinet se deslogea,   1440
Devers Burdeaux s'achimina,
Si enmenont lour prisoner
Et tout lui noble chivaler.
Tant ont chivaché et esré
Que à Burdeaux sont arrivé.   1445
Noblement furent festoiez
De tout le poeple et bienveignez.
As crois et as processions
Et en chantant les orisons

Thus on both sides they talked and spoke kindly together. The English then made great rejoicings, and the Prince lodged this night amongst the dead, upon the plain under a small tent, and his men all around him. On this night he slept right little, in the morning he removed, and took the way towards Bordeaux; and so took with them their prisoners and all the noble knights. So fast did they ride and travel, that they arrived at Bordeaux. They were nobly received and welcomed by all the people. With crosses and processions and chanting of orisons, there came to meet

Vindrent tout en l'encontre d'eaux 1450
Tout li college de Burdeaux,
Et les dames et les pucelles,
Vieilles et joefnes et ancelles.
A Burdeaux fist hom tiele joie,
Si luy vray Dieux mon coer esjoye, 1455
Que merveille fut à veoir.
Là demora, sachez pur voir,
Lui Prince passé tout l'iver.
Puis envoia son messagier
Devers le noble roy, son piere, 1460
Et à la roÿne, sa miere,
Et les nouvelles de son fait
Tout ensi que Dieux li ot fait;
Et manda que hom li tramessist,
Vessealx dont amener poïst 1465
Le roy de France en Engleterre
Pur fair pluis de honour à la terre.

---

them all the college of Bordeaux, with dames and damsels old and young with servant maids. Such rejoicings were there at Bordeaux, so may God gladden my heart, that it was marvellous to behold. There the Prince, know you for truth, took up his quarters and remained all the winter. Then he sent his messenger to the noble King, his father, and the Queen, his mother, with tidings of his deeds, all that God had done for him; and asked that vessels should be sent him, to convey the King of France to England, to increase the honour of his country.

Coment le roy d'Engleterre et la roÿgne firent grant joie des novels queux le noble Prince lour avoit maundé, et en loerent Dieu ; et maunderent vesseaux à Burdeaux, et le Prince amena le roy Johan et les autres prisoners en Engleterre, et en maunda novels au roy, son piere, lequel lui vint à l'encontre et les convoia jesques à Loundres ; et là firent très-grantz festes, reveaux et grantz justes, et demenerent grantz dedutz et grant joie par l'espace de quatre ans et plus.

Quant le roy la novelle oÿ,
    Moult grandement s'en esjoÿ,
Loant Dieu en joinant ses mains,   1470
Disant : « Beau Piere soverayns,
De toutz ces biens soiez loez. »
Et la france roïne assetz

How the King of England and the Queen greatly rejoiced at the news which the noble Prince had sent, and praised God, and sent ships to Bordeaux; and the Prince brought King John and the other prisoners to England, and sent news to the King, his father, who came to meet him and conduct them to London, and there made very great festivities, revels and great tournaments; and how great rejoicings continued for the space of four years and more.

When the King heard the news, he was very much delighted, praising God, joining his hands and saying : « Merciful sovereign Father, be thou praised for all thy benefits. » And the noble Queen also praised God

Looit Dieu et la Vierge pure,
Qui luy avoit cele porture   1475
Envoié come de son filtz,
Lui Prince, qui tant fut hardiz.
Le message tost delivrerent,
Vessealx et barges lui manderent,
Tant que ce fut un grant acounte.   1480
Que vous alongeroit l'acounte ?
A Burdeaux vindrent li vessel,
Dount lui Prince fist grant revel.
Gaires ne volt pluis demorer,
Tout son arroy ad fait trusser.   1485
En mer entrerent li baron
Et tout li chivaler de noun;
Le roy et toutz les prisoners,
De ceaux dont il lour fut mestiers,
Firent eins les vessealx entrer.   1490
Tant siglerent, à voir counter,

---

and the pure Virgin, who had sent her this blessing, namely the Prince, her son, who was so hardy. The message soon they delivered and sent him ships and barges; so that it would be a long story. Why would I lengthen the account? At Bordeaux the ships arrived, whereat the Prince made great rejoicing. Scarcely would he longer delay, he caused to load all his array. The barons and all the knights of name, the King and all the prisoners, whom they wanted, they caused to enter into the ships. They sailed so prosperously, to tell the truth, that they

Qu'ils sont venuz en Engleterre ;
Et sitost qu'ils ont pris la terre,
Au roy manderent les novelles,
Queux li furent bones et beles ;   1495
A l'encontre lui fist mander
Toutz ses barons pur honorer.
Lui-méismes soi corps y vint,
Oue lui countes pluis que vint.
Jesques à Loundres convoierent   1500
Lui Prince, que li festoierent.
Là furent-ils bien festoiez
Des dames, et si bienveignez
Qu'onques ne fut fait tiele joie,
Si lui vray Dieu mon coer esjoye,   1505
Come elle fut fait à ce temps.
Là fut lui noble roy puissants
Et la roÿne, sa muliere,
Et sa miere, qu'il ot moult chiere ;

---

arrived safely in England ; and so soon as they had landed, they sent to the King the news, that were good and fair to him. He ordered all his barons to meet him, as a mark of honour. He came in his own person, and with him more than twenty earls ; they escorted the Prince, whom they greeted, to London. There were they well entertained by the ladies and so welcomed, that never, so the true God glad my heart, was there such rejoicing shown, as was made at this time. There was the noble powerful King, with the Queen, his wife, and his mother, whom he held right dear;

Mainte dame et mainte damsele, 1510
Très-amoureuse, frike et bele,
Dancer et chasier et voler,
Faire grantz festes et juster,
Faisoient eu regne d'Artus
L'espace de quatre ans ou plus. 1515

Coment le roy d'Engleterre refist un voiage en Fraunce ovesque son baronage et lui noble Prince et ducs Henry et des autres plus de dis mille, et chivacha parmy Artoys et plusours pays de Fraunce jesques devant Parys; et là furent logés sur les champs, mais ne combatoient mye, ainz tournerent lour chivachie par devant Chartres, où la pays fut accordée et puis jurée, et le roy Johan de Fraunce fut delivré, et tout Guiane par celle pais fut surrendue et

---

they caused many a dame and damsel, very lovely, frisky and fair, to dance and hunt and hawk, and make great festivities and jousts, as in the reign of Arthur for the space of four years or more.

How the King of England made another expedition into France, with his barons and the noble Prince and Duke Henry and more than ten thousand others, and rode through Artois and many provinces of France as far as Paris; and there were encamped in the fields, but came to no engagement; then they changed their route for Chartres, where peace was agreed and sworn to. And how King John was set at liberty, and all Guienne by this peace was surrendered to the hands of the

*livrée es mains du roy d'Engleterre et du Prince,
son filtz.*

Puis refist lui roys un voiage
En France ovesque son barnage,
Et li noble Prince autresi,
Et de Lancastre ducs Henri,
Et des autres plus de x. mille   1520
Dont je ne voil dire le stille ;
Car c'est droit que je me delivre ;
Mais, ensi come dit le livre,
Il chivacha parmy Artois
Et Pikardie et Vermendois,   1525
Et Champaigne, Burgoine et Brie,
Parmy Bayon, je vous affie,
Et vint jesques devant Parys.
Là fut le noble roy de pris

King of England and the Prince, his son.

THEN the King, with his nobles, made again an expedition into France, with the noble Prince, his son, and Henry, Duke of Lancaster, and more than ten thousand others, whose names I will not record, as it behoves me to proceed; but, as the report says, he rode through Artois, Picardy and Vermandois, Champagne, Burgundy and Brie, through Boulogne, I assure you, till he came as far as before Paris. There was the noble King of worth with the

Et lui noble Prince vaillantz. 1530
Là furent logez sur les champs,
Et embataillez pur combatre,
De cela ne poet hom debatre ;
Mais ils ne combatirent mye.
Puis tournerent lour chivachie 1535
Devant Chartres. Là accordée
Fut la paix que puis fut jurée ;
Et là fut en cette paix faire
Li Prince de très-noble affaire,
Car par li et par son enhort 1540
Furent les nobles roys d'accord,
Et fut delivrés de prison
Luy roy Johan, qui ot grant noun ;
Et là fut par la paix baillie
Toute Guyane en la baillie 1545
Du noble [roy] et de son filtz,
Li Prince, qui tant fut hardiz.

---

valiant Prince. There were they encamped on the fields, and drawn up in battle array, this can no man gainsay ; but no engagement took place. Then they altered their line of march before Chartres. There was agreed to a peace, which was then sworn to, and in concluding this peace the noble Prince had much to do, for through him and his persuasion, were the noble Kings agreed; and King John of great renown was set free from prison. And by that peace, all Guienne was delivered to the power of the noble [King] and his son, a prince of so hardy courage.

Et celle paix que je vous di
Ce fut en l'an que Dieux nasqui,
Mil trois centz ovesque sessante, 1550
Au temps que le russinol chante,
Oep jours en joli mois de may,
Que oiseux ne sont pas en esmay.

Coment le roy d'Engleterre et le Prince, oue tout poer, s'en retournerent en Engleterre; et après furent les deux roys ensemble à Caleis, et ly Prince et touz les barons et chivalers de noun si bien de l'un roialme com del altre, et là jurerent la paix d'ambedeux parties saunz jammés renoveler la guerre; et après ce chescun s'en retourna hastivement à soun pays.

EN Engleterre s'en tournerent
Et lour grant arroy amenerent. 1555

And this peace, of which I tell you, was concluded in the year from Christ's birth, one thousand three hundred and sixty, at the time when the nightingale sings, on the eighth of the merry month of May, when the birds are no longer in dismay.

How the King of England and the Prince, with their forces, returned to England; and afterwards both Kings met at Calais, and the Prince and all his barons and knights of name, as well of the one kingdom as the other, swore there on both sides to observe the peace and not renew the war; and how afterwards each returned quickly to his own country.

To England they then returned, and brought with them their great array. Right nobly and right well did

Moult noble feste lour fist-hom,
Et moult bien les festoia hom.
Après le jour de la Toussains,
Droit en ce temps, je suis certains,
Furent toutz les deux roys ensemble   1560
A Caleis, ensi qu'il me semble,
Lui Prince oue toutz li baron
Et toutz li chivaler de noun,
De tout le roialme d'Engleterre
Et auxi bien, à voir retrere,   1565
De tout le roialme de France.
Là furent de volenté france.
Là jura chescun sur le livre
Et auxi bien tout à delivre
Sur le saint digne sacrement   1570
Que la paix tout principalment
Tiendroient sanz jamès fauxcer
Et sanz guerre renoveler.

---

their countrymen entertain them. After the day of All Saints just at this time, I know well, both Kings met together at Calais, as it seems to me, the Prince with all the barons and all the knights of name, of all the realm of England, and so also, to relate the truth, of all the realm of France. There were they with good will. There each swore upon the book, and also without reserve upon the holy worthy sacrament, that he would keep faithfully all the terms agreed on, without ever playing false and renewing the

Ensi d'accord furent tout doy
Par paix fesant lui noble roy. 1575
Le roy de Fraunce s'en reala,
Qui pluis gaires ne demora;
Et li roy vint en Engleterre,
Et lui Prince de noble affere;
A graunt joie s'en retournerent 1580
Et les hostages enmenerent.
Quei vous ferroy-je un long acounte
De ce dont hom doit faire counte?

Coment le noble Prince se maria à une dame de grant pris. Aprés ce s'en ala ladite dame ovesque luy en Gascoigne, et là prist possessioun de la terre et du païs, et illoeques regna par vij. ans, et tenoit moult grand et beal hostel, et fist grauntz justes et

---

war. Thus were both the noble Kings agreed in concluding peace. Then the King of France with scarce any delay returned home; and the noble King came into England with the Prince of noble deportment; with great joy they came back and brought their hostages with them. Why should I make a long story of what all men ought to know?

How the noble Prince married a lady of great worth. Afterwards he went with her into Gascony, and took possession of all the country; and there reigned seven years, shewing very great and courteous hospitality, and made great jousts and revels,

reveaux, et là avoit deux filz; et touz les barouns et seignours de Gascoigne à lui venoient, et lui fesoient hommage, et de bon coer l'amoient.

Après gaires ne demora,
Luy francs Prince se maria, 1585
A une dame de grant pris
Qui de s'amour l'avoit espris,
Que bele fut, plesante et sage.
Et après celui mariage
Ne volt gaires plùis atargier, 1590
Ains s'en ala sanz detrier
En Gascoigne encontre saisson
Pur prendre la possession
De sa terre et de son païs.
Li Prince, qui tant fut gentils, 1595
Sa mullier ovesque li mena,
Pur ce que durement l'ama.

---

and there he had two sons; and all the barons and nobles of Gascony came to him and did homage, and loved him heartily.

Almost immediately afterwards, the noble Prince married a lady of great worth, who had won his affection, and was lovely, agreeable and wise. And after this marriage he would no longer tarry, but without any delay went into Gascony, in the wrong season, to take possession of his territory and his country. The Prince, who was so gentle, took with him his wife, because he dearly

De sa mullier ot deux enfants;
En Gascoigne regna vij. ans
En joye, en pais et en solas.   1600
Ore ne vous mentiray pas,
Quar tout li Prince et lui baron
De tout le pays environ
Vindrent à lui pur faire hommage.
A bon seigneur loyal et sage   1605
Le tenoient communalment;
Et j'ose dire proprement
Que puis le temps que Dieux fut nez
Ne fut tenuz si beaux hostez
Come il fist, ne plus honorable,   1610
Car toutz jours avoit à sa table
Plus de iiij.xx. chivaliers
Et bien quatre tantz esquiers.
Là fesoient justes et reveaux
En Anguileme et à Burdeaux.   1615

---

loved her. He had by his wife two children; in Gascony he reigned seven years in joy, peace and quietness. Now I will tell you no untruth; for all the lords and barons of all the neighbouring country came to him to render homage. They looked upon him with one feeling as a good lord, loyal and wise, and I may truly say that since the birth of Christ, never was such good entertainment nor more honourable than then; for every day at his table he had more than eighty knights, and four times as many esquires. There made they jousts and revels in Angoulême

Là demuroit toute noblesse,
Toute joie et toute leesse,
Largesse, franchise et honour.
Et l'amoient de bon amour
Tout si subgit et tout li sien,   1620
Car il lour fesoit moult de bien.
Moult le prisoient et amoient
Cils qui entour lui demoroient,
Car largesse le sustenoit
Et noblesse le gouvernoit,   1625
Sens et temperance et droiture
Rayson et justice et mesure.
Homme poet dire par raisoun
Que tiel Prince ne trouvast-hom,
Qui alast serchier tout le monde   1630
Sicome il torne à la reounde.
Li veisin et li enemy
Avoient grant doute de ly;

---

and Bordeaux. There was found all nobleness, all joy and merriment, bounty, freedom and honour. And all his lieges and his people loved him passionately, for he did them much good. Those who were about his person valued and loved him much, for liberality was his staff and nobleness his director; judgment (had he), temperance and uprightness, reason, equity and moderation. Rightly might men say, that search the whole world, as it turns round, you could find no such Prince. Both neighbours and enemies had great awe of him; for so high was his

Car tant fut haute sa vaillance
Que partout regnoit en puissance, 1635
Si que hom ne doit mye ses faitz
Oblier en ditz ne en faitz.
Or n'est pas raison que je faigne
D'un noble voiage d'Espaigne;
Mais bien est raisons que hom l'emprise : 1640
Car ce fut la plus noble emprise
Que onques cristiens emprist,
Car par force en son lieu remist
Un roy qu'avoit desherité
Son frere bastard et maisné, 1645
Ensi comme vous purrez oïr,
S'un poy vous voillietz escoultir.

Coment par la bataille en Bretaigne le duc avoit conquis et gaigné sa terre et la puissance d'Engleterre,

---

courage, that he reigned everywhere in power so that men ought never to forget him either in deed or in word. Nor is there any reason that I should pass over a noble expedition into Spain; but it is right that men praise him for it, for it was the most noble expedition ever undertaken by Christian men; for by his power he restored to his place a king whom his younger and bastard brother had disinherited, as you shall also hear, if you will attend a little.

How by the battle in Britanny and the English power the Duke had gained possession of his land, and Charles de Blois and

et Charles de Blois et autres seignours furent occis, et monsieur Bertrem Klaykyn et plusours altres vaillants furent pris à meisme la bataille.

ORE est bien temps de comencer
Ma matiere, et moy addresser
Au purpos où je voil venir,   1650
A ce que je vys avenir
Après la bataille en Britaine,
Que le duc ovesque sa compaine
Conquesta et gaigna sa terre
Par la puissance d'Engleterre.   1655
Et là fut mort Charles de Blois
Et maint baron noble et curtoys
Et de France et de Pikardie,
De haute et puissante lignie.
Là fut messire Bertram pris   1660
De Claykyn, qui ot grant pris,

---

other nobles were killed, and Messire Bertrand du Guesclin and several other valiant men were taken in the same action.

Now it is good time that I commence my narrative, and address myself to the point I would arrive at, to what I saw take place after the battle in Britanny, where the Duke with his company, by the might of England, conquered and gained possession of his territory. And there died Charles de Blois with many a noble and courteous baron, both of France and Picardy, of high and noble lineage. There was taken prisoner Messire Bertrand du Guesclin, who had great worth, and many of high

Et maint haut baron de parage
De noble et de puissant linage,
Dount je ne voil les nouns nommer,
Car trop me purroie tarder 1665
A revenir à mon purpos ;
Et pur pluis abregier mes motz,

Coment après la bataille en Britaigne monsieur Bertrem de Claykyn traist hors du roialme de Fraunce la grande compaignie et plusours altres chivalers et esquiers pur faire voiage ès parties d'Espaigne à cause de la guerre qu'avoit longement duré entre Espaigne et Aragon, et pur faire paix entre les deux roys par gré du pape.

Vous savez que monsieur Bertrans,
    Qui moult fut hardi et vaillantz,
Traist hors du roialme de France 1670
Par sa proesce et sa puissance

---

rank and noble and powerful birth, whose names I will not record, for it would delay me too long. To return to my story; and to farther abridge my words,

How after the battle in Britanny, Messire Bertrand du Guesclin led out of the realm of France his great company and many other knights and esquires, to make an excursion into parts of Spain, on account of a war which had long lasted between Spain and Aragon, and to make peace between the two kings, by the Pope's will.

You know that Messire Bertrand, who was right hardy and valiant, led forth from the realm of France by his

Toute la grande compaignie
Et moult de la chivacherye
Par le gré du pape de Rome;
Et fist à li aler maint homme, 1675
Barons et bachilers et countes,
Chivalers, esquiers, viscontes.
Au temps que je fay mencion,
Entre Espaigne et entre Aragon
Avoit guerre moult merveillouse, 1680
Que avoit duré moult cruose
Le temps que xiiij. ans et plus.
Et pur ytant fut esléus
Messire Bertram de Claykyn,
Qui ot le coer hardi et fyn; 1685
Et le bon Jacque de Burbon,
Qui counte de la Marche ot noun;
Et d'Audenham le mareschal,
Qui ot le coer preu et loial;

---

prowess and power all the great company and many knights, agreeably to the will of the Pope of Rome; and made many accompany him, barons and bachelors and counts, knights, esquires and viscounts. At the time I speak of, a very marvellous war was carried on between Spain and Aragon, that had lasted, with much bloodshed, for fourteen years and more. And for this undertaking were chosen Messire Bertrand du Guesclin, who had a heart hardy and bold; the good Jacques de Bourbon, whose title was Count de la Marche, with d'Audenham the marshall, who had a heart

Eustace de Abrichecourt, 1690
Qui fut homme de noble court;
Monsieur Hugh de Calvelée,
Qui voluntiers fiert de l'espée;
Et monsieur Maheu de Gournay
Et maint autre chivaler vray,. 1695
Qu'ils iroient en ce païs
Et feroient par lour grant pris,
Que paix seroit entre les roys,
Et que le pays et destroys
Feroient de Gernade ouvrir, 1700
Et que pur aler conquerir
Purroient tant homme de bien
Et tant bon seigneur terrien.
Ensi furent-ils toutz d'accord.
Quei vous feroy-jeo long record ? 1705
Pur celle accord prist grant argent
Dans Bertrem et toute sa gent.

---

valiant and loyal; Eustace d'Abrichecourt, a man of high nobility, Sir Hugh de Calverley, who willingly struck with the sword; and Sir Mathew de Gournay, with many other true knights, who all went into this land; and thought by their high worth to make peace between the kings, and to open the country and the passes to Granada ; and that so many good knights and so many lords of the land might go and conquer it. Thus were they all agreed. Why should I make a long story ? For this alliance did Messire Bertrand and his people receive much pay.

Coment monsieur Bertrem Claykyn et sa compaignie passerent les ports de Aragon, et ont maundé au roy Petre de Castille la novelle et qu'il vousist overir la passage qu'ils purroient aler en une sainte voiage desus les enemys Deu; et le roy en avoit indignacioune, et se apparailla pur defendre sa terre et pur contrester la compaignie; mais ils entrerent en Espaigne: dount le roy Petre fut coroucez, et disoit qu'il emprendroit vengeance, mais bientost après le roy Petre par grant desloialté fut ousté de sa regalie, et s'enfuit hors de soun roialme, et ceux de Castille coronerent le bastard Henry roy de Espaigne.

Q UANT orent lour voie acoillie,
    Ly et toute sa compaignie
Les ports passerent d'Aragon,   1710
Et puis en bien courte faisson

How Messire Bertrand du Guesclin and his company passed the defiles of Aragon, and the tidings were sent to Pedro, King of Castile, that he should open the pass that they might go on pilgrimage against the enemies of God; and the King was wroth, and set himself to defend his country and resist the company; but they entered into Spain: whereat King Pedro was much enraged, and said that he would take vengeance; but soon after was the King Pedro most disloyally ousted from his throne and fled from his kingdom, and they of Castile crowned Enrique the bastard, king of Spain.

W HEN Messire Bertrand and his company had entered
    on their way, they passed the defiles of Aragon, and

Manderent au roy de Castelle
Par un messager la novelle
Coment il vousist accorder
Le pays d'Aragon, et jurer 1715
Qu'il voille overir la passage
Pur entrer en un saint voiage
Desus les enemis de Dieu,
Où tut bon fait d'armes ait lieu.
Cil, qui fut orgoillous et fiers, 1720
Et qui poy cremoit les daungiers
Auxi ne de ceux ne d'autrui,
En prist en son coer grant anui,
Et dit que poy se priseroit
S'envers ceux gentz obéissoit. 1725
Lors fist assembler son effort
Et si l'apparailla moult fort,

---

then in very short terms sent to the King of Castile by a messenger these tidings, how he would grant peace to the country of Aragon, and swear that he would open the passage for to admit a holy expedition against the enemies of God, in which every good feat of arms had place. He, who was both proud and fierce, and who little feared danger, neither from one side or the other, took it much to heart, and said that he should little esteem himself if he yielded to those people. Then he gathered his forces together, and set them right stoutly to defend his

Pur defendre le soen païs.
Lors manda et grantz et petitz,
Gentilx hommes, franks et vileyns,   1730
Et bien quidoit estre certeyns
D'encontre eux sa terre defendre.
Beaux douls seigniour, voillez entendre.
Englois et François et Breton,
Normands et Pikards et Gascons   1735
Entrerent toutz dedeins Espaigne.
Auxi fist la grande compaigne.
Le bon de Calverlée Hugon
Et Gourney, le soen compaignoun,
Et maint bon chivaler hardy   1740
Passerent là sanz nul detry,
Et conquistrent par lour emprise
Toute la terre que conquise
Avoit lui roy Petre jadys.
Moult en fut en son coer malys   1745

---

territory; he summoned great and small, gentle men, free and villeins, and thought himself well able to defend his land against them. Very kind sirs, ye shall hear. English and French and Bretons, Normans, Picards, Gascons, all entered into Spain, and so made there the great company. The good Hugh de Calverley, and Gournay, his companion, with many good valiant knights passed there without any delay, and by their emprise gained all the country that King Pedro had formerly acquired. Much pain had in his

Dan Petre d'Espaigne lui roys;
Dist qu'il ne se prise une nois
Si de tout ce n'en prist vengeance.
Mais poi li vailli sa puissance,
Car n'y ot pas un mois passé   1750
Que par la grant desloialté
De ceux qui li doient servir
Lui covient d'Espaigne partir
Et deguerpir son grant roial,
Car toutz lui furent disloial   1755
Cils qui le devoient amer :
Si que hom doit dire, à voir counter,
Ne doit estre sires clamez
Qui de ses hommes n'est amez.
Apparant est par celi roy,   1760
Qui tant estoit de fier arroy
Qu'il n'avoit doubte de nul homme,
Mais quidoit bien, ce est la somme,

---

heart Don Pedro, King of Spain; he said that he held himself nought, if he took not vengeance for all this. But little availed his power; for scarce did a month elapse, before by the great disloyalty of those who should have served him, he was forced to quit Spain and abandon his great realm; for all those who should have loved him, proved disloyal : so that men might say, to speak truth, that one should not be called lord, who is not loved by his subjects. That is clear in the case of this king, who had so formidable an array that he had fear of no man ; but

Que nul grever ne li peust
Pur grant puissance qu'il eust.   1770
Mais il ne fut gaires de temps
Qu'il n'avoit amis ne parents,
Cosyn germeyn, uncle ne frere,
Que de lui ne se desappere.
Son frere bastard coronerent,   1770
Toute la terre li donerent,
Et toutz li tindrent à seignour
En Castille, grant et minour.

Coment le roy Daun Petre s'en ala vers Seville, et là fist trusser son tresour en mer, et tant sigla qu'il vint au port de Calonge sur la mer, et le bastard chivacha parmy Castille, et prist possessioun des cités et hommages des seigniours de la terre, lesqueux touz s'accor-

---

thought clearly that none could grieve him for the vast power that he had. But scarcely did any time elapse, ere he had neither friend nor parent, cousin-german, uncle or brother, who had not left him. They crowned his bastard brother, and gave him all the land; and all in Castile, great and small, held him as their lord.

How the king Don Pedro took his route towards Seville, and there packing up his treasure put to sea, and so sailed that he came to the port of Corunna on the sea; and how the bastard rode through Castile, and took possession of the cities, receiving homage of the lords of the land, all of whom agreed that

*derent que Henri seroit roy de Castille, horpris un
loial et vaillant chivaler, qui fut appelez* Ferant de
Castres.

A quoi faire vous celeroie
La matiere et alongeroie ? 1775
Dan Pedre n'osa plus attendre,
Ainz s'en ala, à voir entendre,
Trestout droit à Seville, lors
Où demoré fut ses tresors.
Niefs et galayes fist tourser, 1780
Et son tresour y fist porter.
Hastivement en mer se mist,
Sicome la matiere dist ;
De jour et de noit tant sigla
Qu'au port de Calonge arriva, 1785
Lequel si est dedeinz Galice.
Et le bastard ne fut pas nyce ;

Enrique should be king of Castile, except one loyal and valiant knight, who was called Fernando de Castro.

WHY should I continue to relate the matter at length? Don Pedro dared no longer wait, but went, to understand the truth, direct to Seville, where then were deposited all his treasures. He caused to load ships and galleys, and placed in them his treasure. He put to sea in haste, as it is said ; sailed day and night till he reached the port of Corunna, which is in Gallicia. Nor was the

Parmy Castille chivacha.
Unques cité n'y demora
Dount il n'éust possession. 1790
N'y remist counte ne baron
Que toutz ne li firent hommage,
Fors que un soul qu'homme tint à sage.
Ferant de Castres l'appeloient
Par noun cils qui le conissoient. 1795
Moult parfut vaillantz et gentieux,
Et jura, si li vailli Dieux,
Que jà jour ne relinqueroit
Cely qui estoit roy de droit;
Et si toutz faire le voilloient 1800
Cils qui le pooir en avoient,
Si ne purroit-il consentir
Un bastard roialme tenir.
Mais toutz les autres du païs
S'accorderent tout que Henris 1805

---

bastard wanting, but rode through Castile; nor was any city left, of which he took not possession. Nor did there count or baron demur to tender him their homage, save only one, who was deemed wise. *Fernando de Castro* was he called by name by those who knew him. Right valiant he was and generous, and swore, so God help him, never would he desert him who was king by right; and if all the rest who had the power chose to do this, yet could not he consent that a bastard should hold the kingdom. But all the others of the country were of one accord that Enrique

Le demorast roy de Castille
Et de Toulette et de Seville,
De Cordual et de Lions,
Par l'accord de toutz les barons.
Ensi fut Castille conquise   1810
Par la puissance et par l'emprise
De monsieur Bartram de Claykyn.
Ore purrez-vous oïr la fyn
Coment depuis ce jour avint,
Ne passa mye des ans vint.   1815

Coment le roy Petre estant à Calonge sur la mer, moult dolentz des adversités queux lui sount avenuz, se souvint qu'il avoit alliances ovesque le roy d'Engle-

---

should remain king of Castile, of Toledo and of Seville, of Cordova and of Leon, by the will of all the barons. Thus was Castile conquered by the power and the emprise of Messire Bertrand du Guesclin. Thus you will be able to hear the end, how from the day it took place, not more than twenty years have passed.

How King Pedro was at Coruña on the sea, bewailing the ill fortune that had befallen him, when he remembered that he had an alliance with the King of England, and applied for

terre et s'appointa par lui et sa puissance bien estre socouruz et de ses dolours amers relevez.

Or comence noble matiere
  De noble et puissante mestiere;
Car pité, amour et droiture
Mist ensemble sa noriture,
Ensi com vous purrez oïr.   1820
Bien m'avez oï gestier
La matiere de par devant.
Moult fut le roy Petre dolant,
A la Calonge sur la mer,
Et plein de dolorouse amer;   1825
Car cils lui avoient failli
Qui li devoient estre amy.
Moult parestoit plein de tristour,
Et ne scieut aviser quel tour

---

succour from him and his forces, and how his bitter grief was relieved.

Now commences the noble subject of a great and mighty matter; for pity, love and uprightness together attended his education, as you shall also hear. Rightly have you heard me tell in rhyme what had happened before. Very sad was Don Pedro at Coruña on the sea, and filled with bitter grief; for they had failed him who should have been his friends. Full sad then was he there, nor knew which way to turn, where he might find succour

Dont il poïst socours avoir 1830
Ne pur or fin ne pur avoir.
Un jour fut lui roys avisez
Qu'alliances et amistés
Avoit éu de moult long temps,
Dont bien se tenoit pur contens, 1835
Ovesque lui roy d'Engleterre,
Qui tant estoit de noble affaire
Que Dieux lui ot doné vertus,
Que puis le temps le roy Artus
Ne fut roy de tiele puissance. 1840
Et si pur ycelle alliance
Et pur amour et pur linage
Et pur Dieu et pur vasselage
Le voilloit faire socourir,
Unquore li purroit garir. 1845

---

either for fine gold or for property. One day the King was advised that he had for a very long time alliance and friendship, with which he was well content, with the King of England, who was of so noble a deportment, and endowed with such power, that since the time of Arthur, never was there king of such might. For this alliance sake, then, for friendship and parentage, for God and his prowess sake, he wished to gain his assistance that he might warrant him.

Coment le roy Petre appela à lui son conseil, et Ferant de Castres ly conseilla d'envoier al Prince et de lui requerir des socours.

L ORS ad son conseil appelé
  Et la matier lour ad monstré,
Et chescun dist qu'il disoit bien.
Adonc un seigniour terrien
Parla, qui moult fut plain d'avys,   1850
Ferant de Castres lui gentils ;
Et dist : « Sire, entendez à moy.
Par celle foy que je vous doi,
Tout primers, si vous m'en croiés,
Au Prince droit vous manderez   1855
D'Aquitaine, qui est ses filtz.
Moult parest prudhomme et hardiz
Et des gentz d'armes si puissant
Que je croy qu'il n'est hom vivant

How King Pedro summoned his council, and Fernando de Castro advised him to send to the Prince and request of him succour.

T HEN he summoned his council and laid before them
  the matter, and each thought that he said well. Then a noble landed lord, a man full of good counsel, Fernando de Castro the gentle, spoke and said : « Sire, give heed to me. By that faith I owe you, at once, if you believe me, send straightway to the Prince of Aquitaine, who is his son. A man right preux and hardy is he, and so strong in men-at-arms, that there is no man living, save God alone,

Fors que Dieu, qui li fesist tort ; 1860
Et si vous luy trovés d'accort
De vous aider, soiez certains
Qu'Espayn raverez en vos mains
Avant que cest an soit passé. »
A tout ce fut bien accordé. 1865

Coment le roy daun Petre escript ses lettres au Prince en ly requerant à ses bons socours et que ly plerroit d'envoier niefs pur lui emparler, et envoia ses messages oue meisme lettyrr.

Daun Petre, le roy de Castille,
Erraument escript et secille,
Empriant au Prince humblement
Que pur Dieu tut primerement

---

who can wrong him. And if you find him ready to help you, be certain that you will again have Spain in your hands, before this year is over. » To all this it was well agreed.

How the King Don Pedro wrote his letter to the Prince, seeking his good help, and asking him to send ships to confer with him, and sent his messengers with the letters.

Don Pedro, the King of Castile, wrote immediately, and sealed his letter, humbly entreating the Prince, that

Et pur amour et pur pité, 1870
Pur alliance et pur amisté,
Et pur cas de linage auxi,
Et pur droit qu'il ad sanz nul si,
A très-noble Prince puissant,
Honorable, preu et vaillant, 1875
Qu'il lui plese à socourir
Droiture, et li qui requerir
Ly voet en noun de pacience ;
Et qu'il vousist par sa vaillance
Envoier niefs pur ly passer 1880
Et pur lui salvement mener,
Car il voleit parler à lui.
Li messages vint sanz detri.

Coment ly messages du roy Petre trova le Prince à Burdeaux et luy ad presenté les lettres, et le Prince

---

for God's sake first, for love and for pity, for the alliance and for friendship, and for relationship and for the right which he had without any objection, to the right noble Prince, honourable, preux, and valiant, for it was his pleasure to aid the right, and him who asked it on the plea of suffering; also that he would by his own power send ships for his passage, and to convey him in safety, for he wished to confer with him. The messenger went without delay.

How the messenger of King Pedro found the Prince at Bordeaux, and presented the letters to him, and the Prince marvelled,

s'en merveilla, et sur ceo appela à ly ses chivalers et meillours conseillers, et lour mounstra les lettyrs, lesqueux ly disoient lour avis touchant cest fait; et sur ce ordeignez furent gentz d'armes pur querir le roy Petre.

A Burdeaux le Prince trova,
Qui moult forment s'esmerveilla. 1885
Quant il avoit la lettre lue,
Sitost come il eut survéwe,
Lors appela ses chivalers
Et toutz ses meillours conseillers;
Les lettres lour ad tutz monstrez 1890
Ensi come ils furent dittez,
Et lour dist : « Beaux seigniours, par foi,
Merveille ai de ceo que je voi.
Fols est qui s'affie en puissance.
Vous avez bien véu que France 1895

---

and summoned his knights and best counsellors and shewed them the letters; and how each gave their opinion on this affair, whereupon some men-at-arms were appointed to seek King Pedro.

At Bordeaux he found the Prince, who marvelled greatly. When he had read the letter, so soon as he had surveyed it, he called together his knights and all his best counsellors, and showed to all the letters, just as they were written; and said to them : « Good lords, by my faith, marvel have I at what I see. Foolish is he who trusts in his might. You have well seen that France was the chief

Estoit le pluis riche païs
Des cristiens, solonc m'avis,
Et ore ad droit Dieux consentu
Que nous avons éu vertu
Pur le notre droit conquester.   1900
Et auxi ai-je oÿ conter
Que li leoperdz et lour compaigne
Se desployerent en Espaigne;
S'estre pooit en notre temps,
Hom nous en tiendroit plus vaillantz.   1905
Un bon conseil sur ce point,
Seigniours, nous viendroit bien à point :
Ore en dites votre purpos. »
Adonques li a dit Chaundos,
Et puis Thomas de Felton ;   1910
Cils deux estoient compaignoun
De son conseil li plus privé.
Et lui disoient pur verté

---

land of christians, according to my understanding; and now has God given consent that we have had courage of our own right to gain it. And also I have heard tell that the leopards and their company spread themselves in Spain; if this might be in our time, men would hold us the more valiant. Good counsel upon this point, my lords, would be very seasonable for us : tell me now your opinion. » Then spoke Chandos, and after him Thomas de Felton ; these two were companions in his most privy counsel, and spoke

Que ce accomplir ne purroit,
S'ascun alliance n'avoit   1915
Au roy de Navarre, qui lors
Tenoit le passage des ports.
Par le conseil qu'ils accorderent,
Au roy de Navarre manderent,
Le counte d'Armynak auxi   1920
Et toutz les barons sanz nul si
Du noble païs d'Aquitaine.
Et lors, c'est bien chose certaine,
Tut le grant conseil fut ensemble.
Chescun disoit ce qui li semble   1925
Bon affaire de cele emprise;
Et sachez que bien fut comprise
Par tiel conseil et tiel accorde,
Sicome je oi en mon recorde,
Que hom fist vessealx apparailler   1930
A Bayonne sanz detrier,

---

to him in truth, that this could not be accomplished, unless they had an alliance with the King of Navarre, who then held the passage of the defiles. Upon the counsel they gave, they sent to the King of Navarre, and the Count d'Armaignac also and all the barons without fail of the noble land of Aquitaine. And then, as is well known, all the great council was together. Each said what appeared to him the b⸱t to be done in this enterprise; and know that it was undertaken by such counsel and accord, as I have it in my memory, that vessels were equipped at Bayonne without

Gentz d'armes et archiers auxi,
Pur aler quere sanz detri
En Espaigne le roy Peron.
Monsieur Thomas de Felleton,   1935
Lui grant seneschall d'Aquitaine,
Devoit estre lour chiefteigne;
Mais entre eux qu'ils deussent trusser
Lour vessealx et eux aprestier,

Coment le roy daun Petre arriva à Bayone, et amena ovesque lui sez filz et filles et ce que ly fut lessé de soun tresour, et ly Prince s'en ala encontre lỳ, et firent grant deduit; et après ce le Prince et le roy de Navarre graunterent de socorir le roy Petre.

Luy roy daun Petro à Bayone   1940
Arriva en propre persone,
Et amena filles et fieux
Et tut le remanant que Dieux

---

delay, men-at-arms and archers also, to go at once into Spain and seek Don Pedro. Sir Thomas de Felton, the great seneschal of Aquitaine, was appointed their leader; but amongst those whose duty it was to equip and get ready the ships,

How the King Don Pedro arrived at Bayonne and brought with him his sons and daughters and all that was left to him of his wealth, and the Prince went to meet him, and made great rejoicings; and afterwards the Prince and the King of Navarre granted assistance to Don Pedro.

The King Don Pedro in his own person arrived at Bayonne, and brought daughters and sons and all

Ly eust lessé de son tresor,
Pierres, perles, argent et or. 1945
Quant ly Prince en scieut novelles,
Ly semblerent bones et belles ;
Countre ly à Baione ala
Et noblement le festoia
En grant joie et en grant deduyt, 1950
Et là firent maint bel conduyt.
Que vous purroy-je detrier
La matiere et plus alonger ?
Tout furent d'accord sanz detri,
Et le roy de Navarre auxi, 1955
De roy daun Petre conforter
Et en Espaigne remener.
Puisque pur Dieu et pur pité
Et pur droiture et amisté
Si humblement li requeroit, 1960
Bien socouruz estre devoit ;

---

that God had left him of his riches, stones, pearls, silver and gold. When the Prince heard the tidings, they seemed to him good and joyful; he went to meet him at Bayonne, and entertained him nobly with great joy and festivity ; and there he comported, himself well. Why should I delay my story and lengthen it more ? All were agreed without delay and the King of Navarre as well, to comfort King Don Pedro and bring him again to Spain. Since for God and pity's sake, for justice and friendship, he so humbly sought it, it was

Toutz furent d'accord sur ce point,
Et dès lors ne s'aresta point.

Coment le Prince revenoit à Burdeaux, et fist apparailler ses gentz, et Chaundos ala quere les compaignons de la Graund Compaignie, lesqueux venoient; et plusours altres Englois pristrent congé du bastard Henri, et venoient au Prince hors de Espaigne; et le bastard, quant il avoit oÿ noveles de ceste emprise, voloit avoir encombrez les Engleis, et fist trencher lour chemyns, qu'ils ne deussent avoir passez vers le Prince.

Luy Prince, qui tant ot vertus,
A Burdeaux s'en est revenuz   1965
Et fist ses gentz apparailler.
Maint noble et vaillant chivaler

---

right to render him assistance; all were agreed on this point, nor after that did they delay further.

How the Prince returned to Bordeaux, and got ready his forces, and Chandos fetched the companions of the Great Company, who came, and many other English took leave of the bastard Enrique, and came to the Prince out of Spain; and the bastard, when he heard the news of this enterprise, wished to have harrassed the English and caused to cut off their route, that they might not pass towards the Prince.

The Prince, who had such virtue, then returned to Bordeaux, and got his forces in readiness. Many a

Manda par trestout son païs,
N'i demora grant ne petitz ;
Et Chaundos ne demora mye,   1970
Car à la Graunde Compaignie
Ala quere les compaignons
Jesques à quatorze penons,
Sanz les autres, qui retournerent
D'Espaigne, quant ils escouterent   1975
Que ly Prince aïder voilloit
Le roy daun Petre de son droit.
Congé pristrent du bastard Henri,
Lequel lour dona sanz detry
Et les paia moult voluntiers,   1980
Car ne ly fesoient mestiers.
Roy de Castille fut à ce temps,
Et bien s'en tenoit pur contens
Que nul tollir ne li péust
Pur grant puissance qu'il éust.   1985

---

noble and valiant knight did he send for through all the land, nor did any delay great or small. Nor was Chandos inactive, for of the Great Company he collected companions to the number of fourteen pennons, not reckoning those who returned from Spain, when they heard that the Prince wished to aid the King Don Pedro in his right. They took leave of the bastard Enrique, who gave it them without delay, and paid them very willingly, for he had no longer need of them. King of Castile was he then, and with that was well content, that none could wrest it from him on account of

Lors s'en s'en revint, à brief mot court,
Dan Eustace d'Abrichecourt
Devereux, Cressewell et Briket,
Qui savoient de lui parler fait,
Et puis le sire d'Aubeterre,   1990
Qui voluntiers pursuivent guerre,
Et le bon Barnat de la Salle.
Toutz les compaignons de la Galle
Retournerent en Acquitaine ;
Mais avant eurent moult de payne :   1995
Car quant le bastard scieut de vray
Que le Prince sanz nul delay
Vouloit le roy daun Petre aider,
Moult lour purchacea d'encombrer.
Trencher lour fist toutz les chimyns,   2000
Et toutz les soirs et les matyns
Maint embusshe sur eux saillir
Et par maintes fois assaillir

---

the great power that he had. There then came back at short notice, Sir Eustace d'Abrichecourt, Devereux, Cresswell and Briquet, who knew how to speak of their deeds; and then the lord d'Aubeterre, who willingly carried on war, with the good Bernard de la Salle, all the companions of Wales returned to Aquitaine; but first they encountered much trouble; for when the bastard knew certainly that the Prince without delay willed to assist King Don Pedro, much he planned to encumber them. He caused all the roads to be cut up, and every night and day set men in ambush to sally out

Des geneteurs et des villains ;
Mais Dieux, qui est Roy soverains,   2005
Les reamena en sauveté
Tout droit à la principalté :
Dont li Prince fut moult joyous,
Car moult parestoit coveytous
De son desire accomplir.   2010
Et lors ad fait sanz alentir
Apparailler or et argent
Et deniers pur paier sa gent.

Du temps quant ly très-noble Prince comencea cest graund emprise.

SEIGNOUR, le temps que je vous dy
   Ce fut après que Dieux nasquy,   2015
Mille ans trois centz sessante et sis,
Que chanter laist l'oisel gentils;

---

and attack them, oftentimes with light cavalry and peasants ; but God, who is the King of kings, reconducted them in safety right on to the quarters of the Prince, making the Prince right joyous : for he was very anxious to accomplish his desire. And then, without further delay he, caused to prepare gold and silver and money to pay his forces.

Of the time when the right noble Prince commenced this great undertaking.

SIRS, the time I tell you of, was from the birth of Christ one thousand three hundred and six years, when the gentle bird could sing, three weeks before the

Trois semaignes devant le jour
Que Jhesu-Crist par sa douceour
Nasqui de la Virge Marie, 2020
Qu'en cely temps, ne doutez mye,

De la très-grant ordeignaunce faite à Burdeaux par le Prince pur le voiage d'Espaigne.

Luy francs Prince moult noblement
Fist ordeigner son paiement.
Adonques véissez à Burdeaux
Forger espées et coteaux, 2025
Cotes de fer et bacynettes,
Gleyves, haches et gantilettes.
Moult parfut noble li arrois,
S'avoir y déust xxx. roys.

---

day when Jesus Christ of his goodness was born of the Virgin Mary, that at this time, doubt not,

Of the very great ordinance made by the Prince at Bordeaux for his voyage into Spain.

THE frank Prince right nobly ordered all payment to be made. Then might you see at Bordeaux the forging of swords, long and short, iron plates and bacynettes, glaives, axes, and gauntlets. Right noble was the array, as if there had been thirty kings.

Coment l'assemblée fust faite à Dasc, et les Compaignouns se logerent en Bascle et entre les mountains pluis que deux moys pur attendre le passage, et là demorerent tout l'iver jesques au moys de feverere.

A Dasc fut faite l'assemblée   2030
Du Prince à la chiere membrée.
Là s'assemblerent li baron
Et les chivalers d'environ.
Toutz les Compaignons et serjens
Se logierent en celi temps,   2035
En Baskle et entre les montaignes
Se logierent les Grantz Compaignes.
Pluis que deux moys y demurerent,
Moult de suffrete y endurerent,
Tout pur attendre le passage   2040
Qu'ils puissent aller lour voiage.

How the rendezvous was made at Dax, and the Companions were quartered in the Basque country, and among the mountains more than two months to be ready for the passage; and they remained there all the winter until the month of February.

AT Dax the gathering was made of the Prince with the fierce face. There assembled the barons and the knights from every side. All the Companions and soldiers lodged themselves at that time in the Basque country, and among the mountains were quartered the Great Companies. There they remained more than two months, they endured much suffering, waiting till the passage was open that they might proceed on their expedition. There stayed

Là demorerent tout l'yver
Jesques au moy de feverer,
Tant que tout l'ost fut assemblé
Et li lointaigne et ly privé ; 2045
Mais, à ce que je entendy,
Luy Prince de Burdeaux party.

Coment le Prince se departi de Burdeaux, et la très-noble dame la princesse fist très-amers dolours et complaintes à cause de son departir, et le Prince conforta la dame moult noblement ; et bientost après la très-noble dame enfaunta un filtz que fust nomez Richard, et le Prince et maint gent en avoient grant joie.

Après le Noel xv. jours
Ot là très-ameres dolours
En son coer la noble princesse ; 2050
Elle regretoit la dieuesse

---

they all the winter until the month of February, so that all the forces were assembled both from far and near. At which time, as I have heard, the Prince departed from Bordeaux.

How the Prince moved from Bordeaux ; and the very noble lady the Princess was bitterly grieved and sorrowful at his departure ; and the Prince comforted the lady right nobly ; and soon afterwards the right noble dame brought forth a son, who was named Richard, and the Prince and many people were much rejoiced thereat.

Fifteen days after Christmas, the most bitter sorrow had in her heart the noble Princess ; she lamented the

D'amours, qui l'avoit assenée
A si très-haute majestée ;
Car elle avoit le plus puissant
Prince de ce siecle vivant.   2055
Sovent disoit : « Las ! quei feroie,
Dieux et Amours, si je perdoie
La droite flour de gentilesse,
Le flour de très-noble hautesse,
Celi qui eu monde n'ad pier   2060
De vaillance, à voir recorder ?
Mors, tu me seroies proschaine.
Ore n'ay-je coer, sanc, ne vayne,
Que ne me faille et tout li membre
Quant de son partir ne remembre ;   2065
Car tut li monde dist ensy
Qu'unques nul hom ne s'enbaty
En voiage si perillous.
Hé ! très-doulx Piere glorious,

---

goddess of love, who had destined her to so high majesty ; for she had the most puissant Prince at that time living. Often did she say : « Alas ! what would I do, God and Love, if I should lose the true flower of magnanimity ; him who in the world has no peer for courage, to record the truth ? O death, thou wouldst be at hand. Now I have no heart, no blood, no veins, but every member fails me when I think of his departure ; for all the world agree, that never man embarked on an expedition so perilous. O most kind and glorious Father, comfort me with your

Confortez-moy par vo pité. »   2070
Là quant ad ly Prince escouté
Ce que la france dame dist,
Moult très-noble confort luy fist
Et luy ad dit : « Dame, lessez
Le plorer, ne vous esmaiez ;   2075
Car Dieux est puissant de tout faire. »
Luy Prince de très-noble affaire
Doulcement la dame conforte,
Et là, si Dieux me reconforte,
Prist de luy congié doulcement,   2080
Et luy dist amiablement :
« Dame, encor nous nous reverrons
En tiel point que joie en aurons
Et nous et tut li notre amy,
Car mon coer le me dit ensy. »   2085
Moult doulcement s'entr'accolerent
Et en baisant congié donerent.

---

pity ! » There the Prince had heard what the noble lady had said ; right much noble comfort did he give her and said : « O lady, cease your lament, nor be dismayed, for God is able to do all things. » Thus the right noble Prince gave sweet comfort to his lady, and there, so God give me peace, took his leave kindly of her, and said affectionately : « Lady, we shall meet again in such case that we shall have joy, both we and all our friends; for my heart tells this to me. » Very kindly then did they embrace, and took leave with kisses. Then might you see dames in tears,

Là véissez dames plorer,
Et damoiseles dolouser.
L'une ploroit pur son amy,   2090
Et l'autre auxi pur son mary.
La Princesse ot de dolour tant,
Qu'adonques fut grosse d'enfant,
Que de la dolour delivera
D'un beal filtz et enfanta,   2095
Lequel filtz *Richard* ot à noun,
Dont grant joie partut fist hom;
Et li Prince, si Dieux m'avoie,
En ot auxi à coer grant joie;
Et dient tut comunalment :   2100
« Vez-ci moult beal comencement. »

Coment ly Prince s'en est departiz de Burdeaux, et venoit à Dasc, et là demura tant que novelles ly venoient que le duc de Lancastre, son frere, venoit

and damsels to grieve; the one wept for her lover, and the other also for her husband. The Princess suffered such grief, being then great with child, that from sorrow she was delivered and brought forth a lovely son, who was named *Richard*, at which all were much rejoiced; and the Prince, so God help me, was also right glad at heart; and it was commonly said : « See here a right good beginning. »

How the Prince departed from Bordeaux and came to Dax, where he staid till the the news reached him, that the Duke of Lancaster, his brother, was coming to him; and there he

devers ly; et lors li attendi illoeqes. Le duc s'en hasta devers le Prince, son frere, en chivachant parmy Constantyn et Britaigne, et duc Johan li festoia moult noblement.

Lors se parti, à voir entendre,
 Lui Prince, plus ne volt attendre.
Pluis longement n'y mist sojour.
Moult parfut riche son atour.   2105
A Dasc vint et là sojourna ;
Car novelles on li porta
Que le duc de Lancastre vint,
Qui grant gent governe et maintint.
Lors s'avisa qu'il demourroit   2110
Et li soen frere attenderoit.
Et sachez que li noble ducs,
Qui moult ot en li de vertus,

---

awaited him. The Duke hastened towards the Prince, his brother, journeying through Cotentin and Britanny, and the Duke John entertained him right nobly.

Then the Prince departed, to understand the truth, not wishing to tarry, or make any longer sojourn ; very rich was his array. He first came to Dax and there he remained, for one brought him tidings, of the coming of the Duke of Lancaster, who commanded and maintained a great many people. Then he bethought himself to stay and await his brother. And know too that the noble Duke, who had

Quant il oï dire ses ditz
Que li Prince estoit departiz 2115
De Burdeaux, moult ent fut dolantz,
Car n'i quidoit venir à temps.
En Constantyn fut arrivez
Lui noble ducs et redoutez ;
Moult se hasta à chivacher 2120
Et tut li noble chivaler.
Constantyn passa et Bretayne.
Contre li ad beal compaigne ;
Car de Bretayne vint duc Johans,
Ovesque li ot des pluis grantz 2125
Barons de trestout son païs,
Ceux qui pluis tenoit à amys :
Clisson et Canolle et plusours,
Queux li fesoient grantz honours.
En son païs les festoia ; 2130
Mais moult petit y demora,

---

many virtues, when he heard the report that the Prince had moved from Bordeaux, was very sad, for he thought that he had come too late. In Cotentin was he then arrived, the noble and redoubted Duke, whence he hastened to march, he and all his noble knights; and passed thence into Britanny, where he was met by a noble company; for there came the Duke John, and with him very many barons from all his land, those he most looked upon as friends : Clisson, Canolle, and many more, that they might do him honour. In his land he entertained them; but very

Car il le covenoit haster
Pur le Prince, qui volt passer.
Congé ad pris sanz detrier
Au duc Johan et à sa mulier. 2135

Coment le duc de Lancastre tant chivacha qu'il est venuz à Burdeaux, et là trova la princesse qui luy festoia moult doucement, et luy ad demaundé des novelles d'Engleterre; et en aprés luy noble duc de Lancastre s'en chivacha parmy les Landes tant qu'il est venuz à la cité de Dask, et là trova le Prince, son frere, lequel ly vint à l'encontre, et s'encontrerent moult amiablement; et le Prince ly ad demaudé des novels d'Engleterre, et moult grant joie demenerent ensemble, et le counte de Foys lors estoit illoeqes.

Quei vous feroie long demain?
Tant chivacha et soir et main

---

little did the Duke tarry; for it was his aim to hasten to the Prince, who was wishing to proceed. Leave then he took without delay, of Duke John and his lady.

How the Duke of Lancaster marched on till he came to Bordeaux, where he found the Princess, who received him most kindly, and asked him news from England; and afterwards the noble Duke of Lancaster marched through the Landes until he came to the city of Dax, where he found the Prince, his brother, who came out to meet him; and they met most affectionately, and the Prince asked of him news from England, and they were very joyful together, and the Count de Foix was there at that time.

Why should I delay further? The noble Duke of Lancaster rode on night and morning, until he

Que droit à Burdeaux est venuz
De Lancastre lui noble ducs,
Et là il trova la Princesse,
Qui de tout honur est maistresse,   2140
Qui le festola doulcement ;
Et moult très-amiablement
Li ad demandé de la terre
Coment hom fait en Engleterre ;
Et le duc li ad tout conté.   2145
Et puis sachez de verité
Que li duc gaires n'attendi
Que de Burdeaux s'en departi.
Parmy les Landes chivacha
Et moult durement soy hasta   2150
Tant qu'il vint à Dasc la cité,
Où son frere le Prince ad trové,
Qui à l'encontre de li vint,
Et des chivalers plus que vint.

---

arrived at Bordeaux; there he found the Princess, of all honour the mistress, who received him very kindly ; and very affectionately she asked him of England, what was going on there ; and the Duke told her every thing. And then know for truth, that the Duke tarried but little ere he left Bordeaux. He rode through the Landes ; and made very great haste, until he reached the city of Dax, where he found the Prince, his brother, who came out to meet him with more than twenty knights. Know also that at this

Et si sachez que à cest foitz 2155
Y estoit lui conte de Foys.
Grant joie ensemble demenerent
Auxitost qu'ils s'entre-contrerent.
Lors s'acolerent en baisant,
Et li Prince dist en riant : 2160
« Ducs de Lancastre, frere douls,
En notre pais bien veignez-vous.
Dites quei fait le roy, no piere,
Et la roïgne, notre miere,
Toutz nos freres et notre amy. » 2165
— « Sire, dist-il, la Dieu mercy,
Ils ne font trestoutz fors que bien.
No piere dist que s'il faut rien
Qu'il poet faire, si li mandez.
No miere vous salue assez. 2170
Touz nos freres se recomandent
A vous, et par moy ils vous mandent

---

time the Count de Foix was there. Great joy had they together; so soon as they met they embraced kissing each other; and the Prince said smiling : « Sweet brother, Duke of Lancaster, be welcome in mutual peace. Say how fares the King, our father, and the Queen, our mother, all our brothers and all friends? » — « Sire, said he, thanks to God, they are all nought but well. Our father said that, if you require anything in his power, to inform him. Our mother also salutes you ; all our brothers commend themselves to you, and by me they send you word, that they willingly

Qu'ils voluntiers fuissent venu,
Si bon congé éussent éu. »

Coment le duc de Lancastre et le Prince furent venuz à Dask en grant deduit en attendant le passage outre les ports : c'est assavoir le pas de Rouncevalle, et le counte de Foitz se retourna en son païs; et homme disoit que le roy de Navarre estoit alez oue le bastard Henri, et monsieur Hugh de Calvelée eust pris certeines villes en Navarre, et sur ce le roy de Navarre tramist ses messages au Prince; et après vint monsieur Martyn de Lacarre au Prince et lour approcha le passage.

ENSEMENT tout parlant en vinrent   2175
A Dasc et par les mains se tinrent,
Et si sachés que celle nuyt
Demenerent moult grant deduyt.

---

would have come, if they had received permission.

How the Duke of Lancaster and the Prince came to Dax with great joy, waiting till the passages were open beyond the defiles, the pass namely of Roncesvalles, and the Count de Foix returned home; and men said that the King of Navarre was gone with the bastard Enrique, and that Sir Hugh de Calverley had taken certain towns in Navarre, and on this the King of Navarre sent his messengers to the Prince, and afterwards came Don Martin de Lacarre to the Prince; and how they approached the passage.

THUS in converse they came to Dax, holding each other by the hand, and you may know that that night they

De lour parlement pluis ne say,
Ne plus ne vous en conteray.   2180
Lui counte de Foys s'en tourna
Ou païs où il demura ;
Et lui Prince à Dasc demeure
En attendant le temps et l'eure
Que il poïst passer les ports,   2185
Que vous seroit long li records.
Encore ne savoit-il pas
Se il passeroit par le pas
De Rainchevaus ; car hom disoit
Que li roy de Navarre estoit   2190
Alliez ou le bastard Henry,
Dount hom maint furent esbahy ;
Mais en ce temps et ce termyne
Mirand et le Point la Reïne
Ot pris Hughes de Calverley,   2195
Dount Navarre fut esfraé.

---

made a very great entertainment; but of their conversation I know no more, nor can I tell you further. The Count de Foix returned to his territory, where he remained, and the Prince stayed at Dax, waiting the time and the hour, when he might pass the defiles, which would be a long story. Besides he knew not yet whether he might go by the pass of Roncesvalles; for it was said that the King of Navarre was in alliance with the bastard Enrique, at which many men were astonished; but, just at this season, Hugh de Calverley had taken Miranda and Puente la Reina, at which

Luy roy tramist son messager
Au Prince tost sanz atargier,
Et li ad mandé tout le fait
Ce que Hughes lour avoit fait.   2200
Après vint messire Martyn
De Lacarre, qui ot coer fin.
Tant fist par son sens, qu'il ot sage,
Qu'il lour approcha le passage.

Coment le roy de Navarre devers le Prince à Saint-Johan-du-Pé-des-Portz, et le duc de Lancastre lui vint à l'encontre, et lors furent les sermentz renovellez, et après ce fut ordeigné que l'avant-garde passeroit.

ASSEZ vous purroye counter   2205
   Pur la matiere destourber ;
Mais bientost puis ce jour avint
Que ly roy de Navarre vint

Navarre was alarmed. And the King sent his messengers to the Prince without delay, and sent him an account of all that Hugh had done. Afterwards came Don Martin de Lacarre, of noble courage, who so managed by his wisdom, that they were able to approach the pass.

How the King of Navarre moved towards the Prince to Saint-Jean-Pied-de-Port, and the Duke of Lancaster came to meet him, and then were the oaths renewed, and after this it was ordered, that the advanced guard should pass.

ENOUGH might I tell you, which would interrupt the narrative ; but shortly after this day it was that the King

A Seint-Johan-du-Pé-des-Portz,
Et à l'encontre lui vint lors   2210
De Lancastre le noble ducs
Et lui Chaundos, qui moult fut prus.
Devers le Prince li amenerent
En un lieu où ils le troverent.
Piers Forard avoit à noun   2215
Le lieu, la ville et la maison.
Là fut le roy Petre venuz,
Et là fut sur le corps Jesus
Touz lour sermentz renovellez,
Et là fuist chescun accordez   2220
De tout ce qu'il devoit avoir.
Ore voe-je faire mon devoir
De bouter avant ma matiere ;
Car lendemayn, c'est chose clere,

---

of Navarre came to Saint-Jean-Pied-de-Port ; and then came to meet him the noble Duke of Lancaster and Chandos, who was right preux ; they led him towards the Prince, to a place where they found him ; the name of the town and the house was called *Peyrehorade* : thither had Don Pedro come, and there were renewed upon the body of Jesus all their oaths ; and there was each agreed on all that should be done. Now is it my part to go forward with my story. For next day, as is well known, it is a clear thing, the King

Luy roy et lui ducs et lui Chauudos 2225
Se departirent à briefs motz :
Car accordé ensi estoit
Que l'avant-garde passeroit
Tout primer le lundi proschein.
Et cils, sanz faire long demain, 2230
Sont à Saint-Johan arrivez.
Illoeques furent hostellez.
Et lendemain fist hom crier
Que chescun voille apparailler
Pur passer le proschein lundy, 2235
Voir cils qui furent esly
Pur passer ovesque l'avant-garde.
Ore est droit que je preigne garde
A l'avant-garde deviser ;
Les seigniours primers doi nomer. 2240

---

the Duke and Chandos, departed at once : for thus it was determined, that the advance guard should pass, on the next following Monday ; and these, without much delay, arrived at Saint-Jean, and there took up their quarters. And on the day following made a proclamation, that each should be in readiness to pass on the next Monday ; that is, all those that were chosen to pass with the vanguard. Now is it right that I take care to tell you of the vanguard ; first, I must name the lords.

Coment le duk de Lancastre amena l'avant-garde de seignours et d'autres esteantz en sa compaignie.

Le duc de Lancastre, qui prus
Fut et hardi et corageus,
Et si ot en sa compaignie
Moult de noble chivalerie.
Là fut le bon Thomas d'Uffort,　　　　　　2245
Qui le coer ot hardi et fort;
De Hastynges le bon Hugon,
Et Beauchamp, le sien compaignoun,
Guilliame, qui moult fut gentils,
Au counte de Warrewyk filtz;　　　　　　2250
Le sire de Neofvyll auxi,
Et maint bon chivaler hardi,
Que maintenant ne voil nomer,
Car aillours en vorray parler.

How the Duke of Lancaster led the vanguard, and of the nobles and others who were in his company.

The Duke of Lancaster, who was preux, hardy and courageous, had in his company many noble knights. There was the good Thomas d'Ufford, who had a heart hardy and brave; the good Hugh of Hastings, and William Beauchamp, his companion, who was right gentle, son to the Earl of Warwick; the Lord of Neville also, and many valiant knights, whom now I will not name, for elsewhere

Après vous doi nomer Chaundos, 2255
Qui fut conestable del hos,
Qui menoit touz les compaignons,
Desqueux vous voil nosmer les nouns :
Primers fut le sire de Rays,
Qui fut bon et preus en ses faitz ; 2260
Après le seigniour d'Aubeterre,
Qui voluntiers pursuoit guerre ;
Messire Garsis de Castelle,
Qui ot le coer preu et loielle ;
Et Gilbard de la Mote auxi, 2265
Et de Rochewarde Ammery ;
Et messire Robert Camyn ;
Cressewell et Briket le fyn ;
Et messire Richard Taunton,
Et Guilliame de Felleton, 2270
Et Willecok le Boteller,
Et Peverell, qui ot coer fier ;

I shall have to speak of them. Next I should name to you Chandos, who was Constable of the host, and led all the companions, whose names I will tell you : first was the Lord de Raix, good and preux in his deeds ; next the Signor d'Aubeterre, who willingly joined in the war ; Messire Garsis de Castelle, who had a heart preux and loyal ; Gilbert de la Motte also, with Aimery de Rochechouart, and Sir Robert Camyn, Creswell and Briquet the noble, with Sir Richard Taunton, and William de Felton, Willecok le Boteller, and Peverell, of a fierce spirit ; John Sandes, a

Johan Sandes, hom de renoun ;
Et Johan Alein, son compaignon,
Et puis après Shakell et Haulé. 2275
Tout cil peignoun, sanz demoré,
Furent à Chaundos compaignon,
Et mis par desoubz son peignon.
Après furent li mareschaulx,
Qui furent prodhomme et loiaulx. 2280
L'uns fut Stephen de Cosinton,
Qui moult estoit noble person ;
Et l'autre le bon Guychard d'Angle,
Qui ne doit estre mis en l'angle,
Ainz est bien droit que hom s'en remorge, 2285
Ovesque eux le peignon Saint George,
Et moult d'autre chivalerie
Avoient en lour compaignie.

---

man of renown, with John Allein, his companion. Then followed Shakell and Hawley. All these pennons, without demur, were the companions of Chandos, and enrolled themselves under his banner. After came the Marshals, who were men preux and loyal. The one was Stephen de Cosinton, who was a right noble man, and the other the good Guichard d'Angle, who must not be put in a corner, but is it right that men should remember him. They had the banner of Saint George, and many other knights, with them in their company.

Coment l'avant-garde passa outre les portz à la noumbre de x. mille chivalx oue graund peyne et dureté, et les gentz se logerent dedeinz Navarre.

SEIGNIOUR, or vous ay devisé
L'avant-garde et toute nomé, 2290
Qui ne se sont pas alenty;
Mais ils passerent le lundy,
Quatorsieme jour en fevrer.
Mais puis que Dieux le droiturer
Suffri mort pur nous en la crois, 2295
Ne fut passage si estrois;
Car home veoit gentz et chivaux,
Qui moult y suffroient des maux,
Trebucher parmy la montaigne.
Là n'y avoit point de compaigne, 2300
Li piere n'attendoit l'enfant.
Là avoit froidure si grant

How the vanguard passed through the defiles to the number of ten thousand horses with great suffering and hardship, and the forces quartered themselves in Navarre.

SIRS, I have told you of the vanguard, and their names, nor were they dilatory; but on the Monday made the passage, the fourteenth day of February. But since the time when the righteous God suffered death upon the cross for us, never was there passage so narrow; for there were to be seen man and horse, enduring great sufferings, stumbling amongst the mountains. There they had no assistance, nor could the father help the child. So intense was

De niege et de giellée auxi,
Que chescun estoit esbahy;
Mais oue la grace de Dieu   2305
Tout passa en temps et en lieu
Bien x. mille chivalx et pluis.
Et les gentz qui furent des vis,
Dedeinz Navarre se logierent;
Et lendemain s'apparaillerent   2310
Toutz ceux qui estoient, sanz faille,
Oue le Prince en sa bataille.

Des seignours que furent oue le Prince en sa bataille et d'autres à la nombre de xx. mille chivalx, et coment ils passerent outre les portz, et le roy de Navarre les conduist et amena.

ORE est bien droit que je vous nomme
De ces nobles barons la somme,
Tout primers li Prince et lui roy   2315
Daun Petre, que bien nomer doy,

---

the cold the snow and the hail, that all were dismayed; but by the grace of God they passed in time and together, about ten thousand horse and more and the survivors, quartered themselves in Navarre. And the next day all those, who were in the Prince's company, without fail, prepared themselves for the passage.

Of the Lords, who were with the Prince in his company and of twenty thousand other horse, and how they made the passage, and the King of Navarre conducted and brought them.

IT is quite right now that I tell you the sum of those noble Lords: first of all the Prince himself and Don Pedro

Et li roy de Navarre auxi.
Cils trois passerent sanz detri ;
Messire Lowys de Harcourt
Et Eustace d'Abrichecourt,   2320
Messire Thomas de Felton
Et de Pauteney le baron,
Et toutz les freres de Pomiers,
Qui estoient nobles chivalers,
Et puis le seigniour de Clichon   2325
Et le bon seigniour de Curton.
Lui sire de la Waure y fu,
Qui ot en li moult grant vertu.
S'i fut monsieur Robert de Knolles,
Qui n'eust mie trop de parolles ;   2330
Lui visconte de Rocheward
Y fut auxi, si Dieux me gard,
Et de Bourcier le droit seignour,
Et maint bon chivaler d'onour,

---

whom I should name, with the King of Navarre also. These three passed without hinderance; Messire Louis de Harcourt, Sir Eustace d'Abrichecourt, Sir Thomas de Felton, the Lord de Pouteny, all the brothers of Pomiers, who were noble knights, next the Lord de Clisson, and the good Lord de Courton. The Lord de la Warre was there, a knight of great virtue. So was Sir Robert de Knolles, a man of few words; the Viscount de Rochechouart was there also, so God keep me, with the good Lord de Bourchier, and many knights of honour; the Seneschal of Aquitaine,

Et li seneschall d'Aquitayne, 2335
Qui estoit noble capitaine ;
Cils de Paitou et d'Angomois,
Cil de Saintonge à ceste foitz ;
Cil de Pergos et de Cressyn,
Qui ot le coer hardi et fyn. 2340
Et je vous nomerai encor
Le grant seneschall de Bygor,
(Ceux que je di furent sanz faille
Oue le Prince en sa bataille,)
Et d'autres très-bien quatre mille, 2345
Dount je ne vous di pas le stille ;
Mais si Dieux m'alegge mes maus,
Bien furent xx. mille chivalx,
Qui toutz passerent le mardi.
Et li roy de Navarre auxi 2350
Ovesque li Prince passa,
Et le conduist et l'amena

---

who was a right noble captain, him of Poitou and of Angoumois, him of Saintonge at this time, of Périgord and of Quercy, who had a heart fine and valiant. And I will name also the great Seneschal de Bigorre, (these that I have mentioned were without fail in the Prince's company,) with about four thousand others, of whom I do not give the list ; but so God deliver me from my ills, there were about twenty thousand horse who all passed on Tuesday. The King of Navarre also passed with the Prince, and conducted

Outre le passage des portz.
Et Dieux, qui est misericors,
Consenti qu'ils fussent passé ; 2355
Mais moult y suffrist de durté
A passer, c'est chose certaine,
Lui noble Prince d'Aquitaine.

Coment le roy de Maiogre, le counte d'Arminak et plusours altres vaillantz seignours et chivalers estoient en l'arere-garde, et passerent outre le pas et se logerent en la conke de Pampilon.

LE merkredy, si Dieux me garde,
Passa auxi l'arere-garde 2360
De Maiogre lui noble roys,
Et li vaillant counte curtoys
D'Arminak, qui tant fut gentils,
Berart de la Bret li hardis,

---

and brought him through the pass of the defiles. And God, who is merciful, gave his consent to the passing; but it is certain that in the passage the noble Prince of Aquitaine endured many hardships.

How the King of Majorca, the Count d'Armagnac and many other valiant lords and knights, were in the rear guard and made the passage, and were all quartered in the cuenca of Pampeluna.

ON the Wednesday, so God help me, passed also the rear guard. The noble King of Majorca and the valiant and courteous Count d'Armagnac, who was so gentle, Bernard d'Albret the hardy, with the Lord de

Et de Muscyden le seigniour, 2365
Et d'autres chivalers d'onour,
Dont nobles estoit li renons;
Et si avoit d'autres peignons:
Monsieur Bertrukat de la Bret,
Et auxi sachés bien du fet 2370
Que là fut lui bourt de Berteils
Et le bourt Camus, dont les fès
Je ne vois pas entreoublant.
S'i fut Naudons de Baigerant,
Bernard de la Sale et Lamy; 2375
Toutz ceux estoient sanz nul sy
En l'arere-garde ordeigné.
Et passerent pur verité
Le mercredi outre le pas.
Or ne vous mentiray-je pas; 2380
En la conque de Pampilon
Se logea ceste gent chescun.

Mucidan, and other Lords of honour, whose renown was noble and so had other pennons: Sir Perdiccas d'Albret, and also in fact know that there was the bastard of Verteuil and the bastard Camus, whose deeds I am not going to forget. So was there Naudon de Bergerac, Bernard de la Salle and Lami; all these were without doubt appointed to the rear guard, and in truth made the passage upon the Wednesday. Now I will tell you no falsehood; in the cuenca of Pampeluna all these troops lodged. There

Là troverent et vin et payn,
Tant que toutz en estoient playn.

Coment en après passerent le sieur de la Bret et le captal oue ij. centz combatantz, et ly host fut contre ensemble, et le bastard Henri en eut novelles.

EN après sanz longe demoure 2385
De la Bret le noble seignioure
Ovesque le noble captal,
Qui ot le coer pru et loial,
Chescun a cc. combatantz
Des gentz d'armes preus et vaillantz. 2390
Or fut ly host toute ensemblée.
La novelle en fut aportée
A Henri le bastard d'Espaigne,
Qui estoit, li et sa compaigne,

---

they found wine and bread, so that all had enough.

How after this passed the Lord d'Albret and the Captal with two hundred combatants, and how all the army was assembled, and the bastard Enrique had news of it.

AFTERWARDS (passed) without much delay the noble Lord d'Albret, with the noble Captal, who had a heart preux and loyal, each with two hundred fighting men-at-arms, preux and valiant. Now was the army all assembled. When the news was brought to Enrique the bastard of Spain, who was with his army quartered at San Domingo,

A Saint-Dominique logiez. 2395
Or ne fut pas trop esmaiez,
Mais par le conseil qu'il avoit
S'est avisez qu'il manderoit
Au Prince une lettre tantostz.
Il le fist en disant ces motz 2400

Coment le bastard Henri envoia ses lettres au Prince pur savoir quelle part il vouloit entrer en Espaigne, et qu'il lui seroit au-devaunt pur ly doner la bataille.

EN la lettre com vous orrez :
« A très-puissant et honorez
Et noble prince d'Aquitaine.
Chier sire, c'est chose certaine,
Come nous avons entendu, 2405
Que vous et vos gentz sont venu
Et passez par decea les portz,
Et que vous avés fait accordz

---

he was not much dismayed; but by the counsel that he had, he was advised to send letters to the Prince directly; which he did in these words

How the bastard Enrique sent his letters to the Prince to know in what part he would enter Spain, and that he would meet him to give him battle.

IN the letter, as you shall hear : « To the all powerful and honoured and noble Prince of Aquitaine. Dear Sire, it is certain, as we have heard of you, that you and your forces have come hither, and have passed through the defiles; and that you have made accord, and are in alliance

Et estez alliez aussi
Ovesque le notre enemy, 2410
Dont nous donons grant merveille.
Je ne say qui le vous conseille;
Car unques rien ne vous mesfis,
Et envers vous rien ne mespris
Pur quoy vous nous deussez haïr 2415
Ne que vous nous deussez tollir
Tant poy que Dieux nous ad presté
De terre par sa volunté;
Mais pur ce que nous savons bien
Qu'il n'i ad seigniour terrien 2420
En cest monde, ne creature,
Qui Dieux ait donée aventure
Tant en armes come ad à vous;
Et bien savons que vous et tous
Les votres accourez sanz faille 2425
Fors que pur avoir la bataille;

---

moreover with him who is our enemy; at which we have great marvel. I know not who counsels you, for I never wronged you, nor have I erred in any thing towards you, that you should hate us, or that you should take from us that little land, which God hath of his will given us; but for that we know well, that there is no landed lord, nor creature in this world, to whom God has given such success in arms as he has done to you; and we know well that you and all your host assemble without fail, but as to how you may come to an engagement; I promise you

Vous promès amiablement
Que vous nous voillez soulement
Lesser savoir par quel partie
Entrerez en no seigniourie, 2430
Et vous avons en covenant
Que nous vous serrom au-devant
Pur vous bataille delivrer. »
Lors fist ses lettres sealler,
Et les tramist par son heraud, 2435
Qui chimina sanz nul defaut;
Tant come il le Prince trova,
Tantost les lettres lui bailla.

Coment le Prince receut les lettres du bastard et les monstra au roy Petre et à ses barons, et ad appelé son conseil pur estre avisez de la response de meisme les lettres; et à ceo temps monsieur Thomas de Felton demanda congé du Prince pur aler espier l'ost

---

sincerely, that if you will only let us know on what side you purpose entering our kingdom, we will make an agreement, that we will be before you to give you battle. » Then he sealed the letters, and sent them by his herald, who travelled without hindrance, until he found the Prince, and to him directly he delivered them.

How the Prince received the letters of the bastard and shewed them to King Pedro and his barons, and called his council to be advised of the answer to the same letters; and at this time Sir Thomas de Felton asked leave of the Prince to go and spy

du bastard, et avoit congé ; et adonques s'en chivacha parmy Navarre oue certeins chivalers, esquiers et archiers, et passerent la ryvere au Groyngn, et se logierent à Naveret ; et en le meisme temps le roy de Navarre fust pris par traïson, et monsieur Martyn de Lacarre fut fait governour du païs de Navarre, et s'en ala counter novel au Prince de la prise du roy de Navarre, et ly supplia à garder et governer le païs, et le Prince graunta de luy aider. Et adonques comaunda le Prince que l'ost se deust apparailer pur departir lendemain, et lors passa l'ost le pas de Sarrys, et chimina parmy Espuske jesques à Sauveterre.

ET li Prince, si Dieux m'avoie,
 Fist de la lettre moult grant joie,   2440
Et la monstra à ses barons,
Et lour devisa les raisons.

---

the bastard's army ; and he had leave ; and then rode through Navarre with certain knights, squires and archers, and passed the river to Logroño, and lodged at Navarrete ; and at the same time the King of Navarre was taken by treason, and Don Martin de Lacarre was made governor of the country of Navarre, and he came to bring tidings to the Prince of the capture of the King of Navarre, and petitioned him to defend and govern the country, and the Prince agreed to assist him ; and then the Prince commanded his army to be ready to march the next day ; and then the host passed through the pass of Souraïde, and marched through Guipuzcoa to Salvatierra.

THE Prince, so God lead me, was greatly pleased at the letter, and showed it to his barons, and talked it over

Là fut roy Petre mandez,
Et tout le conseill appelez
Pur la response conseiller, 2445
Coment le purroit renvoier
Et respondre par devers lui ;
Mais en ce temps que je vous di,
Monsieur Thomas de Felleton
Au Prince demanda un doun, 2450
Qu'il li pléust tant seulement
De li granter primerement
Qu'il poïst aler chivacher
Pur aler lour host espier ;
Et li Prince lui accorda. 2455
Adonques Thomas appela
Les compaignons, sachez pur voir,
A tantz come il voillent avoir,
Thomas d'Ufford et Felleton,
Guilliam, qui ot coer de lyon ; 2460

---

with them. There was King Pedro sent for, and all the council summoned, to consider of the answer that in return they should sent back to him. But at this time that I tell you, Sir Thomas de Felton asked of the Prince a favour, that it might only please him to grant him first of all that he might go and spy their host; and the Prince granted it him. Then Sir Thomas summoned his companions, know it for truth, so many as he wished to have, Thomas d'Ufford and William Felton, who had a

Hugh de Stafford et Knolles
Y furent à curtois parolles;
Et là survint à l'assemblée
Monsieur Simon de Burelée.
Bien furent, sicom j'oÿ dire, 2465
Oept-vintz lances sanz contredire,
Et si furent ccc. archier.
Lors se pristrent à chivacher
Parmy Navarre jour et nuyt;
Guydes avoient et conduyt. 2470
A Groingn passerent la rivere,
Dont l'eawe fut radde et fiere;
Et se logierent à Naveret
Pur entendre et oïr du fait
Coment lour host se governoit. 2475
Entrewes que là se fesoit,
Fut li roy de Navarre pris
Par traïson, dont esbahis

---

lion's heart, Hugh de Stafford and Knolles, were there, of courteous speech; there came also to the meeting Sir Simon de Burleigh; they were at least, as I have heard, eight score lances, without contradiction, and three hundred archers. Then began they their march through Navarre day and night. Guides had they and conduct. At Logroño they passed the river, of which the water was deep and rapid; and they lodged at Navarrete, to understand and hear in fact, what the army was doing. Meanwhile the King of Navarre was taken by treason, at which the

Fut li Prince et ses consiaux.
Ore fut governour et baus 2480
De tout le païs de Navarre
Monsieur Martyn de Lacarre ;
Par le conseil de la reÿgne,
Qui de toutz biens avoir est digne,
Vint au Prince, si li counta 2485
La prise ensement qu'ele va,
Et li supplia à garder
Le païs et le governer.
Le Prince grant mervaile en ot
Quant il oÿ de mot en mot, 2490
Et respondi de bone guyse :
« Je sui moult dolantz de la prise.
Or ne le puis-je pas reavoir ;
Mais vous savez bien tout pur voir :
Trestout le meultz que je puis faire, 2495
C'est que me parte de sa terre.

Prince and his council were much astonished; Messire Martin de Lacarre was then the governor and bailli of all the country of Navarre; by the advice of the Queen, who is worthy of all that is good, he came to the Prince and told him of the capture as it happened, and besought him to defend and take the government of the country. Great marvel had the Prince, as he heard it word by word, and answered in good part : « I am much grieved at his being taken, nor am I able to recover him; but you all well know that the best I can do is to go from his

Si bien m'avint, sera pur luy,
Si Dieu plest, autant que pur moy.
Je ne sai pluis quei conseiller. »
Lors comande à apparailler   2500
L'ost pur partir le grant matyn.
Dont pria messire Martyn
Qu'il li fesist guydes avoir;
Et il le fist; sachez pur voir.
Lors passa le pas de Sarris,   2505
Qui moult fust estroitz et petitz;
Moult y soffri li host de payne.
Et puis, c'est chose bien certaine,
Parmy Espuke chimina;
Mais poi de vivres y trova   2510
Pur son host tout parmy la terre,
Tant que il vint en Sauveterre.

---

country. If good happens to me, it will be for him, if it please God, as much as for myself. I know not what more to advise. » He then commanded his troops to be ready to march early on the morrow; and he prayed Don Martin to take care to have guides, and he did so, know for truth. He next marched through the pass of Arruiz, that was very narrow and small; the army there suffered very much. And thereafter, as is very certain, their route lay through Guipuzcoa; but little food did he find for his army through all the country, until he came to Salvatierra.

Coment le Prince, oue son host, est venuz en Espaigne et se logea ès villages près de Sauveterre, et quidoit avoir assailli la ville; mais se rendirent au roy Petre. Et illoeques sojourna le Prince vj. jours, et ses gentz furent à Naveret, et espioient l'ost du bastard, et prirent le chivaler du gaite de meisme l'ost, lequel fut prisoner à monsieur Simon de Burelée; et altres deux ou trois furent pris, queux lour disoient la verité del host du bastard; et eux en manderent novels au noble Prince.

O<small>R</small> fut l'ost venuz en Espaigne,
 Qui s'espandi par la champaigne.
Près de Sauveterre ès villages   2515
Se logea lui noble barnages.

How the Prince, with his army, came into Spain, and lodged in the villages near Salvatierra, and thought to have attacked the town; but it surrendered to King Pedro. And there the Prince remained six days, and his troops were at Navarrete, and watched the bastard's army, and took the knight of the out-post of the same host, who was prisoner to Sir Simon de Burleigh; and two or three others were taken, who reported truly of the bastard's army, and they sent the tidings to the noble Prince.

N<small>ow</small> the army had arrived in Spain, and spread themselves through the country. In the villages near Salvatierra the noble barons were lodged; [the Prince]

La ville quidoit assaillir;
Mais bien sachez sanz alentir,
Que au roy daun Petre se rendirent
Touz auxitost que li choisirent.   2520
Illoeques sojourna vj. jours
Lui Prince oue païs entours,
Et entre ce jour et ce temps
A Naveret furent ses gents,
Où bien souvent hors chivachoient   2525
Et l'ost du bastard espioient,
Tant qu'il avint que sur lour gait
Un noet emprissent lour fait.
Tout à chival en eux s'ofrirent
Et le chivaler de gait prirent   2530
Et des autres ou deux ou trois.
Lors prist à lever lui effrois;

---

thought to attack the town; but know well that without delay they surrendered to King Don Pedro as soon as they saw him. There and in the neighbouring country the Prince sojourned six days. Also, at this time some of his troops who were at Navarrete, often made excursions from thence, and watched the army of the bastard. And so it was, that one night they undertook an attack on the out-posts. All on horseback they rushed upon them, and took prisoner the knight of the out-post and some two or three others. Then took place the affray; and the knight that I speak

Et monsieur Simon de Burlée
Fut prisoner celle journée,
Le chivaler que je vous di. 2535
Lors se revindrent sanz detri
A Navaret, où se logeoient,
Et par prisoners qu'ils avoient
Sorent del host la verité;
Errant l'ont au Prince mandé. 2540

Coment le bastard se deslogea, et si vint encontre le Prince et Thomas de Felton; et ses compaignouns se deslogierent de Navarrete, et chivacherent devant l'ost du bastard pur espier plus justement de lour fait, et venoient devant Vitoire, et ent envoierent novelles au Prince; et le Prince vint devaunt Vitoire, et le bastard auxi vint et se logea de l'autre lès de la montaigne, et le Prince est venuz sur les champs, et

---

of was made prisoner in this fight by **Sir Simon de Burleigh**. Then they returned without delay to Navarrete, where they lodged; and from the prisoners whom they had, they learned the true state of their army, which they promptly sent to the Prince.

How the bastard moved and came to meet the Prince, and Thomas de Felton and his companions moved from Navarrete and rode towards the bastard's army, to watch more correctly their proceedings, and came before Vitoria; and they sent tidings to the Prince, and he came before Vitoria, and the bastard also came and lodged on the other side of the hill,

illoeques trova ses chivalers et lour fist moult bone chiere.

ET le bastard sot d'autre part
 Les novelles de l'autre part,
Et dist qu'il se deslogeroit
Et que à l'encontre lour viendroit.
Et quant Thomas de Felleton   2545
Le sot et tut son compaignon,
De Navaret se deslogierent.
Toutz jours devant l'ost chivacherent
Pur reporter plus justement
Les novelles certeinement,   2550
Tant firent des lors demorée
Que les Espaniards sount passé ;
Et bien avoient en memoire
Qu'ils viendroient devant Vitoire,

---

and the Prince came into the plain and there found his knights, whom he bade very welcome.

WHEN the bastard, on the other hand, heard the tidings of his opponents, he said that he would advance and come to meet them. And when Sir Thomas de Felton and his companions heard this, they advanced from Navarrete. All day they rode in advance of the army to report exactly and with certitude the news. And so long did they tarry, that the Spaniards passed them ; and they recollected well that they would arrive before Vitoria, under the

Au lés pardeceà la montaigne. 2555
Devant Vitoire sur la plaine
Sire Thomas de Felleton
Se logea et son compaignon.
Au Prince manderent le fait
Tout ensi qu'ils avoient fait ; 2560
Et quant li Prince ad entendu
La chose tout ensi qu'el fu,
Coment le bastard vint tut droit
A luy, qui combatre voilloit,
Lors dist : « Si m'aide Jhesu Cris, 2565
Moult parest cils bastard hardys.
Aloms vers le seigniour, pur Dieu,
Devant Vitoire prendre lieu. »
Lendemain vint devant Vitoire.
Là n'estoit pas véus encore 2570
Lui bastard, ains fut sur la playne
De l'autre lés de la mountayne.

---

the side of the hill ; there Sir Thomas de Felton, with his company quartered themselves, in the plain before Vitoria, and sent tidings to the Prince of all they had done. When the Prince had heard all the matter as it was, how the bastard came direct to him that he might fight, he said : « So help me Jesus Christ, this bastard is very bold. Let us advance, sirs, to meet him, and take our station before Vitoria. » They arrived there the next day. The bastard was not yet to be seen there, but was on the plain on the other side of the hill. When the Prince, who was right

Quant li Prince fut sur les champs,
Qui moult estoit prus et vaillantz,
Illoeques trova ses chivalers. 2575
Moult les ad véu voluntiers,
Et si lour dist : « Beus seigniours dous,
Pluis de cent foitz bien veignez-vous. »

Coment les coureurs du Prince couroient et reporterent le fait des enemis, et le Prince fist ses gentz rengier et ordeigner ses batailles, et fist les ordeigner pur les banieres esploier; et plusours seigniours et altres furent faitz chivalers.

ENSEMENT, come ils devisoient,
Les coureurs par les champs couroient, 2580
Et les coureurs des enemys
Avoient veu, ce lour fut avis.

---

preux and valiant, arrived on the field, there he found his knights. He saw them with much pleasure and said : « Good and kind sirs, welcome more than a hundred times. »

How the scouts of the Prince ran and reported the doings of the enemy, and the Prince drew out his forces in order of battle, and made them order the banners to be displayed ; and many lords and others were made knights.

THEN also, as they talked, the scouts ran through the fields and brought back news to the Prince that, in their opinion, they had seen the scouts of the enemy. Then was the

Adonques est li host esmeue,
Et trestout est li host venue.
Alarme y oïst-hom crier.   2585
Li Prince fist ses gentz rengier
Et ses batailles ordeignier.
Là se pooit-hom regarder
Ce que rien ne covient de dire ;
Car home y pooit voir reluire   2590
Or fyn et asure et argent
Et goules et sable ensement,
Synnoble et purpre et hermyne.
Là eut mainte baniere fyne
De soie et de sendal auxi ;   2595
Car puis le temps que je vous dy,
Si très-noble chose à véoir
Ne fut, à recorder le voir.
Là fut l'avant-garde ordeignée
Très-noblement à cel journée.   2600

---

army put in motion, and all the host was gathered together. The cry was raised : « To arms ! » the Prince drew out his forces, in order of battle. There might a man behold what no language can express; for there might be seen glistening fine gold, azure, and silver, gules also and sable, vert, purpure and ermine. Many a fine banner of silk and also of sendal was there ; for from the time I speak of to you, never was so noble a sight ever recorded to have been seen. The vanguard was right nobly ordered on

Là véist-hom chivalers faire
Des esquiers de noble affaire.
Le roy daun Petre chivaler
Fist le Prince trestut primer,
Et Thomas de Holand après, 2605
Qui de faire armes estoit près,
Et puis Huon de Courtenay,
Philippe et Peron que bien say,
Johan Trivet, Nicolas Bonde ;
Et li ducs, où toutz biens abonde, 2610
Fist chivaler Raoul Cammois,
Qui fut beux en faitz et curtois,
Et Gautier Ursewik auxi,
Et puis Thomas d'Auvirmetri,
Monsieur Johan de Grevedon. 2615
Là eut xij. ou environ,
Ly noble ducs et redoutez,
Qui bien doit estre renomez.

---

this day, There might be seen esquires of noble estate made knights. The Prince made the King Don Pedro the first knight, and afterwards Thomas de Holland, who was apt at deeds of arms, and then Hugh de Courtenay, Philip and Peter I well know, John Trivet and Nicholas Bond; the Duke also, abounding in good, made Ralph Camoys a knight, who was doughty in deed and courteous, Walter Ursewick also, and then Thomas d'Abernethy, Sir John de Grevedon. About twelve in all were knighted by the noble and redoubted Duke, who rightly deserves renown.

Et bien sachez tut entresait
Là eut maint bon chivaler fait 2620
Dount je ne say les nouns nomer;
Mais à ceo que j'oï counter,
Ly Prince ovesque touz ses gentz
En fist ce jour plus de deux centz.

Coment l'ost du noble Prince fut rengie en attendant la bataille; mais ne pleut à Deu que les enemys venissent mye celi jour, car l'arere-garde del host dudit Prince fut derere par vij. leues de païs; et à vespres l'ost dudit Prince se logea, et fut criez que lendemain touz se retourneroient à ceste playne et que chescun seroit sur sa garde.

A quoy faire vous mentiroie 2625
Et la matiere alongeroie?
Rengiez furent là tout le jour
Et prest pur attendre l'estour;

Know also well besides, there was many a good knight made whose names I know not; but this I can tell you, that the Prince and all those with him made this day more than two hundred.

How the army of the noble Prince was drawn up in expectation of battle; but it pleased God that the enemy should not come on this day, for the rear of the Prince's army was seven leagues behind; and at evening the army of the Prince encamped, and it was ordered that on the next day each should return to the field and be on the alert.

WHY should I tell you an untruth and lengthen the matter? All the day was the army drawn

Mais ne plut pas au Filtz Marie
Que cely jour venissent mye 2630
Des enemys, car par seint Piere
L'arere-garde fut derere
Pluis de vij. leuges du païs :
Dount lui Prince fut moult marris.
A vespres s'alerent logier. 2635
Adonc fist le Prince crier
Que chescun droit en cely playn
Retournast droit à lendemain,
Et que chescun fut sur son garde,
Et nul se passast l'avant-garde 2640
Et se logeast oue sa baniere ;
Mais par la foi que doi saint Piere,
Monsieur Thomas de Felleton
Et Gwilliame, son compaignon,

---

up, and waiting the enemy's attack ; but it pleased not the Son of Mary that the enemy should come on this day ; for, by Saint Peter, the rear was behind more than seven leagues of the country at which the Prince was sore displeased. In the dusk of the evening they went to their quarters. Then the Prince ordered to be announced that each should return the next day just on this spot, and be on the alert, nor should any pass the advanced guard, but remain with his own banner. But, by the faith I owe Saint Peter, Sir Thomas de Felton, and William, his compa-

Pluis de ij. leuges du païs 2645
S'ala logier, moy fut avis.

Coment le counte dan Tille, frere au bastard, demanda congé de chivacher pur espier et reporter le fait del host du Prince, lequel avoit congé; et s'en chivacha sur celi fait et plusours seigniours et autres, à le noumbre de vj. mille en sa compaignie.

ORE est bien temps que je vous counte
De dan Tille, le noble counte,
Qui appela disant ensi
Son frere, le bastard Henri : 2650
« Sire, fit-il, ore m'escoutez.
Il est bien voir, com vous savez,
Tout de vray que notre enemy
Sont logez assez près de cy ;

---

nion, (marched) more than two leagues of the country, and there posted themselves, such was my impression.

How the count Don Tello, brother of the bastard, asked leave to go and watch, and report the doings of the Prince's army, who had leave, and rode out on this enterprize with many lords and others, to the number of six thousand in his company.

Now it is time that I tell you of the noble count Don Tello, who spoke to his brother Enrique the bastard : « Sire, said he, now hear me. It is very true as you know it is true that all that our enemies are encamped very near here;

Et pur ytant si vous voilliez 2655
Et le congé vous m'en doniez,
Le matinet chivacheray,
Et le vray vous reporteray
Des enemis coment ils font. »
Ly bastard errant li respont 2660
Que à ceo faire bien s'accordoit
Et qu'en sa compaignie iroit
Sancez, lequel estoit son frere;
Et si iroit, c'est chose clere.
D'Odenhem le bon mareschal, 2665
A vj. mille hommes à chival
Seroit faite la chivachie.
Ensi fut la chose establie.
Monsieur Bartrem y fust alez
De Claykyn; mais arivez 2670
Estoit celi jour, ce dist hom;
Car tout droit venoit d'Aragon.

---

wherefore, if you wish it, and will give me permission, to morrow I will ride out and bring you back the truth of what they are doing. » The bastard straightway answered him, that he quite agreed with this proposal, and that Sancho, his brother, should accompany him. And also as is clear, the good Marshal d'Audenhem, would go, with six thousand men on horseback which would compose the expedition. So was the matter arranged. Messire Bertrand du Guesclin was to have gone, but he had on this day arrived, as they said, having come straight

Ensi fut compris lour arrès.
Durment manacent les Englois,
Disant que par lour grant outrage   2675
Les feroient morir à hountage.

Coment le counte dan Tilles, oue ses gentz, s'en est approchés al host du Prince, et primerement encontra monsieur Hugh de Calvelée, et fist grant dàmage as Englois, et ensement fortement supprist l'avant-garde, si n'eust esté li noble duc de Lancastre.

OR voille Dieux aider le droit !
Et li Prince logiez estoit
Devant Vitoire et environ,
Ne avoit borde ne maison   2680
Que tout ne fust de sa gent plaine ;
Mais ce est bien chose certaine,

---

from Aragon. Thus was composed their array. They threatened the English sorely, saying that for their great outrage they should cause them to die with disgrace.

How the Count Don Tello, with his forces, approached the army of the Prince, and encountered first Sir Hugh de Calverley, and caused great loss to the English, and the vanguard would have been taken by surprize, had it not been for the noble Duke of Lancaster.

Now, God defend the right! The Prince was posted before Vitoria and round about, nor was there hovel nor house, that was not filled with his troops. But it is very

Le Prince ne se gardoit mie
Lendemain de la chivachie
Que dan Tilles li apprestoit : 2685
Car sachez que pas ne dormoit.
A la mynoet se leva,
Le pluis grant chimyn chivacha
Tut droit contremont la montaigne,
Tant qu'il amena sa compaigne 2690
Tut contreval une vallée.
Primer Huon de Calvelée
Encontra, qui se deslogeoit
Et devers le Prince venoit.
Ses somers et son cariage 2695
Firent les coureurs grant damage.
Dont monta la noise et li cris,
Et les coureurs par les logis
Couroient aval et amont ;
En lour litz maintz tuez sont. 2700

---

certain, that the Prince the next day did not observe the expedition, prepared by Don Tello ; for the count did not sleep. At midnight he rose, rode a long distance, right over the hill, until he had conducted his troops into the opposite valley. First he encountered Sir Hugh de Calverley, who removed and marched towards the Prince. The light troops did much damage to his sumptors and carriages, the noise of which spread far. And the scouts ran, up and down through the camp ; many were slain in their beds. There so God

Là eust esté, si Dieux me garde,
Forment supprise l'avant-garde,
Si n'éust esté li francs ducs
De Lancastre, plein de vertus ;
Car sitost qu'il oÿ le cry,　　　　　　　　　2705
Hors de son logement sailly
Et prist le pas sur la montaigne.
Là se ralia sa compaigne
Et toutz autres que meulz meulz,
Et si dist-hom, si m'aide Dieux,　　　　　　2710
Que Espaniardz quidoient prendre
Celle montaigne, à voir entendre ;
Mais au duc et à sa baniere
S'assemblerent à lie chiere
Toutes les banieres del hos.　　　　　　　　2715
Là venoient le Prince et Chaundos,
Et là fut lui host ordeignée.
Là véissez, sanz demorée,

---

help me, the vanguard would have been taken by surprise, had it not been for the bold Duke of Lancaster, who was full of courage; so soon as he heard the cry, he sallied out of his lodge and took his way to the hill. There he rallied his company and very many others. It was said, so God help me, that the Spaniards thought to take this hill, the truth to understand; but all the banners of the army rallied joyfully around the Duke and his banner. Thither came the Prince and Chandos, and there the army was drawn up. There might you see, without delay, the

Les coureurs rebatre par force;
Ghescun de bien faire s'esforce. 2720

Coment le grant bataille des Espaignardz chivacha, et encontrerent Felton et plusours chivalers et altres esteant sur une mountaigne, et monsieur Guillaume de Felton se fery entre les enemys come chivaler corageous, et si occist moult chivalrousement un Espaignard, et se combati moult vaillamment; et les enemys jettoient launces et dartes, tant qu'ils tuerent son chival desouth ly, et au derrein le très-noble chivaler fut occis.

L ORS chivacha le grant bataille
Des Espaignardz, sachez sans faille.
Si ont encontrez Felleton
Et messire Richard Taunton,

---

light troops beaten back; each striving to do his utmost.

How the great army of the Spaniards marched away, and encountered Felton and many knights and others, who were upon a hill; and Sir William Felton rushed upon the enemy as a bold knight, and so killed right chivalrously a Spaniard and fought right valiantly; and the enemy hurled lances and darts, so that they killed his horse under him, and at last the very noble knight was slain.

T HEN rode off the great army of the Spaniards, know
without fail, and encountered Felton, with Sir Richard

Degory Says, Raoul de Hastyngs, 2725
Qui la mort ne counte ij. gyngs,
Et messire Gaillard Beguer
Et maint bon vaillant chivaler.
Bien estoient cent combatantz
Ensemble, quei petitz quei grantz, 2730
Sur une petite montaigne.
Là allierent lour compaigne ;
Mais monsieur Guillaumes li prus,
Moult hardis et moult corageus,
Se fri entre les enemys, 2735
Come hom sans sens et sans avis,
A chival, la lance baissie ;
Amont, sur la targe florie,
Un Espaignard ala ferir,
Que tout parmy le coer sentir 2740
Lui fist le fer trenchant d'acier.
Jus à la terre tresbuchier

Taunton, Degory Says, Ralph de Hastings, who did not value death at more than two cherries ; and Sir Gaillard Beguer, with many a good knight. There were together great and small at least one hundred fighting men, who took up their station upon a small hill. But Sir William the preux, bold and full of courage, rushed amid the enemy, like a man without sense or counsel, on horseback, with lance in rest ; and struck a Spaniard on his shield-fleury with the cutting steel so as to pierce his heart. To the earth he prostrated him in sight of all the

Le fist veant tute la gent.
Come-home plein de hardiment
Lor couroit sus l'espée traite ; 2745
Et Castillains par lour poeste
Lui suirent sus de tutes partz,
Et li jettoient launces et dartz.
Son chival ont desoubz li mort ;
Mais à pé se defendoit fort, 2750
Come hom qui ot coer de lion,
Monsieur Guillaumes de Felton ;
Mais sa defence poy vailly,
Car mort fut : Dieux en ait mercy !

Coment les Espaignardz, entour le nombre de vj. miile, assaillirent moult fortement les Englois, qui ne furent mye à le noumbre de c. esteaunt sur une mountaigne, et les Englois combatoient moult noblement ;

---

people. He, like a man full of hardihood, then rushed upon them with his drawn sword, whilst the forces of the Castilians followed him on every side, and hurled their lances and javelins at him. His horse was killed under him ; but Sir William Felton, like a man with a lion's heart, defended himself valiantly on foot ; but little did his defence avail him, for he fell, God have mercy on him !

How the Spaniards, to the number of about six thousand, attacked very resolutely the English, in number no more than one hundred, who were on the hill, and how the English fought

mais au derrein par graund force ils furent pris et amenez devers le bastard Henry.

<blockquote>

ET les autre ensemble se mirent   2755
   Sur un montaigne, qu'ils prirent.
Là lour fesoient maint estour
Les Espaignardz, qui sanz sojour
Moult durement les assailoient
Et lances et darts lour lachoient   2760
Et fors archigais esmolluz ;
Et cils, qui moult eurent vertus,
Come gent de hardi corage
Lour monstroient lour vasselage :
Car pluis de cent foitz celi jour   2765
S'avalerent sanz nul sojour,
Les glaives trenchants en lour mains,
Et par force, soiez certeins,

</blockquote>

---

right nobly; but at last by superior force they were taken and brought before the bastard Enrique.

THE rest of the English were together upon a hill they had taken; the Spaniards there attacked them without intermission, and assailed them very fiercely ; hurling at them lances and darts, and strong and sharp javelins. And these who were right valiant, like a people of hardy courage, showed then their boldness : for to day more than an hundred times they drove them down without ceasing, their sharp swords in their hands ; and by force

Ils les fesoient reculer,
Ne jà ne les poïst grever. 2770
Et Castelain, si Dieux me garde,
Ne pot geter launce ne darte,
Ne féussent Francs et Breton,
Normand, Pycard et Burguynon,
Qui y survindrent par un val : 2775
Et d'Audenham le mareschal
Et monsieur Johan de Noefville,
(Cils estoient ensemble mille,)
Tout auxitost come ils les virent,
Tut à pé maintenant se mirent. 2780
Englois et Gascoins bien veoient
Que là plus durer ne pooient ;
Car ils n'avoient nul socours.
Et François plus tost que le cours
Les vindrent à pé assaillir, 2785
Et les autres sans alentir

---

be assured did they make them recoil. Nor could the Castilians hurt them, as God is my defender, whether they hurled lance or dart; had there not been French and Bretons, Normans, Picards and Burgundians, who came upon them by a valley. And the Marshal d'Audenhem, and Sir John de Neville, together with a thousand men, so soon as they saw them, they all immediately dismounted. The English and Gascons saw well that they could no longer hold out, for they had no succour. And the French, with great speed, advanced on foot to attack them, whilst the others without delay

Se defendoient fierement ;
Mais ils ne furent mye cent
Encontre pluis de vj. milliers.
. . . .
Et là fesoient d'armes tant   2790
Que unques Olyver ne Roland
Ne pooient pluis d'armes faire,
Ensi com j'ay oÿ retraire ;
Mais lour defense poy valut,
Car par grant force il lour falut   2795
Qu'ils se rendissent prisoner.
Là furent pris, à voir juger,
Hastynges et Degory Says,
Gaillard Beguer, qui fut parfaitz,
Les troys freres de Felleton   2800
Ovesque ly Richard Taunton,
Mitton et des autres assetz
Dount je ne say les nouns nomez.

---

defended themselves stoutly; but they were not one hundred against more than six thousand. But there such feats of arms were done by the knights, that never Oliver or Roland could have done greater deeds, as I have heard recounted. But their defence availed little, for they were forced by superior numbers to yield themselves prisoners. Then were taken, as one can judge, Hastings and Degory Says, Gaillard Beguer, who was perfect, the three brothers Felton, with Richard Taunton, Mitton, and many others, whose names I

En ce point furent ce jour pris,
Dount moult fut li Prince martis ; 2805
Mais il quidoit certainement
Que tut l'enemi proprement
Fust devalé outre le pas;

. . . .

Son host ensemble departir; 2810
Car il fut alez socourir
Ses autres gentz, si ceo ne fust :
Car moult bien faire le déust ;
Mais il ne fut mye ensi fait.
Et cils que eurent fait lour fait, 2815
Auxi tantost que hom lour counta
Que le Prince fut près de là,
Pluis tost qu'ils purroient se partirent
Et à eux retourner se mirent.
Les prisoners ovesque eux maynent, 2820
Et moult durement les demaynent.

---

know not, in this case, were taken on this day, at which the Prince was greatly grieved. But he thought certainly, that all the enemy's army would naturaly have passed below beyond the pass... and he would not divide his army otherwise he would have gone to aid his other forces, if this had not been so : for much it behoved him to help them; but nothing of the kind was done. And they who had performed this feat, so soon as they were told that the Prince was at hand, departed with all speed, and hastened their return. Their prisoners they took with them, and treated them very hardly.

Coment le bastard fist grant joie de la revenue du counte dan Tilles et des autres, et de la prise des Englois, et fortement manacea le Prince et ses gentz; et coment il fut conseillez au bastard pur destruire les Englois, et le Prince oue ses gentz fut devaunt Vitoire tout dis en attendaunt la bataille.

<blockquote>

Au retourner lour fist grant joie
Le bastard Henri, si Dieux m'avoye;
Et lour dist : « Bien soiez venuz,
Beaux seigniours, bien vous sui tenuz. »   2825
Et puis disoit par motz exprès :
« Toutz les autres viendront après.
Mal quide ma terre tollir
Le Prince et moy quide assaillir :
Pourytant li feray savoir   2830
Que grant covetise d'avoir

</blockquote>

How the bastard rejoiced greatly at the return of the count don Tello and the rest, and at the capture of the English, and threatened the Prince and his people; and how the bastard was advised to destroy the English, and the Prince with his troops lay before Vitoria all that time expecting an engagement.

At their return, so God help me, the bastard Enrique made great rejoicing, and said to them: « Right welcome good Sirs, be ye well preserved; » and then said in plain words : « All the rest will come afterwards. The Prince thinks wrongly to take away my land and attack me : therefore I will let him know that great desire of gain has made him

Li ad fait cest voiage enprendre.
Qui prisoner le purroit prendre,
Tant li donroie argent et or
Que faire en purroit un tresor. » 2835
Quant li mareschal l'entendi,
Moult doulcement li dist ensi :
« Sire, dist-il, quei dites-vous ?
Encore n'avez-vous pas toutz
Les bons chivalers desconfitz ; 2840
Mais bien soiez certains et fis,
Quant à ceux vous combateretz,
Que gentz d'armes les troveretz.
Mais si bon conseil voillez croire,
Vous le purrez, c'est chose voire, 2845
Bien desconfire sanz coup frir :
Si vous voillez faire tenir
Le pas où ils doient passer,
Et bien votre host faire garder,

---

take this voyage. I would give to him who might take him prisoner, so much silver and gold as to form a great treasure. » When the Marshal heard this, he answered very mildly : « Sire, said he, what say you? You have not yet vanquished all these good knights; but be well assured and confident that when you shall fight with them, you shall find them to be men-at-arms. But if you will be well advised, you may perceive how you may gain the victory without a blow : if you will only seize on the pass through which they must march, and bid your army keep it well, so shall you have

Si ne lour facez jà bataille ; 2850
Par grande faute de vitaille
Les verrez d'Espaigne partir,
Ou de faym les verrez morir. »
Ensi fut conseillez li roys
Bastard du conseil des François. 2855
Et li Prince devant Vitoire
Fut rengiez sur les champs encore,
Qui tut dis illoeque attendoit
Si le bastard descenderoit,
Ses batailles toutes rengies 2890
Et ses banieres desploïes.
Sur les champs soi logea la nuyt.
Là n'avoient pas grant deduit ;
Car maint y ot, par saint Martyn,
Qui n'avoient ne pain ne vin. 2895
Pas ne fut trop bons li sojour,
Car sovent y avoit estour,

---

no battle ; from great want of provisions you shall see him quit Spain, or his army die of famine. » Thus was the bastard king counselled by the French, and the Prince was still drawn up on the plains before Vitoria, his line of battle ready formed and his banners displayed there waiting all the time, to see if the bastard would come down. On the field they encamped at night. Little entertainment had they, for many were there, by St. Martin, who had neither bread nor wine. Not very easy was their stay, for often were there attacks, and skirmishings made by the

Escarmuches de geneteurs,
Et des Englois y ot plusours
Et des uns et des autres mortz. 2900
Moult parfut le temps lays et ors
Et de pluie et de vent auxi.
Seigniour, cel temps que je vous dy,

Du temps quant ces choses par-devant escriptes furent faites, et coment le Prince se deslogea et chimina parmy Navarre, et passa le pas de la Garde, et vint à Viane et illoeques se logea, et après ce passa le pont del Groyng, et se logea devant le Groyng ès vergiers, et le bastard retourna de Saint-Vincent et se logea sur la ryvere devaunt Naddres, et le Prince tramist audit bastard une lettir.

CE fut en Mars, n'en doutez mye,
Que sovent pluit, vente et nivie, 2905

---

lancers; and many of the English of one party or the other died. The weather was very nasty and dirty with much wind and rain, Sirs, at the time that I tell you of.

Of the time when the things above written happened, and how the Prince removed and marched through Navarre, and passed the passage of La Guardia and came to Viana, where he stayed, and afterwards passed the bridge of Logroño and encamped before Logroño in the orchards, and the bastard returned from San Vicente and encamped on the river before Najera, and the Prince sent to the bastard a letter.

IT was in March, doubt not, when often it rains, blows and snows; never was there a worse season; and the

Unques ne fut plus malvais temps;
Et le Prince fut sur les champs,
Où moult falloit soeffrir des malx
Pur gentz d'armes et pur chivalx.
Et le lundi se dislogea   2910
Le Prince et s'achimina,
Parmy Navarre est retournez,
Un pas passa qui apellez
Fut par noun le *pas de la Garde*.
Tant chimina, si Dieux me garde,   2915
Qu'à Viane logier se vint.
Et après ce moult tost avint
Qu'il passa le pont de le Groyng.
Li Prince, qui moult ad grant soyng,
Et desires de la bataille,   2920
Celi jour se logea sanz faille
Devant le Groyng eins ès vergiers
Et par-desoubz les olyviers.

Prince was on the field, where he had to suffer greatly, both for his men-at-arms and his horses. And on Monday the Prince moved his quarters, and marched and returned through a pass that was called the pass of La Guardia. So far did he march, so God help me, that he came to Viana. And afterwards very soon it happened that he passed the bridge of Logroño. The Prince, who has a very great care and desire of battle, encamped on this day without fail before Logroño within the orchards and underneath the olive trees. And the bastard king by his

Et le roy bastard par espie
Sciet que l'ost du Prince est logie 2925
Devant le Groyng eius ès gardyns.
Lors n'aresta soirs ne matins,
De Saint-Vincent retourne arere,
Et se logea sur la rivere
Desoubz Naddres en une vynoble. 2930
Bel host avoit, puissant et noble.
Li Prince adonques li tramist
Une lettre, qui ensi dist.

Coment le Prince tramist au bastard ses lettres respon-
sales sur la tenure cy-ensuant.

« Très-puissant et très-honurez
Henry, lequel yestes clamez 2935
Duc de Tristemare, autrement
S'appelle pur le temps present

---

spies knew that the Prince was encamped before Logroño in the gardens; then he stopped neither night nor day, but returned from San Vicente, and encamped on the river below Najera in a vineyard. He had a noble and powerful host. The Prince then sent him a letter, which was couched in this manner.

How the Prince sent an answer to the bastard's letter, of the
following tenor.

« Right puissant and right honored Enrique, who art called Duke de Transtamare, and also calls himself

En ses lettres roy de Castielle.
Bien avons oÿ la novelle
De voz nobles lettres presentes, 2940
Qui sount graciouses et gentes,
Desqueux le tenour est pur voir
Que voluntiers vouldriez savoir
Purquoi nous sumes alliés
Et de notre foy fiancés 2945
Ovesque le votre enymy,
Quel nous teignons pur notre amy.
Sachez que nous le devons faire
Pour les alliances parfaire
Queux ont esté du temps passé, 2950
Et pur amour et pur pité,
Et pur droiture sustenir ;
Car vous deveriez bien sentir
En votre coer que n'est pas droitz
Qu'un bastard déust estre roys 2955

---

for the time present in his letters King of Castile. We have well heard the contents of your noble letters present, that are both gracious and gentle, of which the tenor is for truth, that you would willingly know why we are in alliance and have pledged our faith with your enemy, whom we hold for our friend. Know that we ought to do this to uphold the old alliances which have been in time past, and for love and for pity and to maintain the right; for you ought to understand in your heart that it is not right that a bastard should be king; nor should men agree to the

Pur un droit heir desheriter.
Nul hom ne se doit accorder
Qui soit de loial mariage.
D'un autre point vous faisons sage,
Que pur ce que hom vous prise tant 2960
Et que hom vous tient pur si vaillant,
S'accorder ambedeux purroie,
Moult voluntiers m'employeroye
Et feroie tant de ma part
Qu'en Castille averez grant part; 2965
Mais raison et droit si se donne
Que lesser vous faut la corone,
Et ensi se purroit nurrir
Bon paix entre vous, sanz mentir.
Et quant del entrée en Espaigne, 2970
Sachez que moy et ma compaigne,

---

disenheriting a rightful heir, who is of lawful wedlock. Let me advise you on another point, since that you are so highly esteemed, and held to be so valiant, that you should on each side come to terms, to which I would willingly lend assistance, and would agree for my part, that in Castile you shall have a great share; but reason and justice demand that you give up the crown, thus might there be truly fostered a good peace between you. But as to my entering into Spain, know that myself and my company, will,

Ovesque l'aïde de Dieu,
Y entrerons par lequel lieu
Que nous y plerra à entrer,
Sanz nule congé demander. »   2975

Coment un heraud porta les lettres du Prince et les presenta au bastard, et le bastard sur ce demaunda son conseil, et chescun en disoit son avis, et sur ce firent lour ordinance encontre le Prince.

ENSI fut la lettre dictée,
Et puis après fut seallée ;
Et la bailla à un heraud,
Qui ot le coer joiant et baud,
Et moult demenoit grantz reveaux :   2980
Car hom li dona beaux joiaux,
Robes d'ermyn, manteaux furrez.
Et lors ne s'est pluis arrestez,

---

by the help of God, enter just in that place that it shall please us to enter, without asking any leave. »

How a herald bore the Prince's letters, and presented them to the bastard, and the bastard called his council, and each gave his advice, and on this made their decision against the Prince.

THUS was the letter worded, and afterwards sealed, and they gave it to a herald, who had a heart joyous and light, and exulted much: for men had given him beautiful jewels, robes of ermine and mantles of fur. Then he stayed

Congié prist et s'en departi.
Vers son maistre le roy Henri 2985
Vint et la lettre li dona.
Le bastard, quant la regarda
Et aperceut la volunté
Que le Prince li ad mandé,
Bien sciet que moult ot de vaillance; 2990
Et sanz plus faire demorance,
Appela son conseil ensemble
Et demanda : « Quei vous en semble
De tout ce conseil bon à faire ? »
Chescun en disoit son affaire. 2995
Messire Bartrem de Claykyn,
Qui ot le coer hardi et fin,
Li dit : « Seigniour, ne vous doutez,
Car temprement combaterez;
Mais cognoissez le grant pooir 3000
Que li Prince mayne, pur voir.

---

no longer, but took his leave and departed. He came to his master King Enrique, and gave the letters. When the bastard had looked into them, and had perceived what was the Prince's will, he knew that he was a valiant man; and without making further delay, he called his council together, and demanded of them all : « What appears to you the best to do ? » Each said as he thought. Messire Bertrand du Guesclin, who had a fine and noble heart, said : « Sire, do not doubt but that you shall shortly have to fight ; but remember the great army that the Prince

Là est flour de chivalerie,
Là est flour de bachelerie,
Là sont les meillours combatantz
Qui soient eu monde vivantz, 3005
Si que vous avez bien mestier
Que vous facez apparailler
Voz gentz et mettre en ordinance. »
— « Daun Bartrem, ne aiez dotance,
Respondi li bastard Henris ; 3010
Car j'aurai, et j'en suis tut fis,
Bien iiij. mil chivalx armez,
Qui seront sur les deux costez
Des deux eles de ma bataille ;
Et si verrez, sachez sans faille, 3015
Bien quatre mille genetours ;
Et des gentz d'armes, des meillours
Que hom poet trover par tute Espaigne,
Auray deux mille en ma compaigne.

---

brings for truth. There is the flower of chivalry, there is the flower of bachelry, there are the best men-at-arms that are in the world alive, so that you have good need to draw out your forces and get them ready for action. » — « Messire Bertrand, have no fear, answered the bastard Enrique ; for I shall have, I am thoroughly confident, more than four thousand horse, who shall be on the two sides of the two wings of my division, and so shall you see, know without fail, more than four thousand lancers ; and of men-at-arms, better can no man find in all Spain, I shall have two thousand in my company ; and

Et si puis-je avoir, si sachés, 3020
Cinquante mille homes à pez
Et des arblastiers vj. mille.
Entreci jesques à Seville,
Ne demoere franc ne villayn;
Touz sont de moi aider certayn, 3025
Et si me ont promis par lour foi
Que touz jours me tiendront pur roy,
Si que je n'ay mie paour
Que je n'en aye le meillour. »
Ensi deviserent la nuit
En grant joie et en grant deduit. 3030

Coment le Prince se deslogea devant le Groign une matinée, et oue ses gentz rengiez cel jour chivacha deux leuges, et quidoit bien celui jour avoir la bataille, et envoia ses coureurs pur reporter la verité del host

---

know also that I shall muster fifty thousand infantry with six thousand cross bowmen. From here to Seville, there are neither free nor villain, but will be sure to assist us; for so have they faithfully promised that they will always hold me as their king. Thus I have no fear but that I shall have the best of it. » After that they passed the night with much joy and cheerfulness.

How the Prince decamped from before Logroño one morning, and with his men drawn up marched two leagues, thinking that this day he should have to fight; and how he sent his scouts to bring him true word of the bastard's army, that was

du bastard Henry, qui fut logie à Naveret, et les deux hostes, adonques deux leuges d'ensemble.

Et lui Prince n'aresta mye;
Lendemain à l'aube esclarcie
De devant le Groign deslogiez
S'est, que rien n'est atargiez.
En droit bataille ordeignée　　　　　　　　　　3035
Chivacha celle matinée,
Et rengist si joliement
Que unques ne vist si noble gent
Nul hom puis que Jhesu nasqui.
Celi jour fut le vendredi.　　　　　　　　　　3040
Deux leuges chivacha cel jour
Le prince sanz prendre sojour,
Et bien quidoit, sachez pur voir,
Celi jour la bataille avoir.

---

encamped at Navarrete, and the two armies were two leagues apart.

AND the Prince tarried not, but at the next earliest dawn he decamped from before Logroño: so that nothing was delayed. All in battle array he marched on this morning, and so excellent was their order, that never since Jesus' birth had men seen so fine an army. This day was Friday. Two leagues did the Prince ride this day without encamping, and thought, know for truth, that this was to be the day of battle. His scouts he sent out

Ses coureurs envoia partout, 3045
Lesqueux se travaillerent moult
Pur la verité reporter;
Mais au verité recorder,
De l'autre host virent la couvine,
Et perceurent qu'en ce termine 3050
Fut logiez desur la rivere
Près de Naddres en la bruere,
En les vergiers et en les champs.
Moult parestoit lour host puissantz,
Et de rien semblant ne fesoient 3055
Que cel jour chivachier devoient.
Au Prince erraument reporterent
De l'ost ensi qu'ils le troverent,
Qui se logea à Naveret,
Là où homme tout entreset 3060
L'ordonnance de la bataille.
Or furent si, sachez sanz faille,

---

everywhere, who exerted themselves much to bring him back the truth; but to make a true report, they saw the plan of the other army, and perceived that at this moment they were encamped upon the river near Najera on the heath, amongst orchards and in the fields; their army was very strong, nor did they make any show as if they would march on this day. To the Prince they straight reported of the host as they had found them, encamped before Navarrete, where they descried all the order of battle. Now were, know for certainty, the armies quartered,

A deux leuges près d'ensemble
Les hostz logiez, come moi semble.
Cele noet chescun sur son garde   3065
Estoit et de li se prent garde,
Et si coucherent tout armé.
Et devant qu'il fust adjourné,
Tramist le roi Henri espies
Vers Englois en plusours parties   3070
Pur savoir lour deslogement;
Mais, si lui estoire ne ment,
A plus matin se deslogierent
Et à chivachier chiminerent.
Mais le Prince oue le coer fin   3075
N'ala pas le plus droit chemyn,
Ançois prist, sachez de certayn,
Le chimin à la droite main,
Une montaigne et un grant val
Avalerent tout à chival   3080

---

as it seems to me, at a distance of two leagues apart; on this night each was on his guard, and took the greatest care, and so all the army passed the night. But before it was daybreak, King Enrique had sent scouts towards the English in many parties, to find out their removal; but, if my account lies not, very early they decamped and commenced their march. But the Prince with a fine judgment did not march by the direct road, but took, as is certain, the road to the right hand over a hill, and descended a deep valley; all were on horseback, so nobly appointed and so

Si très-noblement ordeignée
Et si coyntement serrée,
Que merveillouse fut à véir.
Et li bastard, sanz alentir,
Avoit très à la myenoit 3085
Ordeigné sa bataille et droit.
A pé estoit monsieur Bartrans
Et li bon mareschal vaillantz
D'Odreham, qui tant fut gentils,
Et li countes Sanses de pris, 3090
Lui counte de Dene ensement,
Qui d'Aragon fut proprement.
Si fut li Beghes de Villaine,
Qui estoit un moult bon chieftaine,
Monsieur Johan de Noefville 3095
Et d'autres plus de iiij. mille,
Dont je ne say nomer les nouns :
Quei d'Espaigne, quei d'Aragons,

---

neatly compact, that it was marvellous to see. The bastard too without delay had at very midnight, drawn out his army in array. And Messire Bertrand was afoot, and the good and valiant Marshal d'Audrehem, who was so gentle, the noble Count Sancho, and the Count de Denia also, who was just from Arragon. So was the Begue de Villaine, who was a good leader, Messire Jean de Neuville, and more than four thousand others, whose names I know not : some from Spain and Arragon, from France and

Quei de France et de Picardie,
De Britayne et de Normandie,   3100
De moultz d'autrez païs lointain.
Puis fut à la senestre main
A chival le conte dan Tille,
Qui avoit plus de xij. mille
Geneteurs, hommes à chival.   3105
Au destre lés fut le roial

De la grande bataille du bastard, qu'avoit ovesque lui xv. mille hommes d'armes et grant nombre des arblasters, et des chivalx armez iiij. mille et cent ; et le priour de Saint-Johan-le-Baptistre et le maistre de Saint-Jakes estoient en sa bataille.

Au roy bastard, que hom dist *Henri*,
Lequel avoit ovesque lui
Bien xv. mille hommes armez
Et des gents du païs assetz,   3110

Picardy, from Britanny and Normandy, and other distant parts. There then was on the left wing, on horseback, the Count Don Tello, who had more than twelve thousand mounted Spanish light horse. On the right side was the royal banner

Of the great army of the bastard, who had with him fifteen thousand men-at-arms, a great number of cross-bowmen and four thousand one hundred horse; and the prior of San Juan Bautista and the master of Santiago were in his army.

Of the bastard King, whom they called *Enrique;* he had with him more than fifteen thousand men-at-arms, with

Arblastiers, villayns et servantz,
A lances et à darts trenchantz
Et à fondes pur getter pieres
Pur garder devant les frontieres.
Unques tel mervaille ne fu, 3115
Ne tiel plenté de poeple vu
Come il ot à cele journée.
Là ot mainte baniere ouvrée
Qui fu de cendal et de soye.
Si le corps Jhesu-Crist m'avoye, 3120
Un petit et sur le costé
Estoient li chival armé
A·nombre de iiij. mille et cents.
Un chivaler de moult grant sens
Les governoit (moult fut subtils, 3125
Appelé fut *Gomez Garils*),
Et le priour de Saint-Johan,
Qui disoit qu'il feroit ahan

---

many people of the country, cross-bowmen, villains, servants, with lances and sharp darts, and slings to throw stones and to the cover their front. Never was such a marvellous sight, never so many people seen, as were engaged in this day's fight. Many were the banners worked, both of cendal and of silk. So help me Jesus Christ, a little towards one wing were the armed horses, to the number of four thousand one hundred. A knight of great sense and very clever commanded them (*Gomez Carillo* was his name), and the prior of San Juan, who said that he would cause the English

Englois soffrir celle journée.
Et là estoit sanz demorée 3130
Le maistre de Saint-Jacque auxi
Et un bon chivaler hardi,
Maistre de Calletrave ot noun.
Il disoit à haute raisoun
Que celi jour tant y ferroit 3135
Que la bataille perceroit.

Coment le Prince descendi de la mountaigne, et monsieur Johan Chaundos adonques fut mis à baniere : dount ses compaignons fesoient grant joie, et eux baillerent de combatre.

OR fut la chose devisée
Et tut lour host est ordeignée,
Et le Prince voet sanz attendre
Jus de la montaigne descendre. 3140

---

to suffer on this day. And there was ready at his post the master of Santiago also, and a good and hardy knight (the master of Calatrava was his name), who said in high terms, that this day he would strike so hard, that he would pierce the enemy's line.

How the Prince came down from the hill, and Sir John Chandos then was created a banneret, at which his company greatly rejoiced, and were eager for the fight.

Now were all things arranged and all the army drawn up; and the Prince wished without delay to come

Quant l'un host l'autre apercevoit,
Chescun sciet bien qu'il n'y avoit
Fors de combatre tout certain;
Nulle ne attendroit demain.
Monsieur Johan de Chaundos   3145
Est venuz au Prince tantos,
Et là porta sa baniere,
Qui fut de soie riche et chiere.
Moult doucement lui dist ensy :
« Sire, fait-il, pur Dieu mercy,   3150
Servi vous ay de temps passé;
Et tut ce que Dieux m'ad doné
De biens, ils me veignent de vous.
Et bien savez que je sui touz
Le votre, et je seray tout temps;   3155
Et s'il vous semble lieu et temps,

---

down from the hill. When one army perceives the other, each well knows that there was nothing for him but certainly to fight; no one would wait till the morrow. Then Sir John Chandos came forthwith to the Prince, and there brought his banner, that was of silk, rich and costly. And said right gently : « Sire, says he, so God have mercy, I have served you in time past; and all the good, that God has given me, has reached me through you; and you well know that I am entirely yours and always shall be ; and if the place and time suit you, that I might be a banneret,

Que je puisse à baniere estre,
J'ai bien de quoi à icel mestre
Que Dieux m'ad doné pur tenir.
Ore en faites votre pleisir.   3160
Veiez-le-cy, je vous present. »
Adonc le Prince sanz attent,
Et le roi Petre sanz detri,
Et le duc de Lancastre auxi,
La baniere li desploierent   3165
Et par le haut la li baillerent;
Et li distrent sanz plus retraire :
« Dieux vous en laist votre preu faire ! »
Et Chaundos sa baniere prist,
Entre ses compaignons la mist,   3170
Et lour ad dit à lée chiere :
« Beaux seigniours, vez ci ma baniere,
Gardez-la bien come la votre ;
Car auxi bien est toute notre. »

I have enough of my own to serve the master that God has given me; now do you your pleasure, see I present it to you. » Then the Prince directly and the King Pedro, with the Duke of Lancaster also, unfurled the banner, and presented it to him by the top ; and said without more ado : « God enable you to profit by it. » And Chandos took his banner, placed it among his companions, and said to them with a glad countenance : « Good sirs, here is my banner, defend it as your own ; for it is as well yours as mine. » His

Les compaignons ont fait grant joie ;   3175
Ils soulement ont pris lour voie.
Et ne vouloient pluis attendre,
Au combatre voillent entendre.
Celle baniere que vous dy
Portoit Guilliames Alery.   3180

Coment les Englois sont descenduz à pé, et le Prince fist ses prieres à Deu tout-puissant, et parla roy Petre certaines paroles, et adonques l'avant-garde passa avant.

ENGLOIS sont à pé descendu,
Qui moult ont le coer esmoü
De gaigner et conquere honour.
Et le Prince lour a dit : « Ce jour,
Seigniours, n'i ad autre termine.   3185
Vous savez bien que de famine

---

companions were right glad, and alone began their march. Nor would they wait longer, but would only hear of fighting. This banner that I tell you of was borne by William Alery.

How the English infantry marched down, and the Prince made his prayers to Almighty God, and King Pedro spoke a few words, and then the vanguard marched forward.

THE English then marched down, with hearts fully bent to gain and obtain glory ; and the Prince said : « To day, Sirs, has no other termination, as you well know, but

Et par vitailles sumes pris,
Et vez-ci là noz enemys
Qui de vitailles ont assetz,
Pain et vin et pissons salés   3190
Et frès, de doulce eawe et de mer;
Mais il les nous faut conquester
Au ferir de glayve et d'espée.
Or faceons tant ceste journée
Que partir puissons à honour. »   3195
Adonc le Prince de valour
Devers le ciel joingnit ses mains,
Et dist : « Vray Piere soverayns,
Qui nous avez fait et creez,
Si vrayment come vous savez   3200
Que je ne sui pas cy venuz
Fors pur droit estre soutenuz
Et proesce et pur franchise,
Qui mon coer semont et attise

---

in famine, for want of food we are well nigh taken. And see here and there our enemies, who have food enough, bread and wine and fish, salt and fresh, from the river and the sea; but those we must now obtain by the dint of sword and spear. Now let us do such a day's work, that we may separate with honour. » Then the Prince of valour joined his hands towards heaven, and said : « O very Sovereign Father, who hast made and fashioned us, so truly as you know that I am not come hither but to defend the right, for prowess and for liberty, that my heart craves

De conquester vie de honour, 3205
Je vous supplie qu'en cest jour
Voilliez garder moy et ma gent. »
Et quant le Prince ou le corps gent
Eut vers Dieu faite sa priere,
Adonc ad dit : « Avant, baniere ! 3210
Dieux nous aïde à notre droit ! »
Et lors le Prince là endroit
Le roy daun Petre par la main
Ad pris, et lui dist pur certain :
« Sire roy, au-jour-de-huit saurez 3215
Si jamès Castille rauretz.
Aiez en Dieu ferme creance. »
Ensement disoit sanz doutance
Ly Prince au coer sufficiant,
Et l'avant-garde va devant. 3220

---

and burns to obtain a life of honour, I pray you that on this day you will guard myself and my people. » And when the Prince had made his prayer to God, then he said : « Advance, banner ! God defend our right ! » Then the Prince straightway took King Don Pedro by the hand, and said to him : « Certainly, Sire King, to day you shall know if ever you shall recover Castile. Have thou firm trust in God, » added the Prince, with a noble heart, nothing doubting; and the vanguard moved forward.

Coment le duc de Lancastre et monsieur Johan Chaundos passerent en l'avant-garde, et là furent fait chivalers, et le duc conforta très-noblement ses gentz.

De Lancastre li noble ducs,
  Qui moult eut en lui de vertus,
Et Chaundos, le bon chivaler,
Fist là chivalers sanz targer
Curson, Priour et Elitoun,   3225
Monsieur Guilliam de Faryndon
Et Ammori de Rocheward,
Cely de la Mote, Gaillard,
Et monsieur Robert Briket.
Là eut-il maint chivaler fet,   3230
Qui furent plain de vasselage,
De noble et de puissant linage.
Li duc de Lancastre einz le champ
Dist à Guilliame de Beauchamp :

How the Duke of Lancaster and Sir John Chandos accompanied the vanguard, and there were made knights, and the Duke encouraged his troops.

THE noble Duke of Lancaster, who had many virtues, and the good knight Chandos made knights without delay Curson, Priour, and Eliton, and Sir William de Faringdon, with Aymery de Rochechouart, and Gaillard de la Motte, and Sir Robert Briquet. Many knights were then made, who were full of courage, of noble and puissant lineage. The Duke of Lancaster in the field said to William

« Veiez, fist-il, noz enemys ; 3235
Mais, si m'aïde Jesus-Cris,
Huy me verrez bon chivaler,
Si mort ne me fait encombrer. »
Puis dist : « Baniere, avant, avant !
Preignons dampne-Dieu à garant, 3240
Et face chescun son honour. »
Et lors li francs ducs de valour
Devant toutz ses hommes se mist ;
Plus de cent revenir en fist
De lour corages plus hardis 3245
Que devant furent, ce m'est vis.
En celle heure fist chivaler
Li duc Johan d'Ipre au coer fier.

Du commencement de la grant bataille, et des seigniours qui furent à la bataille oue le duc de Lancastre, et

---

Beauchamp : « See there, said he, our enemies; but, so help me Jesus Christ, to day you shall see me a good knight, if death prevent me not. » Then he cried : « Banner, advance, advance ! Let us take God to our rescue, and each do to his honour. » And then the noble Duke of valour put himself at the head of all his men; more than a hundred did he cause to become of higher courage than ever they were before, as I am aware. In this hour did the Duke make John of Ipre of high courage a knight.

Of the beginning of the great battle, and of the lords who were there with the Duke of Lancaster, and of their meeting with the

de l'assemblée à la bataille de monsieur Bertram, et coment maint bon chivaler fut tresbuché à terre.

Or commence bataille fier,
 Et prist à lever le poudrer.   3250
Archiers traient à la volée,
Plus dru que plume n'est volée.
Li ducz de Lancastre devant
S'en va come homme vaillant.
Après li va Thomas de Ufford   3255
Et Hugh de Hastynges fort,
Chescun baniere desploïe.
Chescun tenoit launce basie.
Sur la main destre fut Chaundos,
Qui celi jour acquist grant los ;   3260
Estephenes de Cossyngtone,
Johan Devereux, noble persone ;

---

army of Messire Bertrand, and how many good knights were slain.

Now commenced the battle fiercely, and the dust began to rise. Archers made their arrows fly in clouds thicker than feather had ever flown. The Duke of Lancaster in advance bore himself like a valiant man. After him came Thomas de Ufford and the brave Hugh de Hastings, each displaying his banner. Each held his lance in rest. On the right hand was Chandos, who this day acquired great praise; with Stephen de Cosington, Sir John Devereux, a noble man; and there was the good

Et là fut li bon Guychard d'Angle,
Qui ne se tenoit pas en l'angle.
Ovesque li ot ses deux filtz   3265
Et d'autres chivalers de pris,
Qui bien fesoient lour devoir ;
Et là estoit, sachez de voir,
Li très-noble sires de Rès.
Là véist-hom venir tout près,   3270
Après banieres et peignons,
Ensemble touz les compaignons.
Chescun tint la lance en pugnie,
Et fesoient grant envaïe
Pur courre sur lour enemys.   3275
Et les archiers traioient toutdiz
Et arbalastiers d'autre part,
Qui furent oue le bastard ;
Mais tout à pé tant chiminerent
Que tout ensemble s'encontrerent   3280

Guichard d'Angle, who kept not in the back ground. His two sons he had with him; other knights of renown were there who well did there duty; and there was also, know for truth, the right noble Lord de Raix. There might one see following closely the banners and pennons, all the great Companies, every one holding his lance in his grasp; and struggling to the utmost to fall upon the enemy. And all the time the archers, and cross-bowmen on the other side who were with the bastard shot their arrows; but all on foot they marched on, until they encountered the division of Bertrand, who

A la bataille de Bertran,
Qui moult lour fist soeffrir ahan.
Là véissez à l'assembler
Ensemble de glayves bouter.
Chescun de bien faire se payne.   3285
Là ne fut, c'est chose certayne,
Nul coer eu monde si hardis
Que ne puist en estre esbahis
Pur les grantz coups qu'ils se donoient
Des grandes haches qu'ils portoient   3290
Et des espées et cotiaux.
Ce ne fut mie grantz reviaux,
Car vous véissez tresbucher
A terre maint bon chivaler.

Coment mainte baniere fut versée à terre, et monsieur Johan Chandos fut abatuz à terre, et un Castillayn fut cheuz sur ly et lui plaia ; mais par la grace de

---

caused them to suffer much. There then at the encounter might you see swords thrust and crossed, each striving to acquit himself well. Never, in good sooth, was there in the world a heart that would not have been staggered by the heavy blows that were struck by the great axes they carried and by the swords and knives. This was no great disport, for many a good knight might there be seen cast to the earth.

How many a banner was cast down, and Sir John Chandos was struck to the ground, and a Castilian fell on him and wounded him ; but by the grace of God he recovered himself and slew

*Dieu il recoveri et occist le Castillayn, et après ceo
refiert en la mellée et combati moult fortment.*

<blockquote>

Grant fut la noise et la fumiere.　　　　3295
Là n'y ot peignon ne baniere
Qui ne fust à terre versée;
Tiele foitz fut celle journée.
Chaundos fut à terre abatuz.
Par desus li estoit chéuz　　　　　　　　3300
Un Castillain, qui moult fut grantz;
Appelez fut *Martins Ferantz*,
Lequel durement se paynoit
Coment occire le purroit,
Et li plaia par la visiere.　　　　　　　　3305
Chaundos à très-hardie chiere
Un cotel prist à son costé,
Le Castillain en ad frappé,
Qu'en son corps lui ad embatu
Par force le cotel agu.　　　　　　　　　3310

</blockquote>

the Castilian, and after that he was again in the action and fought right strongly.

Great was the noise and the dust. There was not a pennon nor a banner that was not thrown to the ground; such was this fight. Chandos was beaten down, and there fell upon him a Castilian of great stature, *Martin Fernandez* by name, who struggled hard how he might kill him, and wounded him through the visor. Chandos right boldly took a knife at his side, struck the Castilian, and plunged the sharp knife into his body. The Castilian fell down

Le Castillain mort s'estendi.
Et Chaundos sur ses pés sailli ;
Entre ses poings ad pris l'espée
Et se refiert en la mellée,
Qui moult estoit dure et cremeuse   3315
Et au regarder merveilleuse.
Cil qui de ly estoit atayns,
De la mort peust estre certains.

*Coment le duc de Lancastre très-chivalerousement
combatoit, et se mist en très-graunt aventure.*

E<small>T</small> d'autre part, li noble ducz
De Lancastre, plein de vertuz,   3320
Si noblement se combatoit,
Que chescun s'en esmerveilloit
En regardant sa grant prouesce,
Coment par sa noble hautesse

---

dead. And Chandos leaped upon his feet, grasped his sword in both hands, and was again in the battle, that was right hard and fearful and wonderful to behold; and he that was struck by him might be certain of his death.

How the Duke of Lancaster fought right valiantly, and exposed himself to very great danger.

O<small>N</small> the other hand, the noble Duke of Lancaster, full of virtue, fought so nobly, that all marvelled in beholding his great prowess, how in his high daring he

Mettoit son corps en aventure : 3325
Car jeo croy que unques creature,
Poevre ne riches, ne se mist
Cel jour si avant come il fist.
Et ly Prince n'attendoit pas ;
A l'estour plus tost que le pas 3330
S'en venoit, si sachez sanz faille,
Du lès destre de sa bataille.

Coment la baniere au roy de Navarre et monsieur Martin de Lacarre se partirent oue le Captal oue ij. mille combatauntz pur combatre au counte dan Tille ; et devant qu'ils purroient assembler, le counte dan Tille s'en departi.

La baniere au roy de Navarre
Et monsieur Martin de Lacarre
Se partirent ou le Captal, 3335
Qui ot le coer preu et loial,

---

exposed himself to danger; for I think that never man, poor or rich, put himself so forward, as he did on this day. Nor was the Prince behind hand in the fray, but with all speed came up, you must know without fail, with the right wing of his division.

How the banner of the King of Navarre and Don Martin de Lacarre departed with the Captal, with two thousand fighting men, to engage the Count Don Tello; and before they could engage, the Count Don Tello took to flight.

The banner of the King of Navarre and Don Martin de Lacarre departed with the Captal, who had a preux

Et le droit seignour de la Bret,
Qui de bien faire s'entremet,
Ensemble furent bien ij. mille
Pur combatre au counte dan Tille, 3340
Qui fut sur la senestre main
De dan Bertran au coer certain;
Mais je vous puis bien recorder
Qu'avant qu'ils purent assembler,
Dan Tille s'en prist à partir ; 3345
Et le Captal, sanz alentir,
Sur ceux à pé prist son retour.
Moult les travaillerent ce jour.
Come gent de hardi corage
Se defendoient par vasselage 3350
A senestre d'autre costé
Du Prince, c'este verité,
Percy, le seigniour de Clisceoun,
Et monsieur Thomas de Felton

---

and loyal heart, and the good Lord d'Albret, who set himself to do well, together were they two thousand to fight with the Count Don Tello, who was on the left hand of the stout-hearted Messire Bertrand's division; but I ought to tell you that before they engaged, Don Tello betook himself to flight; and the Captal, without delay, marched back again on the foot soldiers. They struggled hard on this day, like men of a daring spirit defending themselves courageously. On the left of the other side of the Prince, it is true, Percy, the Lord of Clisson, with Sir Thomas

Et messire Gautier Hewet, 3355
Qui sovent parler de ly fait.
Cils venoient pour visiter
L'avant-garde et pur conforter.

Coment li très-noble Prince venoit oue sa graunt bataille pur combatre, et l'arere-garde fut comaundée d'estre à une petite mountaigne par devers les chivalx armez, et là fut le roy de Mayogre et plusours seigniours, et la bataille comença de toutes parts, et combatirent tant que les Espaignards s'enfuirent.

Lors s'enforce li ferréis
Et fors fut li abatéis; 3360
Car lui franc Prince d'Aquitaine
Toute sa grant bataille amaine.
Là n'avoit cely qui se faigne.
Une bien petite montaigne

Felton and Sir Walter Hewet, whose deeds are often spoken of, came to visit and encourage the van-guard.

How the right noble Prince came with his great army into action, and the rereward was ordered to the side of a small hill towards the armed chargers, and there was the King of Majorca and many lords, and the battle commenced on every side, and lasted until the Spaniards were put to flight.

Then raged the din of arms and great was the slaughter; for the noble Prince of Aquitaine brought up his main body. There were no cowards there. On the left,

Avoit desoubz la main senestre. 3365
Là ot-hom comandée à estre
L'arere-garde sur le lés
Par devers les chivalx armez.
Là fut le Maiogre le roy,
Que pas oblier je ne doy, 3370
Et le preu conte d'Armynak
Et le seigniour de Saverak,
Messire Berard de la Bret
Et Bertrukat, qui fu en het
De combatre et entalentés. 3375
Et se ne vous ay pas nomez
Monsieur Hugh de Calverlé,
Purquoy vous seroit destorbé
La matiere et plus alongie?
Moult fut la bataille enforcie, 3380
Qui comence de toutes partz.
Archigaies, launces et dardz

---

below, was a very little hill; men had there been posted, the rereward on the side, towards the armed chargers. There was the King of Majorca, whom I ought not to forget, the preux Count d'Armagnac, and the Lord de Severac, Messire Bernard d'Albret, and Perdiccas, who was eager and well able to fight. And if I have not named Sir Hugh de Calverley, why should I interrupt and made my history too long? Right vigorous was the fight that now began on all sides. The Spaniards hurled stoutly arrows,

Lanceoient Espaignards par force.
Chescun de bien faire s'esforce,
Car plus drut traioient archier   3385
Que ne soit pluie en temps d'yver.
Chivalx et hommes lour blisceoient,
Et les Espaignards bien perceoient
Que plus ne purroient endurer.
Les chivals prirent à tourner   3390
Et à la fuite se sont mys.
Quant les vit li bastard Henris,
En ly n'avoit que coroucier.
Par trois foitz les fist reculer
En disant : « Seigniours, aidez-moy   3395
Pur Dieu, car vous m'avez fait roy
Et si m'avez fait serement
De moy aider loialement. »
Mais sa parole rien ne vaut,
Car toutzjours renforce l'assaut.   3400

---

lances, and javelins. Each strove to do his best. The arrows flew thicker than rain in winter time. Horses and men they wounded, and pierced through the Spaniards, that they could no longer endure it, and the cavalry began to give way and betook themselves to flight. When the bastard Enrique saw them, he was much enraged, three times he rushed them back, saying : « Sirs, give me aid for God's sake, for you have made me King, and you have taken an oath to aid me by your loyalty. » But his word availed nothing, for the attack encreased every moment.

Coment le bastard s'enfui, et les Espaignardz furent descomfitz, et après ce les François se combatirent et furent auxi descomfitz, et monsieur Bartrem et plusours seigniours et chivalers furent pris et gentz d'armes mortz, et des Englois le sieur de Ferrers fut occis à mesme celle bataille.

Quei voillez-vous que je vous dye ?
Il n'avoit en la compaignie
Du Prince home, tant fust petitz,
Qui ne fust bien auxi hardiz
Et auxi fiers come un lion.　　　　　　　　　　3405
Home ne poet comparaison
Faire de Olyver et Rolant.
Espaignardz se tournoient fuyant,
Chescun ses frains abandonez.
Dolantz en fut et moult irez　　　　　　　　　　3410

How the bastard fled, and the Spaniards were put to flight, and afterwards the French engaged and were also discomfited, and Messire Bertrand and many lords and knights were taken and soldiers slain, and of the English the Lord de Ferrers was slain at the same battle.

What will you that I now relate ? There was not in the Prince's army one man so small, who was not also hardy and as bold as a lion. Neither might men compare with them Oliver or Roland. The Spaniards then turned and fled each at full speed. Grieved and right angry

Luy bastard quant il les veoit;
Mais fuyer il les covenoit,
Ou ils fuissent toutz pris et mortz.
Lors comence lui grant effortz;
Là véissez le pé taillié, 3415
Occis d'estoch et detaillié.
Luy bastard s'enfuit tut un val;
Mais encore sont en estal
Li François, Bretons et Normandz;
Mais petit dura lour baubantz, 3420
Car moult tost furent disconfit.
Et si sachez trestouz de fit
Qu'hom crioit là à haute gorge
En maint lieu : *Guyane ! Saint George !*
Illoec fut pris monsieur Bertrans, 3425
Et le mareschal sufficiantz
D'Odrehem, qui tant fut hardiz,
Et un counte qui eut grant pris;

---

was the bastard at the sight; but it behoved them to fly, or they had all been slain or taken. Then commenced the great struggle; there might you see the drawn sword smiting point and blade. The bastard fled by the valley, but the French, Bretons and Normans still stood their ground; but little availed their high courage, for they were soon defeated. And so know ye all was over. And men cried with a loud voice in many places for *Guienne ! Saint George !* There was taken Messire Bertrand and the able Marshal d'Audrehem, who was so hardy, and a count of great

Counte de Dene fut nomez.
Ly counte Sanses, n'en doutés, 3430
Y fut pris, qui fut chieftayne,
Oue le Beghes de Villaine,
Monsieur Johan de Noefville
Et des autres plus de ij. mille.
Et pur faire juste report, 3435
Luy Beghes de Villiers fut mort
Et plusours autres, dont de noun
Je ne say faire mencioun;
Mais li report y fut tenuz :
Cink centz homes d'armes, ou plus, 3440
Morurent en la piece à terre
Où homme eut maynte et maynte afere.
Auxi de la part des Englois
Morut un chivaler parfès :

---

price; Count de Denia was his name. The Count Sancho too doubtless, who was in command, was taken there, with the Begue de Villaines, Messire Jean de Neville and of others more than two thousand; and, to make a true report the Begue de Villiers was killed, with many others, whose names I know not how to mention. But it was reported that five hundred men-at-arms, or more, fell upon that field, where men had their hands full. Also on the side of the English fell a perfect knight, the noble Lord de

Ce fut le seigniour de Ferriere. 3445
Li glorious Dieux et seint Piere
Ait les almes des trespassés!
Seigniour, pur Dieu ore entendés.

*De la place où la grant bataille estoit, et de la chase
après la bataille; et coment les Espaignardz, plus
de deux mille, se noierent en une rivere; environ
vij. mille et vij. c. furent mortz, issint que l'eawe
en fut vermaille; et les Englois entrerent en la ville
et là furent prisoners pris; et le Prince, qui se
tenoit oue sa baniere levée, fut moult joious.*

LA place où home combati
Estoit sur un plaine joly 3450
Où il n'eut arbre ne buysson
D'une grant leuge environ,

Ferrers. The glorious God and Saint Peter have the souls of the dead! Sirs, for God's sake now hear.

Of the place where this great battle was, and the pursuit afterwards; and how the Spaniards, more than two thousand, were drowned into a river; and about seven thousand seven hundred were killed, so that the water was red with blood; and the English entered the town, where prisoners were taken, and the Prince, who remained with his banner raised, was right joyous.

THE place where the battle was fought was a beautiful plain, where was neither tree nor bush for a good

Solohe une beal rivere,
Qui moult estoit et radde et fiere ;
Lequel fist ceo jour de maus   3455
Sur Castillains, car li enchaus
Dusque à la rivere dura,
Plus de deux mille en y noia.
Devant Nazareth sur le pont
Je vous fais assavoir que mont   3460
Fut l'enchaus perillous et fiers.
Là véissez-vous chivalers
De paour en l'eawe sallir
Et l'un sur un autre morir ;
Et si dist-hom par grant merveille   3465
Que la rivere en fut vermeille
Du sanc que issoit hors des corps
Des hommes et des chivalx mortz.
Tant fut grantz la disconfiture
Que je croy que unques creature   3470

---

league round, by a beautiful river, that was both rapid and deep, which on this day enhanced the misery of the Castilians, for the pursuit continued down to the river. More than twelve thousand were drowned. On the bridge before Najera I tell you that very perilous and grievous was the chace. There might you see knights for fear leaping into the water, and dying one upon another. And men said that by great marvel the river was red with blood that flowed from the bodies of the dead men and horses. So great was the defeat, that I believe never had

Ne pooit unques avoir vewe
Un peril, si Dieux m'aiue :
Tant fut gros la mortalité.
Li nombres ent fut reporté
Environ vij. mille et vij. centz.   3475
Et si vous di bien que les gentz
Du Prince entrerent en la ville.
Là en eut des mortz plus de mille,
Et là fut pris en une cave
Lui grant mestre de Calletrave   3480
Et le priour de Saint-Johan,
Qui moult lour fist soeffrir d'ahan,
Le mestre de Saint-Jake auxi.
Cils deux s'estoient sans detri
Trait par deux costés d'un haut mur.   3485
Là ne furent pas asséur,
Car gentz d'armes sus se metoient,
Qui à l'assaillir se voloient;

---

man at any time seen such a loss, so, God be my help, great was the slaughter. The number was reported about seven thousand seven hundred. And so, I tell you, the troops of the Prince entered the town. There were more than a thousand dead; and there they took in a cave the grand master of Calatrava, the prior of San Juan, who made them suffer much, the master of Santiago also. These two were without delay covered on both sides by a high wall. There they were not safe, for men-at-arms climbed up, to assail them from thence; humbly then they surren-

Mais humblement se vindrent rendre,
Car ne les oserent attendre. 3490
Eńsi furent-ils mortz et pris :
Dont très-forment fut rejoïz
Lui très-noble Prince vaillantz,
Lequel se tenoit sur les champs
Et ot sa baniere levée, 3495
Où sa gent se fut rassemblée.

Du temps quant ceste bataille estoit.

SEIGNIOUR, le temps que je vous dy
Ce fut droit par un samady,
Trois jours droit eu moys d'averil,
Que tiel doulce oisselet gentil 3500
Preignent à refaire lour chantz
Par prées et bois et par champs.
En celluy temps fut tout sans faille
Devant Nazarz la grant bataille.

---

dered themselves, for they dared no longer wait. Thus were they slain or taken; at which the very high and noble Prince greatly rejoiced. He remained upon the field, and had his banner raised, where his troops reassembled.

Of the time of the battle.

SIRS, the time that I tell you of, was just upon a Saturday, the third day of the month of April, when the sweet gentle birds begin again their song, through meadow, wood and field. At this time was without fail the great battle before Najera.

Coment le Prince se logea à noet oue ses gentz, où le bastard fut logié la noet devant, et là menerent grant deduit et gracioient Dieu, et là troverent vitailles assetz et grant plenté de richesse.

Ensi fut come oÿ avez. 3505
En cele noet fut hostellez
Lui Prince droit eu logement
Où luy roy Henri proprement
Avoit esté logiez la nuyt.
Illoec menoient grant deduyt, 3510
Et gracioient Dieu le Piere,
Le Filtz et sa benoite miere,
De la grace qu'il lour ad fait;
Car bien sachez tout entresait
Que là trouverent vin et pain 3515
(Toutz les loges ent furent plain),

How the Prince with his troops at night encamped, where the bastard was lodged the night before, and were right joyful and gave thanks to God, and there found victuals enough and riches in plenty.

So it was as you have heard. The Prince was encamped on this night, in the very lodging where King Enrique himself had lodged the night before. There they had great rejoicings, and thanked God the Father, the Son and his blessed Mother, for the grace he had bestowed; for know well besides that they found there wine and bread (all the

Cofres, vessel, or et argent,
Dont il pleut bien à mainte gent.

Coment le roy daun Petre est venuz au Prince et le remercia de ce qu'il avoit fait pur luy, et disoit au Prince coment il voloit prendre vengeaunce de ceux qui avoient esté contre luy, et le noble Prince à ce respoundi, et luy disoit son sage avis.

LY roy daun Petre en est venuz
Au Prince, qui moult fut ses druz, 3520
Et lui ad dit : « Beau cosin chier,
Je vous doi bien remercier,
Car ce jour-de-huy m'avez fait tant
Que jamès jour de mon vivant
Je ne le purray deservir. » 3525
— « Sire, fit-il, votre pleisir.

---

quarters were full), coffers, vessels, gold and silver, with which many were well pleased.

How the King Don Pedro came to the Prince, and thanked him for all he had done, and told the Prince how he wished to take vengeance on those who had been against him, and the noble Prince replied and gave him his good advice.

THE King Don Pedro came to the Prince, who was his warm friend, and said to him : « Cousin dear, I ought indeed to thank you, for you have done more for me this day, than I can ever deserve, the longest day I live. » — « Sire,

Merciez Dieu, et noun pas moy ;
Car par la foy que je vous doy,
Dieux l'ad fait, et noun mie nous,
Si que nous devons estre touz   3530
En volunté de li prier
Merci et de lui gracier. »
Daun Petre dist qu'il disoit voir
Et de ce avoit bon vouloir ;
Mais il voilloit prendre vengeance   3535
Des traïtours qui par puissance
Lui ont fait tant de mal sentir.
Lors dist le Prince sanz mentir :

Coment le Prince conseilla le roy Petre de pardoner à ceux qui avoient esté encontre lui ; et le roy daun Petre lui granta, forspris un qui avoit à noun Gome

---

said he, 'with your leave, give thanks to God, and not to me ; for, by the faith that I owe you, God, not we, has done this, so that we ought all willingly to pray his mercy and give him thanks. » Don Pedro answered that he spake truth, and that he was willing to act thus ; but he wished to take vengeance on the traitors who in their might had done him such evil. Then spake the Prince plainly :

How the Prince advised King Pedro to pardon those who had been against him; and the King Don Pedro assented,

Garilles, *lequel fut trayné parmy l'ost et la goule trenchée.*

« SIRE roy, donez-moy un don,
   Je vous pri, si vous semble bon. »   3540
Dist lui roy Petre : « Las ! purquoy,
Sire, demandez-vous à moy ?
Tout est votre ce que je ay. »
Lors dist li Prince sanz delay :
« Sire, du votre ne voil rien ;   3545
Mais je vous conseille pur bien,
Se estre voillez roy de Castelle,
Que par tout mandez la novelle
Que ottroié avez le doun
De doner à touz ceux pardoun   3550
Qui ont encontre vous esté ;
Et ce par male volunté

---

excepting one who was named Gomez Carillo, *who was dragged through the army, and his throat cut.*

« SIRE King, grant me one boon, I pray you, if it seem good. » King Pedro answered : « Sire, why do you ask of me ? All I have is yours. » Then said the Prince without delay : « Sire, of yours I want nothing ; but I advise you for good, if you would be King of Castille, that you send forth word, that you have consented to give pardon to all those who have been against you, and have by ill will or by

Et par malvais conseil auxi
Esté ou le bastard Henry,
De ore en avant lour pardonez ; 3555
Mais que de bonne voluntez
Ils veignent vous merci prier. »
Lui roy daun Petro ottroier
Le volt, mais ce est à grant payne.
Puis dist au Prince d'Aquitayne : 3560
« Beau cosin, je le vous ottroie,
Fors que d'un, mais je ne vorroie
Avoir trestout l'or de Seville
Pur deporter Gomez Carille,
Car certes ce est le traïtour 3565
Qui plus m'ad fait de deshonour. »
Et li Prince li dist ensi :
« Faites votre vouloir de luy,
Et les autres touz pardonez. »
Sanches, frere au bastard, fut amenez, 3570

---

ill advice also, sided with the bastard Enrique ; but, before you pardon them, that they, all of free will, come to pray you mercy. » The King Don Pedro consented, but with much difficulty. Then he said to the Prince of Aquitaine : « Good cousin, I consent to all with one exception ; but I would not for all the gold of Seville, trifle with Gomez Carillo, for he is the very traitor who has done me dishonour. » The Prince answered him : « Do your will with him, and pardon all the others. » Then Sancho, the bastard's

Et plusours autres prisoniers,
Qui il pardona voluntiers
Pur le Prince et pur sa priere.
Et lors se retourna arere
Tout droit où il estoit logiez, 3575
Et illoc fut apparaillez
Gome; traÿner le fist-hom
Et trencher la goule soubz le menton
Adonc devant toute la gent.
Purquoy feroy-je un parlement 3580
De la matiere plus lontayne?
Le Prince le lundi proschayne

Coment le Prince et le roy Petre s'en departirent de Naddres par devers Burghes, et les novelles s'en alerent à toutes parts.

DE devant Naddres se party,
Et le roy daun Petro auxi.

---

brother, and other prisoners were brought up, whom he freely pardoned, for the Prince and his prayer's sake. And then he returned again straight to his camp; and there Gomez Carillo was dressed, then dragged out, and had his throat cut beneath his chin before all the troops. Why should I make a longer story of this matter? The Prince on the next Monday

How the Prince and King Pedro departed from Najera towards Burgos, and the news travelled far and wide.

THEY departed from before Najera, and King Pedro also. They took their way to Burgos; and then the

Par devers Burghes chiminerent ; 3585
Et lors les novelles alerent
Par Espaigne de toutes partz
Que desconfitz fut li bastardz.

Coment la femme du bastard estoit à Burghes ; et quant ele avoit oÿ les novelles, ele s'enfuit moult dolente en Aragon, et fist ses grantz et dolorouses compleintes de la fortune ; et après ce comenda li Prince moult noblement ; et le Prince se vint loger à Bervesques.

A Burghes estoit sa moullier,
Qui n'eut mye temps de targier. 3590
Sitost que novelles savoit,
S'en ala plus tost que pooit,
Et ce qu'ele pooit porter
De bien que elle pooit trusser.

---

tidings travelled through Spain on every side, that the bastard was defeated.

How the wife of the bastard was at Burgos ; and when she heard the news, she fled all wretched into Aragon, and made great and dolorous complaint of fortune ; and afterwards she commended the Prince right nobly, and the Prince removed to Briviesca.

AT Burgos was his wife, who had no time to tarry. So soon as she had heard the news, she with all possible speed, and with what she could carry of those

Tant chimina et jour et nuit 3595
Oue ceux qui li font conduit,
Qu'en Aragon elle est venue.
Moult durement fut deperdue ;
Come dolante et esplorée
Disoit : « Las ! purquoy fui-je née ? 3600
De Castille estoie roïgne
De corone d'or riche et fine ;
Mais poi a duré la fortune.
Hé ! mort, que estes à touz commune,
Que attends-tu ? Morir vorroie, 3605
Car jamès avoir ne purroie
Ne esbatement ne solas.'
Toute foitz que homme dira : « Las !
Veiez-là la roigne d'Espaigne,
Que corona la grant Compaigne ! 3610

---

goods she could pack up, travelled day and night with those who formed her escort until she came to Aragon. Very sadly was she cast down ; as bewailing and full of tears, she said : « Alas ! why was I born ? I was Queen of Castille with a rich crown of gold; but a short time has fortune lasted. O death, who art common, to all men why delayest thou now that I would die, for never more can I have relief nor solace. Men will always say : « Alas ! See there the Queen of Spain, crowned by the great

Hé! Prince, ta puissance fiere
M'ad de haut en bas mis arere.
Moult est bien la dame honorée
Que à ton corps est assenée ;
Car dire poet qu'ele ad la flour   3615
De tout le monde et le meillour,
Et que tout le monde maistrie. »
Ensi dist la dame jolie,
Que se compleindoit en ses dits ;
Et li noble Prince de pris   3620
S'en vint à Bervesques logier,
Et le roi Petre à chivacher

Coment le roy Petre s'en chivacha devaunt Burghes, et les burgeis venoient encontre lui et ly receiverent moult belement. Et après ceo le Prince venoit à Burghes, et là demora par un moys ; et le roy Petre manda

---

Company. Oh Prince, thy proud prowess has brought me down from my high estate. Highly is that lady honoured, who is bound to thee; for she can say that she has the best flower of all the world, and he who is master of all. » Thus said the lovely dame, who made these complainings; and the noble and renowed Prince marched and encamped at Briviesca, and King Pedro rode there.

How the King Pedro rode towards Burgos, and the citizens met and received him very kindly. And afterwards the Prince came to Burgos, and there stayed one month ; and King Pedro

par toute Espaigne, et lour sount venuz les gentz de toutes parties, et lui prierent mercy, et il les pardona.

S^E prist devant Burghes tut droit.
Encontre de li là endroit
Vindrent touz li riches burgeois, 3625
Qui lui disoient : « Bien-veignez, rois. »
Lors fut à Burghes recéuz,
Et li Prince y est venuz
Après le terme de vj. jours,
Et à Burghes fut ly sojours 3630
Bien le terme d'un mois passé.
Par tout Espaigne ad hom crié
Si qu'il n'i ad cité ne ville
Et à Tollette et à Seville,
A Cordevalle et à Lion, 3635
Par tout le roialme environ,

---

sent through all Spain, and there came to him the people from all parts, and prayed him mercy, and he pardoned them.

HE took his way straight to Burgos, from which town all the rich inhabitants came out to meet him; and said : « Oh King, welcome ! » Then was he received into Burgos. The Prince came there also, after the lapse of six days, and sojourned at Burgos, until a month had passed away. Through all Spain the proclamation was made, so that there was no town nor city, both at Toledo and Seville, at Cordova and Leon, through all the realm round

Que chescun venist sanz detry
Au roy Petre prier mercy.
Lors sont de toutes partz venu
Lui estranges et lui conu, 3640
Et li roy tous lour pardona.
Seigniour, ne vous mentiray jà.

Coment le Prince tenoit son jugement devant Burghes, et toute Espaigne fut à sa ordinance; et là vint Ferantes de Castres, et le Prince ly fist grant honour et le festoia moult noblement; et là sojourna le Prince vij. mois et plus, et illoeques furent les serements renovellés.

Luy Prince tint certainement
Devant Burghes son jugement,
Et tint son gage de bataille, 3645
Si que hom pooit dire sanz faille

---

about, that did not come without delay to ask mercy of King Pedro; from all parts they came, strangers with those known, and the King pardoned them all. Sirs, I will tell you no untruth.

How the Prince held his court before Burgos, and all Spain was at his bidding; and there came Fernando de Castro, and the Prince did him great honour, and right nobly entertained him; and there sojourned seven months and more, and there the oaths were renewed.

The Prince in good truth held his court before Burgos, and his wager of battle, so that men might say truly

Qu'en Espaigne ot tiele puissance
Que tut fut à son ordinance.
Là vint de Castres dans Ferrantz,
Qui moult estoit preu et vaillantz. 3650
Lui Prince moult le festoia
Et moult grant honour li porta.
A Burghes, la cité garnie,
Ly Prince oue sa baronie
Sojournerent vij. mois, ou plus ; 3655
Et là fut lour conseil tenus ;
Et là furent renovellé
Les serments qu'ils eurent juré,

Coment le roy Petre s'en ala devers Seville pur purchacer or et argent pur paier au noble Prince et à ses gentz, et le noble

---

that he had in Spain such power, that all were at his bidding. There came Don Fernando de Castro, who was right preux and valiant. The Prince entertained him well, and did him much honour. The Prince and his barony sojourned at the rich city of Burgos seven months, or more ; and there was their council held, and there were renewed the oaths they had before sworn :

How the King Pedro went towards Seville to procure gold and silver to pay the noble Prince and his troops, and the noble

Prince l'attendi entour la Valedolif par vj. mois, et ses gentz soeffrirent grant dureté par defaute de vitaille.

ET que le roy daun Petre droit
Devers Seville s'en iroit,   3660
Pur purchacer or et argent
Pur paier le Prince et sa gent.
Et li Prince devoit attendre
Le roy daun Petre, à voir entendre,
Au Valedolif et là entour;   3665
Et ordeigna un certain jour
Qu'il devoit à ly retourner;
Mais, à verité recorder,
Ly Prince l'atendi vj. mois,
Dont moult endura de destroiz   3670
Son hoost de soif et de faim
Par defaute de vin et pain.

Prince waited in Valladolid six months, and his troops suffered great hardships for want of food.

AND that King Don Pedro should go straight towards Seville, to procure gold and silver to pay the Prince and his troops; and the Prince was to wait for the King Pedro, the truth to hear, in Valladolid and the neighbourhood; and he appointed a certain day when he would return to him; but to record the truth, the Prince waited six months, during which his army suffered greatly by distress and hunger for want of wine and of bread. A proverb I have

Car roy fut de toute Cástielle, 3705
Et chescun son seigniour l'appelle;
Mais sa gent lui ont respondu,
Sachez, li grant et li menu,
Qu'il ne purroit avoir argent
S'il ne fesoit voider sa gent. 3710
Et pur tant le Prince prioit
Amiablement com pooit
Qu'il li pléust à repairer,
Car plus n'avoit de li mestier,
Et qu'il vousist ordeigner gent 3715
Pur resceyvre son paiement.
Le Prince moult s'esmerveilla,
Sitost que la lettre escouta;
Deux chivalers vers ly tramist
Et par lettres savoir li fist 3720
Que il n'avoit tenuz les ditz
Qu'il avoit jurés et promis.

---

had done him; for that he was now King of all Castille, and each called him his lord. But his people had answered him, both high and low, that money he could not have, unless the Prince removed his troops; and therefore he begged the Prince, with as good a grace as he could, to be pleased to withdraw, as he had no further need of him, and that he would appoint persons to receive his payments. The Prince marvelled greatly when he had heard the letters; he sent to him two knights, and by letter let him know that he had not kept his word, as he had sworn and promised.

Coment le Prince prist son purpois de retourner en Aquitaine, car plusours disoient que le bastard y estoit entrez et fait grant damage; et le Prince tant chivacha qu'il vint à la vale de Sorie, et en ce temps Chaundos conceilla oue le conceil d'Aragon.

A quoy faire vos conteroie
La matiere et alongeroie?
Tant vous en purroye conter   3725
Que bien vous purroye taner.
Luy Prince ad bien apercéu
Qu'ensi le roy Petre ne fu
Pas si foiaux come il quidoit;
Lors dist qu'il s'en retourneroit,   3730
Quar plusours disoient ensi
Auxi que le bastard Henri

How the Prince proposed to return to Aquitaine, for many said that the bastard had entered there and done great damage; and the Prince marched back to the vale of Soria; and how Chandos at this time held council with the council of Aragon.

WHY should I recount to you this matter at greater length? So much I might tell you, that I would teaze you. The Prince had well seen that King Pedro was not so trustworthy as he thought; then he said that he would return, for many had told him that the bastard

Estoit entrez en Aquitaine
Et moult fesoit soffrir de paine
Au comun poeple du païs, 3735
Dont le Prince fut moult maris.
Lors prist le Prince son retour
De Mandregay sanz nul sojour;
Tant jour et noet ad chivaché
Qu'il vint eu val de Soryé, 3740
Où il sojourna bien un mois.
Et Chaundos conseilla en trois
Oue le conseil d'Aragon.
Du conseil ne say si poy non.

Coment Chaundos et monsieur Martin de Lacarre venoient au roy de Navarre, et purchacerent le passage du Prince; et le Prince se parti de la vale de Sorie et prist sa voie parmy Navarre, et le roy de Navarre

---

Enrique had entered Aquitaine, and caused much distress among the common people of the land; at which the Prince was greatly wroth. Then he straightway returned from Madrigal without delay; so he travelled day and night till he came to the vale of Soria, where he remained one month. And Chandos, with three others, negociated with the council of Aragon, which I know but little of.

How Chandos and Messire Martin de Lacarre came to the King of Navarre, and obtained a passage for the Prince, and how he left the vale of Soria, and marched through Navarre;

*ly conduist outre le pas, et là prirent congié; et le
Prince vint à Bayone, et là fut par v. jours en grauntz
reveaux, et les burgeis le festoioient moult graund et
noblement.*

Mais pur la matiere abreggier, 3745
Chaundos s'en vint sanz atargier
Par devers le roy de Navarre.
Il et dauh Martin de Lacarre
Purchacerent tant que le roys
De Navarre, qui fut curtoys, 3750
Lessa le Prince repasser;
Et le Prince, sanz arester,
Se parti du val de Sorie.
Parmy la Navarre ad quillie
Sa voie sanz prendre sojour. 3755
Lui roy, qui moult fut plain d'onour,

---

*and the King of Navarre gave him conduct beyond the pass,
and took his leave; and the Prince came to Bayonne, and
was there five days with great revels, and the citizens entertained him much and nobly.*

But to shorten the narrative, Chandos came without delay before the King of Navarre. He with Don Martin de Lacarre so wrought, that the King of Navarre, who was courteous, suffered the Prince to pass again; and the Prince directly left the vale of Soria, and took his route through Navarre without stopping. The King, who

Au Prince grant honour fesoit,
Car toutz les jours li envoioit
Vin et vitaille à grant plenté.
Parmy Navarre l'ad mené, 3760
Et conduit tout outre le pas.
Après, ne vous mentiray pas,
A Saint-Johan-du-Pé-des-Portz
Festoierent par grantz desportz.
D'illoec ensemble congié prirent 3765
Doucement et se departirent.
Lors s'en vint le Prince à Baione,
Dont graunt joie ot mainte persone.
Noblement les nobles burgeois
Le festoioient, et ce fut droitz, 3770
Et là congié done à sa gent;
Et lour dist que lour paiement
Venissent querir à Burdeaux.
Là fut v. jours en grant reveaux.

---

was right honourable, did the Prince great honour; for each day he furnished him with plenty of wine and food. He conducted him through Navarre all through the passes. Afterwards, I will tell you no untruth, at Saint-Jean-Pied-de-Port they feasted right joyously. Thence together they took their leave in good will and departed. Then the Prince came to Bayonne, at which many were right glad. Nobly did the principal townsmen entertain him, as was right; and there he disbanded his troops, and said that they should come to Bordeaux to receive their pay. There he was entertained five days.

Coment le Prince s'en est partiz de Bayone, et est venuz à Burdeaux, et fut reçuz moult noblement à croys et à processions: et la Princesse, oue Edward, son filiz, vint encontre ly oue plusours dames et chivalers, et demenoient moult graunt joie.

D<small>E</small> Baione s'est departiz　　　　　　　　　3775
　Lui Prince, plus n'est alentiz
Tant que il est à Burdeaux venuz.
Noblement y fut rescéuz
A croys et à processions;
Et toutes les religions　　　　　　　　　　　3780
A l'encontre de li venoient,
Moult noblement le festoioient
En loeant et graciant Dieu.
Lors descendi à Saint-Andrew,　　　　　　　3785
La Princesse vint contre ly,
Qui fist aporter oue luy

How the Prince left Bayonne and came to Bordeaux, and was received nobly with crosses and processions; and the Princess, with Edward, her son, met him with many ladies and knights, and they had great rejoicings.

F<small>ROM</small> Bayonne the Prince departed and did not tarry till he came to Bordeaux. There was he nobly received with crosses and processions; and all the conventuals came to meet him, and entertained him most nobly, praising and thanking God. Then he went to Saint-André. The Princess met him, and caused to be brought with her Edward, his

Edward, son filtz le primiers.
Les dames et les chivalers
Pur li festoier y venoient   3790
Et moult grant joie demenoient.
Moult doulcement s'entr'acolerent
Ensemble quant ils s'encontrerent.
Ly Prince, qui ot coer gentil,
Baisa sa moullier et son fil.   3795
Dusque à l'ostiel à pé s'en vinrent,
Ensemble par les mains se tinrent.

Coment le Prince demura à Burdeaux en grant joie et deduit, et chescun s'en resjoï de sa venue par tout le païs d'Aquitaine, et chescun festoia moult noblement son amy.

A quoy faire vous mentiroye ?
A Burdeaux fesoit-hom tiel joie
Que chescun se rejoïssoit   3800
Du Prince qui venuz estoit ;

---

first born son. Ladies and knights came there to greet him, and caused much rejoicing; right sweetly did they embrace when they met together. The Prince, who had a gentle heart, kissed his wife and his son, and they held each other by the hand, until on foot they reached their lodging.

How the Prince stayed at Bordeaux with much joy, and how all throughout Aquitaine every one rejoiced at his coming, and all made merry with their friends.

WHY should I tell you what is not true ? At Bordeaux men were so rejoiced that each showed his delight,

Et cils qui furent ovesque ly
Chescun festoyoit son amy.
Hom pooit savoir que cel nuit
Fist hom en maint lieu grant deduit 3805
Par tout le païs d'Aquitaine,
De ce est bien chose certaine.
Pur venir à conclusion,
Ore vous ai fet mencion
Du Prince et de son grant voiage 3810
Et de son noble baronage :
Pardonés-moy si mal j'ai dit,
Car de rien ne vous ay menti.

Coment le Prince, après ce qu'il avoit demoré un temps à Burdeaux, fist assembler à Saint-Milion touz les nobles de toute la principalté moult debonairement.

---

at the arrival of the Prince and those who were with him ; each made merry with his friend. One should know that on this night, men rejoiced in many places throughout all Aquitaine, of this there is no doubt. To come to the conclusion, now have I made mention to you of the Prince and his great expedition, and of his right noble baronage : pardon me if I have spoken ill, for nothing have I spoken falsely.

How the Prince, after that he had stayed some time at Bordeaux, assembled at Saint-Emilion all the lords of the principality right fairly, as well those who had been with

si bien ceux qui avoient esté ovesque ly en Espaigne, et les festoia moult noblement, et grauntz douns lour dona ; et lors chescun se parti vers soun hosteil.

A Burdeaux demora un temps,
Et bien se tenoit pur content   3815
De ses gentz et de son païs,
Car moult li avoit resjoïz.
Puis fist, en rien contrefaison,
Assembler à Saint-Milion
De toute la principalté   3820
Les nobles, ce fut verité :
Countes, barons, vesques, prelatz,
Là vindrent-ils à grant solas ;
Et ly Prince debonairment
Les mercia moult humblement,   3825
Ceux qui ovesque sa compaigne
Furent et oue ly en Espaigne,

---

him in Spain, and entertained them right nobly, and gave them large presents; and then each returned to his home.

At Bordeaux he remained some time, and was very much pleased with his people and his country, for they had much gladdened him. Then, in nothing we belie, he assembled at Saint-Emilion the nobles of all his principality, it is true : counts, barons, bishops, prelates, came there with much pleasure; and the Prince kindly and humbly thanked them, those who were with his company and with

Et ceux qui demoré estoient,
Qui le païs gardé avoient,
Et lour dist : « Beaux seigniours, par foy,   3830
De tout mon coer aymer vous doi ;
Car vous m'avez très-bien servi.
De bon coer je vous en merci. »
Moult noblement les estora,
Et moult beals dons lour dona,   3835
Or, argent et riches joiaux ;
Et cils en fesoient grantz reveaux.
Du noble Prince se partirent,
Vers lour hostelx lour chimin prirent.

Coment le Prince se vint à Anguleme, et là luy survint sa maladie, et adonques comencerent fauxetés et

---

himself in Spain, and those who had remained to guard the country, and said to them : « Good sirs, by my faith, with all my heart I ought to love you, for you have served me right well. From my heart I thank you. » Right nobly he entertained them, and gave them rich presents, gold and silver and rich jewels; and those made great festivities. They departed from the noble Prince, and took their way homeward.

How the Prince arrived at Angoulême, and there his malady overtook him, and then commenced falsities and treasons

traïsons entre les seigniours du païs ; car ils s'accorderent entre eux de comencer guerre contre le Prince.

Assetz tost après ce avint 3840
Que à Anguleme logier vint
Lui noble Prince d'Aquitaine ;
Et là, c'est bien chose certaine,
Li comencea la maladie
Qui puis dura toute sa vie : 3845
Dont fut damages et pité.
Adonc comencea fauxeté
Et traïson à governer
Ceux qui le devoient aymer ;
Car cils que tenoit pur amis, 3850
Adonc furent ses enemis.

---

amongst the lords of the country, who conspired together to war against the Prince.

SOME short time after this it happened that thither came to sojourn in Angoulême the noble Prince of Aquitaine ; and there, it is well certain, began that malady, which lasted to the end of his life : great pity indeed that it was so. Then began duplicity and treason to rule those who should have loved him; for those whom he held as his friends, became then his enemies. But it is

Mais ce n'est mie grant merveille,
Car l'enemy qui touz jours veille,
Pluis tost grevera un prudhomme
Que un mauvais, ce est la somme ; 3855
Et pur ce sitost que hom savoit
Que li noble Prince estoit
Malades, en peril de mort,
Ses enemis furent d'accort
De la guerre recomencier : 3860
Si comencerent à traitier
A ceux qu'ils savoient de fit
Qu'ils estoient si enemit.

Coment la guerre fut recomencée entre Fraunce et Engleterre, et adonques villes et cités et plusours seigniours du païs se tournerent encontre le Prince, et se trahirent vers le roy de Fraunce, come à lour seigniour

---

no great marvel, for the enemy who is ever watchful, would rather trouble a noble man than one of low birth, so it is: wherefore when men knew that the noble Prince was ill, in danger of his life, his enemies agreed to recommence the war, and so began to treat with those whom they knew for fact that they were his enemies.

How the war was recommenced between France and England, and the towns and cities and many lords of the land turned against the Prince, and sided with the King of France as

soverain, pur appeler le Prince en sa court, en disant qu'il lour avoit fait grant tort.

ADONC recomencea la guerre
Entre la France et l'Engleterre, 3865
Et lors villes et cité
Se tournerent, c'est verité,
Et plusours countes et barons,
Dont je ne doi celer les nouns :
Arminak, Lisle et Peregos, 3870
Labret, Cominges, à briefs motz,
Toutz relinquirent à un jour
Le Prince, lour liege seigniour,
Pur ce que malades estoit
Et que aider plus ne se pooit. 3875
Adonc furent-ils d'accord,
Sicome je oy en mon record,

---

their lord paramount to summon the Prince into his court, saying that he had done them great wrong.

THEN began again the war between France and England, and then towns and cities deserted, as is true, with many counts and barons, whose name I need not hide : Armagnac, Lisle, and Périgord, Albret, Comminges, in a few words, all in a day left the Prince, their liege lord, because he was ill and could no further help himself. Then were they all agreed, as I have it in my memory, that they would separate from the Prince and commence the war.

Que du Prince s'expelleroient
Et que guerre comenceroient.
Ly counte d'Arminak primers						3880
Et plenté d'autres chivalers
Se trairent vers le roy de France,
Et luy dirent sanz demorance
Qu'ils voilloient en appeler
En sa court et eux retourner,						3885
En disant que le Prince tort
Lour fesoit et travailloit fort :
Pur ce venoient de certain
Vers luy com seignour soverain.

Coment le roy de Fraunce appela son grant conseil et lour monstra l'entente du counte d'Armynak, et sur ce le roy de Fraunce envoia prier le Prince de venir

---

The Count d'Armagnac first, with many other knights, went over to the King of France, and said to him without demur that they wished to appeal to his court, and return to their allegiance, saying that the Prince had done them wrong and oppressed them much : wherefore they came before him as to their sovereign lord.

How the King of France summoned his great council, and showed them the intention of the Count d'Armagnac, upon which the King of France sent for the Prince to come and

et respondre en son parlement : dount le noble Prince fut corucez.

Le roy de France en appela 3890
Son grant conseil et assembla,
Et lour monstra toute l'entente
Coment cil d'Arminak le tempte
De la guerre recomencier.
Dont se pristrent à conseiller ; 3895
Et le conseil fut sur ce point,
De ce ne vous mentiray point,
Qu'ils firent le Prince mander
Que il venist sanz arester
Respondre en son plein parlement. 3900
Et contre cel appelement
Ly Prince, qui malades fut,
Quant il ot le fait entendu,

---

answer before his parliament, at which the Prince was greatly enraged.

THE King of France then called a meeting of his great council, and laid before them all the design, how the Count d'Armagnac tempted him to recommence the war; upon which they debated and came to the resolution, of which I will say no untruth, that they should summon the Prince to appear without delay to answer in full parliament. And upon this appeal the Prince, who was sick, when he had

Moult durement fut coroucez.
Adonc s'est de son lit drescez 3905
Et ad dit : « Beaux seigniours, par foi,
Avis m'est, à ce que je voi,
Que François me teignent pur mort ;
Mais si Dieux me doint vrai confort,
Si de ce lit lever me puis, 3910
Encor lour ferai moult d'anuys :
Car Dieu sciet bien que sanz bon droit
Se pleindent de moy ore endroit. »

*Coment le Prince remanda au roy de France, et après
ce comencea guerre en Aquitaine.*

Lors remanda au roy de France
De volunté hardie et france 3915
Que voluntiers certeynement
Il iroit à son mandement,

---

heard what was done, was mightily provoked, and rose up in his bed, and said : « Good sirs, by my faith, it seems from what I see, that the French hold me as dead ; but if God give me true relief, and I can once leave this bed, again will I cause them much annoyance : for God knows well that they complain unjustly of me in this. »

*How the Prince answered the King of France, and afterwards
the war began in Aquitaine.*

Then he wrote back to the King of France in a stern and frank tone, that willingly and certainly would he come

Si Dieux li doinst saunté et vie,
Li et toute sa compaignie,
Le bacinet armé au chief, 3920
Pur li defendre de meschief.
Ensi, c'est bien chose certaine,
Comencea guerre en Aquitaine,
Et lors fist touz les Compaignons
Mettre en toutes les garisons. 3925
Là véissez guerre mortele
Et en plusours lieux moult cruele.
Le frere fut contre le frere
Et le filz fut contre le piere.
Chescun de eux sa part tenoit 3930
A quel part que meulz li plesoit;
Mais en le temps que je vous di,
Ly noble Prince moult perdit :
Car traïsons et fauxetés
Regnoient là de touz costés. 3935

---

at his bilding, if God granted him health and life, himself and all his company, helmed to the head, to keep him from mischief. Then, it is true indeed, commenced the war in Aquitaine, And then made he all the Companies take possession of all the garrisons. There might you see a deadly war, in many places very cruel; brother fought against brother, and the son against his father. Each of them took that side which best pleased him; but at the time I speak of, the noble Prince lost much : for treachery and falsehood prevailed on

Hom ne savoit en qui fiance
Avoir, si le vray Dieu m'avance;
Mais nepurquant se confortoit
Ly Prince au meulz que il pooit.

Coment le Prince envoia en Engleterre pur socours avoir de son piere, et il ly envoia Esmond, counte de Cantebrigge, son filtz, et le counte de Pembrok oue moult noble chivalrie, lesqueux pristrent Bourdell per assaut; et le counte de Pembrok fut fait chivaler, et après ce mistrent siege à la Roche-sur-Yon.

EN Engleterre fist mander 3940
Socours pur li reconforter,
Et li très-noble roy, son piere,
Li envoia Esmond, son frere,
De Cantebrigge de renon,
Qui eut le coer fier com lion, 3945

---

every side. Men, so God help me, knew not in whom to put their trust; but nevertheless the Prince exerted himself to the utmost.

How the Prince sent to England for aid from his father, and he sent Edmund, Earl of Cambridge, his son, and the Earl of Pembroke with many noble knights, who took Bourdeille by assault; and the Earl of Pembroke was made a knight, and afterwards they besieged La Roche-sur-Yon.

HE then demanded succour from England to strengthen him; and the right noble King, his father, sent him Edmund, his brother, the renowned Earl of Cambridge, who had a heart courageous as a lion; him of Pembroke

Le counte de Pembrock auxi,
Qui eut le coer preu et hardi;
Et orent en lour compaignie
Moult de noble chivalerie.
Cils deux vindrent en le frontiere, 3950
Et moult fesoient bele chiere.
Bourdielle prirent par assaut,
Dont eurent le coer lez et baut.
Et là fut chivaler le counte
De Pembrok, dont home fist counte. 3955
Puis mistrent en courte saison
Siege à la Roche-sur-Yon,
Et Chaundos fut à Montauben,
Qui illoc se maintenoit bien.

Coment la Roche-sur-Yon fut pris par le counte de Cantebrigge, et Audelé et Chaundos trespasserent.

---

also, who had a heart preux and hardy; and they had in their company much noble knighthood. These two reached the frontier, and were indeed right welcome. Bourdeille they took by assault, which made their hearts light and gay. And the Earl of Pembroke, so highly esteemed, was there knighted. They then laid siege immediately to la Roche-sur-Yon; whilst Chandos was at Montauban, maintaining himself there well.

How la Roche-sur-Yon was taken by the Earl of Cambridge, and of the death of Audley and Chandos.

Que vous purroi-je recorder 3960
Pur la matiere destourber ?
De toutes partz fut la fortune
En Aquitaine horrible et frune.
La Roche-sur-Yon fut pris
De Cantebrigge et son empris ; 3965
Mais ensi qu'il pleut à celly
Vray Dieux, qui unques ne menty,
Monsieur James de Audelée,
Qui moult fut de grant renomée,
Morut illoec de maladie : 3970
Dont dolantz fut, n'en doutez mye,
Li très-noble Prince de pris,
Car moult li fut saives amys.
Et puis gaires ne demora
Que Chaundos auxi trespassa 3975
Au pont de Lussac, bien savez :
Dont fut damages et pitez,

Why should I tell you that which would interrupt the narrative ? On every side in Aquitaine was fortune adverse. La Roche-sur-Yon was taken by Cambridge and his emprise; but, as it pleased the God of truth, who never lies, Sir James de Audley, who was of very high renown, died there from sickness, at which you need not doubt, the noble Prince was greatly grieved : for he was a wise friend to him. And then, after a very short time, Chandos also passed from this life at the bridge of Lussac, you may know, whereat was great loss and sorrow; for

Car moult en estoit esmaÿs
Ly Prince, qui moult fut marris;
Mais hom voit sovent avenir   3980
Que quant il doit mesavenir,
Li meschief après l'autre vient.
Beaucop des foitz ensi avyent.
Toutz les meschiefs ensi sourdoient,
Et l'un après l'autre venoient   3985
Au noble Prince, qui gisoit
Eu lit où malades estoit.
Mais de tout ce gracioit Dieu,
Et disoit : « Tout aura son lieu ;
Si de ci lever me purroye,   3990
Bien la vengeance en prenderoye. »

Coment les François se rejoïssent moult de la maladie du Prince et de la mort de Chaundos et Audelé, et

---

the Prince, who was much vexed, was sorely dismayed at it. But it is often seen to happen, that when mishaps arise, one follows upon another; many times this is the case. So then all the evils arose and came one after another upon the noble Prince, who lay sick upon his couch. But for all this he thanked God, and said : « All things will have their place, and if from hence I may rise, I will take good vengeance. »

How the French were right glad at the sickness of the Prince and the deaths of Chandos and Audley, and then the King of

*adonques le roy de France en manda novelles à
monsieur Bartrem de Claykyn en Espaigne, et qu'il
deust retourner ; et il s'en vint à Tholouse.*

Q UANT François savoient que Chandos
  Estoit mort, qui avoit grant los,
Moult grant joie firent partout
Et se rejoïssoient moult,   3995
Et disoient : « Tout sera notre,
Auxi vray com le Paternostre. »
Lors fist le roy Charles de France
Mander sanz point de demorance
A monsieur Bartrem de Claykyn,   4000
Qui ot le coer hardi et fyn.
En Espaigne lors il estoit,
Là où le roy bastard servoit ;
Et manda que Chaundos fut mort.
Voluntiers oÿ le recort   4005

---

*France sent tidings to Messire Bertrand du Guesclin in Spain,
that it behoved him to return; and he came to Toulouse.*

W HEN the French knew that Chandos, who had great
  worth, was dead, they everywhere showed their joy
and made great rejoicings, and said: « All will now be ours,
as surely as the Pater-noster. » Then the King Charles of
France sent without any delay to Messire Bertrand du
Guesclin, who had a heart of fine courage. He was then
in Spain, where he served the bastard ; and told him that
Chandos was dead. Gladly did Bertrand hear the news,

Bartrem, en France retourna.
Bientost gaires ne demora,
A Tholouse s'en est venuz.
Là fut d'Anjou li riche ducz,
Qui le festoia doulcement   4010
Et moult très-amiablement,
Et dist : « Dan Bartrem, bien trovez
Soiez-vous et bien arivez.
Nous avons grant mestier de vous ;
Car si vous estez oue nous,   4015
Nous conquesterons Aquitaine,
Car ce est bien chose certaine :
Audelée et Chaundos sont mortz,
Qui nous ont fait tant de discordz,
Et li Prince gist en son lit   4020
Malades, qui poy ad delit ;
Si que vous le conseillerez,
Nous sumes touz apparaillez
De chivachier parmy la terre. »

---

he returned into France. With scarce any delay he arrived at Toulouse. There was the rich Duke d'Anjou, who received him gladly and with great kindness, and said : « Messire Bertrand, well found are you and in good time come. We have great need of you ; for if you be with us, we shall gain Aquitaine : for it is well ascertained that Audley and Chandos, who have opposed us so much, are dead, and the Prince, who little pleasure has, lies on his bed sick. If you therefore advise it, we are all ready to march through the country. »

Coment monsieur Bartrem s'accorda de faire la guerre encontre le Prince, et adonques les François firent assembler lour grant poer, et le duc d'Anjou entra parmy Crescin, et le duc de Barry et le duc de Burbon chivacherent parmy Lymosyn, et furent en purpose d'assieger le Prince, et lors le Prince se leva et fist son poair.

 A ce faire bien s'accorda   4025
Daun Bartrem, qui le conseilla ;
Et là furent-ils tut d'accord,
Si come j'oy en mon record,
Que à deux costés chivacheroient
Et que le Prince assegeroient.   4030
Lors fesoient assembler lour gentz
Assez par milliers et par centz.
Le duc d'Anjou parmy Cressin
Chivacha à moult grant trahin,

How Messire Bertrand agreed to make war against the Prince, and then the French assembled their great forces, and the Duke d'Anjou marched by Quercy, and the Duke de Berry and the Duke de Bourbon marched by Limousin and purposed to besiege the Prince, who then arose and collected his forces.

MESSIRE Bertrand, who advised it, was perfectly willing to do this, and there they were all agreed, as I have heard it reported, to march from two sides and beset the Prince. Then they assembled their forces, by thousands and by hundreds. The Duke d'Anjou with a very great train marched by Quercy; those of Berry and

Cil de Barry et cil de Burbon 4035
Ovesque des gentz grant fuison.
Parmy Limosyn chivacherent
Tant que à Lymoges se logierent,
Et quidoient, au voir jugier,
Venir droit le Prince assegier 4040
En Anguileme, où il estoit
Si malades qu'il se gisoit;
Et ly Prince fut en son lit,
Qui pas n'avoit trop grant delit.
Sitost qu'il en oÿ novelles, 4045
Qui ly semblent bones et beles,
De son lit tantost se leva
Et tout son poair assembla.

Coment en cel temps le duc de Lancastre, ove moult noble chivalrie, fut arrivez en le païs et volt aler pur

---

Bourbon, with a great number of troops, rode by Limousin till they encamped at Limoges, and imagined, to judge the truth, that they might beset the Prince in Angoulême, where he was so sick that he lay upon his bed; and the Prince, who was on his bed, had not too great delight. So soon as he heard the tidings, which seemed good and fair to him, he soon raised himself from his bed and assembled his troops together.

How at this time the Duke of Lancaster, with many noble knights, arrived in the country, and wished to go and engage

combatre les enemys; et quant ils en savoient et que le Prince avoit assemblé son poair, les enemys se retournerent et n'oserent pas attendre. Et en cel temps Lymoges fut rendu par fauxeté, et le Prince y mist assege, et le regaigna par assaut, et là furent plusours gentz d'armes et burgeis pris et mortz.

A ceo temps fut ly riche ducz
De Lancastre, en qui fut vertuz, 4050
Arrivés dedeinz son païs
Et moultz des chivalers de pris,
Et les vouloit aler combatre
Pur son noble païs debatre;
Mais sitost qu'ils oïrent dire 4055
Que le Prince, sanz contredire,
Avoit assemblé son poair,
Ils s'en retournerent pur voir

---

the enemy; and when they knew it, and that the Prince had collected his army, the enemy retreated and dared not await them. And at that time Limoges was given up by treachery, and the Prince laid siege to it, and retook it by assault, and there were taken and slain many men-at-arms and townsmen.

AT this time the noble Duke of Lancaster, who was right virtuous, arrived in the country, with many valiant knights, and he wished to go and fight in order to conquer his noble land; but they, so soon as they heard that the Prince, without doubt, had assembled his forces, they all retreated,

Et ne l'oserent pas attendre.
Mais en ce temps, à voir entendre, 4060
Limoges, la bone cité,
Fut rendue par fauxeté,
Et li Prince celle part vint,
Qui par devant l'assiege tint
Tant que il le gaigna par assaut, 4065
Dont moult il ot le coer haut;
Quar là fut Rogier de Beaufort,
Qui de tenir se fesoit fort,
Et monsieur Johan de Villemur,
Qui dist qu'il garderoit le mur, 4070
Et des gentz d'armes bien iij. centz,
Sanz les burgeis de par dedenz;
Mais touz y furent mortz ou pris
Par le noble Prince de pris :
Dont avoient grant joie entour ly 4075
Toutz ceux qui li furent amy,

---

for a truth, and dared not await him. But at this time, the truth to know, the good city of Limoges was given up by treachery, and the Prince came there, and upheld the siege before it until he won it by assault; in which he showed his high courage, for there was Roger de Beaufort, who was confident that he could keep it, and Messire Jean de Villemur, who promised to guard the wall, and good three hundred men-at-arms, besides the townsmen within; but all were slain or taken by the noble Prince of price; whereat great joy had all around those who were his

Et les enemis en avoient
Grant paour et se repentoient
Que la guerre recomencie
Avoient vers ly, je vous affie. 4080

Coment après ceo que Lymoges fut pris, le Prince s'en revint à Anguyleme, et trova Edward, son filtz, trespassé, dount il fut moult dolentz. Et après ceo s'en vint en Engleterre, et ovesque luy sa femme et son filtz Richard, et moult plusours autres de ses gentz.

A PRÈS que Limoges fut pris,
Ly noble Prince de haut pris
En Anguileme s'en revint,
Dont autre ensegne ly avint,

---

friends, and the enemies were much frightened at it, and repented, I assure you, that they had again begun the war against him.

How after Limoges was taken, the Prince returned to Angoulême, and found his son Edward dead, at which he was very sorrowful. And afterwards came to England, and with him his wife and his son Richard, and many more of his people.

A FTER Limoges was taken, the noble Prince of high price returned to Angoulême, where other news

Car adonc trova trespassé 4085
Son filtz Edward, son primer né,
Dont bien fut dolantz en son coer ;
Mais nul ne poet la mort fuyer.
Tout ly covenoit prendre en gré
Ce que Dieux ly avoit doné. 4090
Après gaires ne demora
Que tout son arrai apresta ;
Et en Engleterre s'en vint
Pur la maladie que ly tint,
Ovesque li sa femme et son fitz 4095
Et moultz des chivalers de pris.

Coment la novelle vint en Engleterre que la Rochelle fut perdu et le counte de Penbrok pris, et sur ceo le roy d'Engleterre fit une très-graunt armée, en quelle fut ly tres-noble Prince et maint vaillant seigniour

---

awaited him; for then he found his son Edward, his first born, dead, whereat he was very grieved in his heart; but none can escape death. It behoved him to take in good part that which God had given him. After that he scarcely tarried, but made ready his array; and came into England, on account of the sickness upon him, and his wife and son and many knights of renown came with him.

How news came to England that la Rochelle was lost, and the Earl of Pembroke taken, and upon this the King of England mustered a large army in which was the right noble Prince

*et chivalers de renoun, queux furent sur la mer
entour ix. semaignes, et ne puvoient avoir vent pur
passer.*

DEPUIS fut la novel venu
Que la Rochelle fust perdu,
Et si fut pris le noble counte
De Penbrok, dont home fit counte.   4100
Donc fit li roy faire une armée,
Qui moult fut de grant renommée.
Et là furent tout li baron
Et toutz les chivalers de noun.
Ly noble Prince illoc estoit,   4105
Qui en grant paine se mettoit
Que armer peust et prendre guerre
Pur aler socourir sa terre.
Mais à ceo que j'oy counter,
Noef semaignes estoient sur mer   4110

---

*and many valiant lords and knights of renown, who were at
sea about nine weeks, and could have no wind to cross.*

AFTERWARDS the news arrived that Rochelle was lost, and
the noble Earl of Pembroke, much esteemed among
men, taken. Then caused the King an army to be collected
that was of great renown, and there were all the barons and
all the knights of name. The noble Prince was there, who
put himself to great pain to arm himself to wage war
and succour his territory. But, as I have heard it said, nine

Que unques ne pouroient avoir vent,
Ains les fallut tout vrayement
Retourner et venir arriere :
Dont moult fesoient mate chiere
Luy roy et le Prince auxi   4115
Et touz les chivalers hardi.

*Coment le Prince se compleindoit en ses grantz maladies,
et pria ses gentz prier pur ly.*

ORE vous ay toute countée
La vie du Prince et rimée :
Pardonés-moy s'un poy briefment
Je l'ay passée legierment ;   4120
Mais il faut que je m'en delivere,
Car homme en purroit faire un livere,
Bien auxi grant comme d'Artus,
D'Alisandre ou de Clarius.

---

weeks were they at sea, without any wind reaching them ; then were they verily obliged to return and come back again : at which they were much cast down the King and the Prince as well, with all the hardy knights.

How the Prince mourned in his great sickness, and besought his people to pray for him.

Now have I told and rhymed all the life of the Prince : pardon me if a little briefly or lightly I have passed it by ; but it is right that I shall get rid of it, for one might make a book of it almost large as that of Arthur, of

Mais pur doner en remembrance 4125
De son fait et reconissance
Et de sa très-haute proesse
Et de sa très-noble largesse,
Et auxi de sa prudhommie,
Coment il fut toute sa vie 4130
Prodhom loialx et catholiques
Et en touz biens faire publiques ;
Et si ot si très-noble fin
En reconissant de coer fyn
Son Dieu et son vrai creatur. 4135
Et disoit as sons : « Beaux seigniour,
Regardez ci, pur Dieu merci,
Nous ne sumes pas seigniour cy.
Tout coviendra par ci passer,
Nul hom ne s'en poet destourner : 4140
Pur ce très-humblement vous pri
Que vous voillez prier pur my. »

Alexander or of Clarus. But (it has been my part) to give a remembrance and recollection of his deeds, and his very lofty prowess, and his very noble liberality, and also his knightly bearing ; how he was all his life prudhomme, loyal and catholic, and did all for the public good. And so had he a right noble end in remembering in his fine heart his God and his true Creator ; and he said to his people : « Good sirs, attend to this, for God's sake, we are no longer masters here. All must pass this way, and there is no man who can avert his fate : wherefore I right humbly beseech you that you would pray for me. »

Coment le Prince fit ovrir sa chambre, et trestoutz ses hommes fit venir devaunt luy, et les regracioit moult noblement de lour service à luy fait, et eux recomenda son filtz, qui estoit moult joefne, et ils plorerent moult tendrement.

Le Prince fit sa .chambre ouvrir
Et trestouz ses homines venir
Qui en son temps servi l'avoient 4145
Et qui voluntiers le servoient :
« Seigniour, fait-il, pardonez-moy,
Car, par la foy que je vous doy,
Vous m'avez loialment servi.
Si ne puis-je de droit demy 4150
Rendre à chescun son gueredon ;
Mais Dieux par son saintisme noun
Ens ès ciels le vous rendera. »
Là chescun de coer larmoia,

How the Prince caused his chamber to be opened, and made all his men come before him, and thanked them right nobly for their service done him, and commended to them his son, who was quite young, and they wept right tenderly.

Then the Prince caused his room to be opened and all his followers to come in, who in his time had served him and served him willingly : « Sirs, said he, pardon me, for, by the faith I owe you, you have served me loyally, and I cannot render to each the half of his right guerdon ; but God, by his holy name, within the heavens will render it to you. » Then each wept heartily, and mourned right

Et plorerent moult tendrement 4155
Touz ceux qui furent en present :
Conte, baron et bacheler ;
Et disoit à touz haut et cler :
« Je vous recomande mon fitz,
Qui moult est joefnes et petitz, 4160
Et vous pri, si servi m'avez,
Que vous de bon coer ly serrez. »

Coment le Prince appela le roy, son piere, et le duc de Lancastre, son frere, et à eux recomenda sa femme et son filtz en suppliaunt de les conforter et maintenir; et trestouz ly promistrent de ce faire, et très-grant dolour fut entre eux.

Lors appela le roy, son piere,
Et le duc de Lancastre, son frère ;
Sa femme lour recomenda 4165
Et son filtz, que fortment ama,

---

tenderly, all who were there present : earl, baron and bachelor; and he said in a clear voice : « I recommend to you my son, who is yet but young and small, and pray that, as you have served me, so from your heart you would serve him.

How the Prince called the King, his father, and the Duke of Lancaster, his brother, and to them commended his wife and his son, entreating them to comfort and defend them; and how all promised him to do this, and there was much sorrow between them.

Then he called the King, his father, and the Duke of Lancaster, his brother; he commended to them his

Et lour supplia là endroit
Que chescun les aider vouloit.
Chescun li jura sur le livre
Et ly promistrent à delivre   4170
Que son enfant conforteroient
Et en son droit le maintiendroient.
Tout li prince et tout li baron
Là jurerent tout environ,
Et li noble Prince de pris   4175
Lour rendi cent mille mercys;
Mais onques, si Dieux m'aïwe,
Si dure dolour ne fut viewe
Come fut à la departie.
La noble Princesse jolie   4180
Tiel dolour en son coer sentoit
Que à poi son coer ne partoit.
Jà de pleindre et de suspirer,
De haut crier et dolouser,

---

wife, and his son, whom he greatly loved, and straightway entreated them so that each was willing to give his aid. Each swore upon the book and promised him at once that they would comfort his child and maintain him in his right. All the princes and barons swore all round to this, and the noble Prince of fame gave them a hundred thousand thanks; but never, so God aid me, was seen such bitter grief as that of the noble amiable Princess at his decease; such pain she felt at her heart, that it almost burst. With moaning and sighing, crying out and condoling,

La gent avoit un mors si grant, 4185
Qu'eu monde ne fust hom vivant,
Qui éust le doel regardé,
Qu'il n'en éust eu coer pité.

De la noble et devoute repentance du Prince, et coment et en quel lieu et à quel temps il trespassa. Et yci fine cest livre que retrahist Chaundos le haraude.

LA eut si noble repentance,
Que Dieux par sa haute puissance 4190
Avera de s'alme mercy;
Car il pria à Dieu mercy
Et pardon de touz ses mesfaits,
Qu'en cest monde mortel eut faitz.
Et lors li Prince trespassa 4195
De cest siecle, et si devia

---

the people had such great anguish, that no man living could have seen the dolour without feeling it in his heart.

Of the noble and devout penitence of the Prince, and how and in what place and at what time he died. And here ends the book that Chandos the herald composed.

THERE had he such noble penitence, that God of his great power will have pity on his soul; for he prayed God for mercy and pardon for all his misdeeds, that he had done in this mortal world. And then the Prince passed away from this age, and so died in the

L'an mille ccc. sesze et sessante
Et du regne le roy, cinquante,
A Londres, la noble cité,
Le haut jour de la Trinité,   4200
Dont il fesoit toute sa vie
Feste en coer oue melodie.
Ore prioms Dieu, le roy des roys,
Qui pur nous morut en la croys,
Qu'il ait de son alme pardon,   4205
Et li ottroie de son doun
La gloire de son paradis.
Amen; et ci fyn je lui ditz
Du très-noble Prince Edward,
Qui n'avoit unques coer coward,   4210
Que retraist li heraud Chaundos,
Qui voluntiers recordoit motz.

---

year one thousand three hundred and seventy-six, in the fiftieth year of his father's reign, in the noble city of London, on the high day of the Trinity, which through all his life he had kept holy in choir with melody. Now let us pray God, the King of Kings, who for us died upon the cross, that he may pardon his soul, and grant him of his gift, the glory of his paradise. Amen! And here ends the history of the right noble Prince Edward, who never had a coward's heart, that the herald Chandos has composed who willingly recorded words.

Cy ensuivent les nouns de ceux qui furent les hautes officiers du très-noble Prince par ly faitz en son temps en Aquitaine.

SEIGNIOURS, vous aurez oy de certaine
Du noble Prince d'Aquitaine;
Ore vous diray briefment, 4215
Sanz un plus longe parlement,
De ses plus hautes officers,
Lesqueux li furent moult chiers
En Aquitaine en son temps,
Desqueux se tenoit bien contens: 4220
Primerment John Chaundos fut conestable,
Et après sa mort le captawe, sanz fable;
Monsieur Gwichard d'Angle fut mareschal,
Et Estephen de Cosinton, qui ot coer loial;
Et monsieur Thomas de Felleton, à voir jugir, 4225
Fut seneschal d'Aquitaine sanz mentir;

Here follow the names of those who were the chief officers of the right noble Prince, whilst he held the province of Aquitaine.

SIRS, you have heard certainly of the right noble Prince of Aquitaine; now I will tell you briefly, without any longer story, of his chief officers, who were right dear to him, whilst he was in Aquitaine, with whom he was well contented: In the first place John Chandos was constable, and after his death the Captal, without fable;. Sir Guichard d'Angle was marshal, and Stephen de Cossington, of a loyal heart; and Sir Thomas de Felton, to judge the truth, was seneschal of Aquitaine; and

Et monsieur Guilliam de Felleton
Fut seneschal de Peyto par noun ;
Et après sa mort, come dit le stille,
Monsieur Baudewyn de Freville ;   4230
Et après monsieur Baudewyn departir
En Engleterre, à voir contir,
Monsieur Thomas de Percy li vaillant
Y fut oue honour moult grant ;
Et de Saintonge fut seneschal,   4235
Monsieur John Harpeden oue coer loial ;
Et monsieur Henri de la Hay
Fut seneschal d'Anguymois, bien say ;
Monsieur Thomas de Roos oue coer fyn
Fut seneschal de Lymosyn ;   4240
Et après son departir en Engleterre
Monsieur Richard Abberbury, à voir retrere,
Et monsieur Thomas Wetenale en verité
Fut seneschal de Roargue le counté ;

Sir William de Felton, by name, was seneschal of Poitou; and after his death, as says the list, Sir Baldwin de Freville; and after Sir Baldwin had departed for England, the truth to tell, the valiant Sir Thomas de Percy was there with great honour; of Saintonge the seneschal was the loyal Sir John Harpeden; and Sir Henry del Hay was seneschal of Angoumois; the fine hearted Sir Thomas de Roos was seneschal of Limousin; and after his departure for England Sir Richard Abberbury, the truth to say, Sir Thomas Wetenhale in good truth was seneschal of the county of Rouergue; and, if I have

Et si ne vous ai nomé unquore 4245
Le seneschal de Cressy et Peregore,
Ce fut monsieur Thomas Walkfare,
Que bon chivaler vous declare ;
Et du counté de Agenoys
Fut seneschal à ceste foiz 4250
Monsieur Richard de Baskerville ;
Et après sa mort, comme dit le stille,
Monsieur Guilliam le Moigne,
Car ce n'est pas mençoigne.
Et de monsieur Guilliam après le departir 4255
En Engleterre, à voir jugir,
Si fut un bon chivaler
Monsieur Richard Walkfare oue coer fier ;
Et de Bigore fut seneschal,
Monsieur John Roche oue coer loial. 4260
Et le sire de Pyan fut seneschaux
Des Laundes de Burdeaux ;

---

not yet named to you the seneschal of Quercy and Périgord, it was Sir Thomas Walkfare, whom good knight I declare; and of the county of Agenois Sir Richard of Baskerville was seneschal at this time; and after his death, as is said, Sir William le Moigne, for this is no false tale. And after the departure of Sir William for England, to judge the truth, the bold hearted Sir Richard Walkfare a good knight (succeeded him); of Bigorre the seneschal was the loyal hearted Sir John Roche; and the sire de Pyan was seneschal of the Landes of Bordeaux; and many other

Et plusours autres très-vaillantz,
Qui furent adonques vivantz,
Furent oue loure Prince, à voir juger, 4265
Lesqueux je ne sai nomer.
Mais je pri à très-haute Trinité
Que del alme du Prince avant-nomé
Et de touz les autres qui mortz sont
Et qu'en après morir deveront, 4270
Ait merci à son jugement;
Et je pri auxi verayment,
Que as vivantz li plese doner
Longe vie et bon fin achever.
Amen, Amen, par sainte Charité 4275
De chescun en son degré.
Amen!

---

right valiant knights, who were at that day alive, were with their Prince, the truth to judge, whose names I cannot tell. But I pray the most high Trinity, that at his judgment he may have mercy on the soul of the Prince before named, and on all the others, who are dead, or who shall hereafter die; and I also pray verily that it please him to give to those alive a long life, and that they may achieve a good end. Amen, amen, by saint Charity, for each in his degree. Amen!

*Cy ensement l'escripture faite sur la tumbe du noble
Prince devant-nommé.*

Vous qui passez de bouche close
    Par là où ce mien corps repose,
Entendez ce que te diray
Si come je dire le say.   4280
Tiel come tu es et tiel je fu,
Tu seras tiel come je su.
De la mort ne pensois-je mye
Tant come j'avoie la vie;
En terre avoi-je graund richesse,   4285
Dount je y fis graunde noblesse,
Terre, maisons et graund tresor,
Draps, chivalx, argent et or;
Mais je suis or poevre et cheitifs,
Parfond en la terre où je gis.   4290
Ma graund beauté est tout allée,
Et ma char est toute gastée.

Here also is the inscription upon the tomb of the Prince above-named.

ALL ye that pass with closed mouth by where this my body reposes, hear this that I shall tell you, just as I know to say it. Such as thou art, such was I, thou shall be such as I am. Of death I never thought so long as I had life; on earth I had great riches, of which I made great nobleness, land, houses and great wealth, clothes, horses, silver and gold; but I am now a poor wretch, deep in the earth I lie. My great beauty is all gone, my flesh is all

Moult est estroite ma maison,
Oue moy n'ad si vermyn noun ;
Et si ore me véissez, 4295.
Je ne quide pas que dissez
Que je eusse unques homme esté :
Si sui-je tut en tut changé.
Pur Dieu priez au celestien Roy
Qu'ait merci de l'alme de moy. 4300
Tut cil qui pur moy prieront,
Ou qui à Dieu m'accorderont,
Dieu les mette en son paradis,
Où nul ne poet estre cheitifs !

---

wasted, right narrow is my house, with me but worms remain ; and if now ye should see me, I do not think that you would say that ever I had been a man : so totally am I changed. For God's sake pray the heavenly King that he have mercy on my soul. All they who pray for me, or make accord to God for me, God give them his paradise, where none are wretched !

NOTES

THE BLACK PRINCE

With the life of the Black Prince by Froissart, by Barnes [1], Collins [2], Ashmole [3], James [4], and Poittevin de la Croix [5], before the reader, it is not necessary to swell the bulk of the present volume, by any lengthened account of the actions of our hero, not mentioned in the preceding poem; at the same time an outline of the more prominent features of his career may be useful, as an index more than anything else, to the dates of the respective periods in which they occurred. With this view the following sketch has been compiled by H. O. Coxe, and somewhat enlarged by the present editor.

Edward, the Black Prince, eldest son of Edward the III., and Philippa, youngest daughter of William, earl of Hainault, was born at Woodstock on Friday, the 15th of June 1330, in the fourth year of

---

[1] Joshua Barnes, *The History of Edward III., together with that of Edward the Black Prince.* Cambridge, 1688, folio.

[2] Arthur Collins, *Life and glorious Actions of Edward Prince of Wales, eldest Son of K. Edward III. and of his royal Brother, John of Gaunt, King of Castile.* Lond., 1740, 8vo.

[3] *The Institution, Laws, and Ceremonies of the noble Order of the Garter.* Lond., 1672, fol.

[4] G. P. R. James, *A History of the Life of Edward the Black Prince, and of various Events connected therewith which occurred during the Reign of Edward III.* London, 1822 (and also, 1836 or 1839), 2 vols 8vo.

his father's reign [1]. On the 18th of May 1333, he was created Earl of Chester, and upon the death of John Eltham, Earl of Cornwall, by charter bearing date the 17th of March 1337, was further raised to the dukedom of Cornwall, being, as Barnes adds, "the first precedent for the creation of the title of duke with us in England." In the following year, he was constituted *custos Angliæ*, on his father's going into Brabant, and held a parliament on the 26th July at Northampton. In the parliament held in May 1343, he was created Prince of Wales. After a lapse of three years he accompanied Edward III. in his expedition into France, and on the 12th of July 1346 received the honour of knighthood at his father's hands upon his landing at La Hogue, and was enrolled amongst the knights of the order of the Garter, founded about two years before. On the 26th of August following, he commanded the van, assisted by Chandos and the Earl of Warwick, at the battle of Crécy [2]. Immediately following this action he laid siege with his father to the town of Calais, and was present at the affray there in the night of the 31st of December. From this period, it being a time of truce, we hear little of him until the naval action off Rye with the Spaniards on the 29th of August 1350. On the 24th of June 1355, the truce with France being expired, we find him preparing for his departure for Gascony, invested as the king's lieutenant with the government of his French possessions. Arrived at Bordeaux, he commenced a series of minor victories; amongst which however are

---

1 The scheme of his nativity by **Thomas** Allen of Gloucester Hall (now Worcester College) may be seen in Ashmole's *History of the Garter*, p. 670. In the Issue Roll, Easter, 9 Edw. III., as translated by Devon, are the following entries :

" 29th May. To Thomas Prior, valet of the Lord the King, to whom the Lord the King (for the welcome and desirable news he brought to the same King concerning Edward, his eldest son) granted him, by his letters patent, 40 marks; etc. *l.* 13..6..8.

" 30th May. To Catherine de Monte Acuto in money, paid to her by the hands of William de Northwode, in part payment of 200 marks which the Lord the King commanded to be paid her for the 500 marks which the said Lord the King granted her for the welcome news she brought him of the birth of his son." (*Issues of the Exchequer*, etc. London, 1837, 8vo. p. 143, 144.—Cf. Rymer's *Fœdera*, 3d. edit., tom. ii. pars iii. p. 69, col. 1). A similar bonus had been given by Edward the II. to the valet of the Queen, for bringing him the tidings of the birth of Edward III. (Ashmole, *History of the Garter*, p. 644).

2 It has been reported that from his wearing on this day a black cuirass, he obtained the name of the *Black Prince*.

to be noticed the taking of the towns of Carcassonne and Narbonne in the same autumn, and Romorantin in the following spring, which terminated in the glorious victory of Poitiers, when with, comparatively speaking, a handful of men, he defeated the hosts of France, his superiors in number by more than eight times. In May 1357, he returned to England and entered London with the king of France as his prisoner, on the 24th of that month. It will be unnecessary to dwell upon the expedition of Edward III. into France, and the peace of Brétigny, followed by the liberation of John on the 25th of October 1560. The marriage of the Black Prince with the countess of Kent [1], on the 10th of October 1361, is the next most important point in our hero's life; almost immediately after which he retired to his principality of Aquitaine. The prosperity of the Black Prince had now reached its summit, and he, of whom history records no dishonourable act, was doomed to be the victim of a man as unworthy of Edward's confidence as he was unlike him in character. From his first connexion with the dethroned king of Castille we may date the downfall of the Prince of Wales. The victory of Nájera on the 3rd of April placed Don Pedro the Cruel on the throne of Spain, but left the conqueror without provisions and without money in a climate that laid the seeds of an illness that eventually brought him to the grave. Returning to Bordeaux harassed in mind and body, he passed a few years in directing his government of Aquitaine [2], and in preparing to carry on the war against Charles V.,

---

[1] « .... qu'il avoit par amours prise à espouse et à compaigne, de se volenté, sans le sceu dou roy, son pere, laquelle damme avoit estet fille dou comte Aimont de Kent, oncle dou roy englès. » (Chron. de Froissart, t. VI, p. 275, § 502.) The case was not new, if it is true " that Thomas Boyerton, sunne to Edward the first, married a meane gentilwoman yn France, at Burdeaux, without his father's counsel for his pleasure, " etc. (*The Itinerary of John Leland the Antiquary*, vol. VI ; Oxford, 1711, 8vo, p. 21.)

[2] The retaking of Limoges, after it had been given up by the bishop of the same see, who had been the god-father of Edward's eldest son, was almost the only action of note in which he took an active part.

Concerning the management of the local affairs of Aquitaine by the Black Prince, we know nothing more than that we have said in our *Histoire du commerce et de la navigation d Bordeaux*, vol. i. p. 195, 199, 203, note 5, 255, 264 ; to which may be added two entries concerning the grant of an *octroi* to the city, *De sex denariis majori et burgensibus Burdegale concessis*, the former in latin, the later in French. (Rot. Vasc. 28 Edw. III. membr. 5, and 49, membr. 1.)

Some authors ascribe to the Black Prince the construction of a beacon known under the name of *Tour de Cordouan* ; but they afford no proof to this statement.

the French King, until unable any longer to bear up against the increasing virulence of his disorder, he returned to England, where he died on Trinity Sunday, the 8th of June, 1376.

Line 18. « Li mieldre jugleor en Gascoigne, » said an old proverb, quoted by Crapelet, p. 89; Chandos herald must have had an opportunity of observing them.

An anonymous one thus enumerates the works of fiction which were circulated in the feudal courts of the south, and interspersed with antics and tricks by « menestrels de bouche et du bas mestier, » as Froissart calls them :

> Apres si levon li juglar ;
> Cascus se vol faire auzir.
> Adonc auziras retentir
> Cordas de manta tempradura.
> Qui saup novella violadura,
> Ni canzo ni descort ni lais,
> Al plus que poc avan si trais.
> L'uns viola[l] lais del Cabrefoil,
> E l'autre cel de Tintagoil ;
> L'us cantet cel del Finz Amantz,
> E l'autre cel que fes Ivans.
> L'us menet arpa, l'autre viula ;
> L'us flautella, l'autre siula ;
> L'us mena giga, l'autre rota,
> L'us diz los motz e l'autrels nota ;
> L'us estiva, l'autre flestella
> L'us musa, l'autre caramella ;
> L'us mandura, e l'autr'acorda
> Lo sauteri al manicorda ;
> L'us fai lo juec dels banastelz,
> L'autre jugava de coutelz ;
> L'us vai per sol e l'autre tomba,
> L'autre balet ab sa retomba,
> L'us passet sercle, l'autre sail ;
> Neguns a soun mestier non fail.
>
> *Le Roman de Flamenca*, l. 584, etc., p. 19. Cf. p. 278 sqq.

North of the Loire, it was the same :

> Assés i ot tableterresses
> Ilec entor et tymberresses,
> Qui molt savoient bien joer ;
> Et ne finoient de ruer
> Le tymbre en haut, si recuilloient
> Sor un doigt, e'onques n'i failloient.
> Deus damoiseles molt mignotes,
> Qui estoient en pures cotes
> Et trescles à une tresce
> Faisoient Deduit par noblesce
> En mi la karole baler, etc.
>
> *Le Roman de la Rose*, l. 756 ; t. I, p. 32.

> N'ot menestrel en la contrée
> Qui riens séust de nul deduit
> Que à la cort ne fussent tuit.
> En la sale molt grant gent ot,
> Chascuns servit de ce qu'il sot :
> Cil saut, cil turne, cil enchante,
> Li uns encontre l'autre chante,
> Li uns sible, li autres note,
> Cil sert de harpe, cil de rote,
> Cil de gigue, cil de viele,
> Cil fleute, cil chalemele.
> Puceles querolent et dancent,
> Trestuit de joie faire tencent.
>
> *Roman d'Erec et d'Enide*, Ms. of the Nat. Libr. fonds de Cangé, n° 26, Reg. 7498-4, folio 15 verso, col. I, v. 1.

They afterwards became so licentious in tongue and conduct, that their name was used to express all that was false or of doubtful credit. Another rhymer vilifies thus their character :

> Bien doit estre vavassors vils
> Qui veut estre menesterez.
> Miex voudroie que fussiez rez
> Sanz ove, la teste et le col,
> Que jà n'i remainsist chevol.
>
> Ce n'apartient mie à vostre oès
> D'avoir garnement s'il n'est nués;
> Ç'apartient à ces jougleors
> Et à ces bons enchanteors,
> Que il aient des chevaliers
> Les robes, que c'est lor mestiers.
>
> *Du Chevalier à la robe vermeille*, l. 206. (*Fabliaux et Contes*, Méon's edit., t. iii, p. 279.— Cf. p. 283, *De Saint Pierre et du Jougleor.*)

Giraud de Cabreira, in his sonnet remaining to us, abuses his jongleur for playing so vilely on the violin, singing so ill, and having a head thicker than a Breton,— whilst Pierre d'Auvergne, in his satire on the troubadours, speaks of Guillaume Adhémar, as « le plus mauvais jongleur qui fut jamais. » (Millot, *Histoire littéraire des Troubadours*, t. iii, p. 171.). There is a very curious account of the home life of a minstrel, Colin Muset, in the *Hist. littéraire de la France*, XIIIth century, t. xxiii, p. 552; and no less interesting are the peregrinations, in 1384, of a certain Walter « le Herpeur, menesterel et joueur de la herpe, Anglois, » and Felix, his wife, in Secousse's *Histoire de Charles II. roi de Navarre*, vol. ii, Paris, 1755, 4to., p. 494-503. Cf. Yanguas, *Diccionario de antigüedades del reino de Navarra*, t. iii, p. 131, 531.

The name *Felix*, which is not uncommon among the Jews, gives us an occasion to conjecture that some of those *jougleurs* belonged to that nation either by descent or by marriage. See *Henrici de Bracton de Legibus et consuetudinibus Angliæ Libri quinque*, etc. Londini, an. Do. 1569, fol., lib. iii, cap. 28, fol. 147 verso.

There is in Devon's *Issues of the Exchequer*, p. 247, an item of a gift to two minstrels from the King of Aragon (15 Richard II.), and p. 452 (24 Henry VI.) similar bounties for others of the King of Sicily and of the Duke of Milan [1]. Price, after having mentioned a gratuity

---

[1] Such wandering minstrels were by appointment officers to princely houses of Italy, they also belonged to a class of society which was not more respected than our present street musicians; at least Petrarch speaks of the generality of them as a despicable lot of vagabonds. See a letter to Boccaccio. (Rer. Senil. lib. V.— De quorumdam ambitione — among his works, Basle, edit. 1581, fol., p. 793. Cf. *Mémoires pour la vie de François Pétrarque*, liv. vi ; t. iii., p. 654-656, ann. 1364.)

of a pipe of wine to Beatrice, wife of Richard, harper of King Henry III. in the 36th year of his reign, says : " Beatrice may possibly have been a *jugleress*, whose pantomimic exhibitions were accompanied by her husband's harp, or who filled up the intervals between his performances. This union of professional talents in husband and wife was not uncommon. In the copy of the ordonnances for regulating the minstrels, etc. residing at Paris, a document drawn up by themselves in the year 1321, and signed by 37 persons on behalf of all the *menestreus, jougleurs et jougleresses* of that city, we find among others the names of " Jehanot l'Anglois et Adeline, fame de l'Anglois, Jauzon, filz le Moine, et Marguerite, la fame au Moine." See Roquefort, *De l'Etat de la poésie françoise dans les XIIe et XIIIe siècles*, p. 288 ; and B. Bernhard, *Recherches sur la corporation des ménétriers ou joueurs d'instruments de la ville de Paris*, in the *Bibliothèque de l'Ecole des Chartes*, t. iii, p. 377-399.

The words *filz le Moine, fame au Moine*, as above, give rise to suspicion, since we read in *Richaut*, l. 928 (*Nouveau Recueil de fabliaux*, t. i, p. 67), that a harlot, having been brought up in a nunnery, had decoyed an abbess and turned *jugleress*.

From the prior's accounts of the Augustine canons of Maxtoke, temp. Henry VI., and the accompt rolls of Winchester College, Edward IV., Warton (*The History of English Poetry*, ed. 1824, vol. i, p. 94, 117 ; and vol. ii, p. 153, note) has copied some curious entries, *de Joculatoribus et Mimis*, which complete du Cange's and Carpentier's quotations. (*Gloss. med. et inf. Lat.*, v^{iis} *Jocularis, Joculator, Ministelli, Tornatrices*, t. iii, p. 896, col. 1 et 2 ; t. iv, p. 413 et 414 ; t. vi, p. 612, col. 2 ; t. vii, p. 210, col. 2.) To conclude, Bishop Percy has a long note upon them, in the first vol. of his « Reliques ; » so also Sismondi, *De la Littérature du midi de l'Europe*, t. i, p. 193 ; Legrand d'Aussy, *Fabliaux ou Contes*, etc. Paris, 1829, 8vo., t. i, pp. 32, 33 ; and the Notes 58, 59 of « *Floriant et Florete*, » a metrical Romance of the fourteenth Century, printed for the Roxburghe club. (Edinburgh, 1873, 4to, p. lviii, lx), where is a plate to be compared with an illustration of the Ms. 7189 of the National Library, representing minstrels playing upon musical instruments before King Peleus. (P. Paris, *Les Manuscrits françois de la bibliothèque du Roi*, t. vi, p. 161.)

19. A rogue contents himself with drawing out his tongue half a foot :

> Renars li a la langue traite
> Bien demi-pié fors de la geule.
> *Renars le Nouvel*, l. 3161. (*Roman du Renart*, t. iv, p. 251.)

In fine, Reynard the Fox is exhibited as having made to Tiebert the cat one hundred « loupes, » wens. (*Ibid.*, *i. e.* t. i, p. 42, l. 1106.)

Elsewhere some people are represented as jeering at another « ... en luy jettant de gros lardons, et tirant la langue en derriere. » (*Les Arrêts d'amours*, edit. of 1731, tom. ii, p. 397, arrêt XLI.)

See also Wright's *History of Caricature and of Grotesque in Art, Literature, Sculpture, and Painting*, etc. London, 1875, post 8vo. p. 147, n° 97, etc.

20. We do not know in what way jesters imitated slugs; but faces are fully illustrated by artists and writers of the times. In a fabliau the devil makes a grimace by twisting his mouth behind a hermit:

> Li deable torna la joe;
> Par guile li a fet la moe,
> Que le preudom ne le vit mie.
> *De l'Ermite*, etc., l. 243. (Méon, *Nouveau Recueil de fabliaux et contes*, t. ii, p. 369.)

Another devil of a fellow does the same:

> Vers aus se retorne un petit
> Et tret la langue et tuert la joe,
> Et li houller refont la moe.
> *De Boivin de Provins*, l. 150. (Méon, *Fabliaux et contes*, t. iii. p. 362 l.)

36. So in the prologue of Marie de France:

> Ki Deus ad doné en science
> De parler la bone eloquence
> Ne s'en deit taisir ne celer,
> Ainz se deit volunters mustrer.
> *Poésies*, etc. Paris, 1820, 8vo., t. i, p. 43.

53. The heroes of ancient history and knights of modern fiction, « De coi cil menestrelz font ces nobles romans, » occur frequently in historical works. We might mention Charlemagne, Roland, Olivier and Percheval, referred to in the metrical chronicle of Adam de le Halle, l. 49, 53; but more striking passages are to be found in

---

† Farther on, we read: « Cele fist molt le grimoart, » which may mean: « This made many faces. » *Du Pescheor de Pont-seur-Saine*, l. 52. (*Ibid.*, p. 473.)

Cuvelier's book, which offers a long enumeration of romantic heroes, to some of whom more than one noble family traced their origin [1]. See *Chronique de Bertrand du Guesclin*. Paris, 1839, 4to. t. i, p. 376, l. 10711, etc.

85. The person selected to superintend the education of the young prince was Walter Burleigh, or Burley, of Merton College, who had been appointed almoner to the Queen.

93. On the death of the Black Prince on Trinity Sunday, Barnes remarks, « which festival in whatever place he was, he constantly all his life held the most sacred and solemn of all the days in the year. In memory whereof his anniversary obit was afterwards appointed to be held at Windsor on the eighth of June for ever, » p. 882.

113. Edward III. did not wait for the death of Philippe de Valois (22 August 1350 [2]) to assume the style of King of France, and bear the arms « écu d'azur aux trois fleurs de lys d'or, » quartering them with those of England. Although he did this as early as the 7th of October 1337, it was not until the 25th of January, 1340, the anniversary of his accession, that in dating important public documents, he added the year of his nominal reign over France to the year of his reign hitherto in England. This style was given up 24 October 1360, after the definitive ratification of the treaty of Brétigny [3].

The Edwards of England inscribed on their coins EDWAR. R. ANGL. DNS. HYB., when, suddenly, the " Greatest of the Plantagenets " altered the legend, and wrote EDWARD. D. G. REX ANGL. Z.

---

[1] « Adsurge, lector, de Holgerio Dano nosti, si quicquam nosti; ab Holgerio Dano, decantatissimo illo paladino (quem primum de Comitatu Lossensi a Carolo Magno investitum memorant) hunc Ludovicum comitem Lossensem proseminatum scias, ac eidem, hæreditario jure, successisse, » etc. (Rymer's *Fœdera*, etc., tomi i. pars 1, ad lectorem, p. xvii.)
Such was the popularity of Ogier the Dane, that it gave rise to a proverb :
  Nonpourquant tantost tourne en fuie,
  Sans ce qu'il oit chanter d'Ogier.
  La Branche des royaux lignages, ann. 1194. (*Chron. nat. fr.*, t. viii, p. 95.)

[2] The image of his burial at the Abbey of St.-Denis is preserved among the *Tombeaux des Rois et Reines de France* of Gaignieres' collection in the Bodleian Library (Oxford).

[3] *L'Art de vérifier les dates*, vol. i, p. 811. — Sir Harris Nicolas, *The Chronology of History*, p. 299.

[4] *Grandes Chroniques de France*, ed. of Paulin Paris, ch. cxxxiv ; vol. vi, p. 218.

FRANC. D. HYB. We may refer to Martin Folkes (*Tables of Silver and Gold Coins*, 1763, 4to.), Ruding (*Silver Coinage*, 4to.), Snelling *On the Coins of Great Britain, France and Ireland; A View of the Silver Coin*. London, 1762, fol., pl. II), Francis Wise (*Numorum antiquorum Scriniis Bodleianis reconditorum Catalogus*. Oxford, 1750, fol., pl. XX), Steph. Martin Leake (*An historical Account of English Money*, London, 1793, 8vo., pl. II), John Yonge Akerman (*Numismatic Manual*, Lond., 1840, 8vo., p. 311); but it would be more becoming to quote the two following works, although it is requisite to mention Ruding's text : Edward Hawkins (*The Silver Coins of England*, London, 1841, 8vo., pl. XXIII, p. 98); and Henry William Henfrey (*A Guide to the Study and Arrangement of English Coins*, London, 1869, 8vo., p. 8 et sqq.).

Edward III. did more, he coined golden crowns entirely copied as to the type of the face and the reverse, from those of Philippe de Valois, and bearing the legend : EDWARDVS DEI GRA AGL. FRANCIE REX. See General Ainslie's *Illustrations of the Anglo-French Coinage*, London, 1830, 4to., pl. II, n° 15. — This coin is of French weight.

The title of King of England and France lasted till the end of the reign of Elizabeth.

James I. assumed the title of MAGN. BRIT. FRANC. ET. HIB. REX, which Charles II continued. The Commonwealth interrupted the mention of *France* : Cromwell did not protect us; but Charles II. was eager to resume all the former titles.

That of king of France remained on money till the end of the reign of George III. It was this prince who in fine took the legend GEORGIVS III. D. G. BRITANNIAR. REX. F. D. (*Fidei defensor*) which has subsisted till now, with the simple change of personal name.

120. « No knight banneret can be made but in the warre, and the king present ; or when his Standard royall is displayed in the field. » (Sir William Segar, *The Booke of Honor and Arms*. London, 1590, 4to., p. 69.) See the form of the creation of Sir J. Chandos, by Froissart, in Kervyn's edition, vol. vii, p. 199, 454, and in the preceding poem, p. 3180. Cf. La Curne de Sainte-Palaye, *Mémoires sur l'ancienne chevalerie*, t. i, p. 359, and below, note to l. 193.

120. The writs to the sheriffs, to provide for the passage, are printed in Rymer's *Fœdera*, last edition, vol. iii. part. i, p. 66, in which

the vessels to be pressed (*arestari*) into the service are described as *naves portagii triginta doliorum et ultra, burgeas, fluvos,* etc.

123. Thomas Beauchamp, third earl of Warwick, son of Guy, Earl of Warwick, Marshal of England in 1343; one of the founders of the order of the Garter. Walsingham reports that, by his valour, he greatly facilitated the disembarkation of the English army at la Hogue; but it does not appear probable that any opposition was made to their landing. See below, l. 553, and Barnes, p. 341. He died on his return from an expedition against the Pays de Caux, the 13th November 1369.

125. William de Bohun, earl of Northampton, son of Humphry de Bohun, earl of Hereford and Essex, by the princess Elizabeth, seventh daughter of Edward I. He succeeded to the Garter stall of his nephew Sir Hugh Courtenay, in 1349, and died in September 1360.

127. Robert Ufford, son of Robert, Lord Ufford, admiral of the fleet (Rymer, t. ii. part iii., p. 158, col. 1); on the 16th of March 1336-7, created earl of Suffolk. G. Fr. Beltz has observed that he had seen no corroboration in the public records of the fact of this nobleman having accompanied this expedition. (*Memorials of the Garter*, etc. London, 1841, 8vo., p. 99.) The text however is borne out by Froissart and the Corpus Christi College MS. quoted by Barnes. He was made knight of the Garter in 1348, and died the 4th of Nov. 1369. In the *Issues of the Exchequer*, edited by Frederick Devon, p. 167, is a note of 3000 florins paid to him for his share of the ransom of the Earl d'Auxerre, taken at the battle of Poitiers.

Ralph, first earl of Stafford, son of Edmund Lord Stafford. He was one of the founders of the Garter, and died 31 August 1372. In the Issue Rolls, Easter Edward III., is a grant of L 1000. made to him for capturing Burseald, a French knight, in the war in Gascony. (Devon, p. 159.)

129. William, Lord Montacute, second earl of Salisbury, son of William, the first earl, succeeded his father, who died of wounds received at the Windsor jousts, in January 1344, being then in his 16th year, and became one of the founders of the Garter in the April following. He was at Crécy, Caen, Winchelsea, etc. He married Joan Plantagenet, the fair maid of Kent, but was obliged by papal

bull to resign her to Lord Holland, her previous husband. He died 5th June 1397.

130. John de Vere, eighth earl of Oxford, son of Alphonse, younger brother of Robert, seventh earl. He served in Scotland and Flanders, in the 19 Edward III., was retained to serve with 80 men-at-arms, 3 bannerets, 27 knights, esquires and 80 archers on horseback. He was at Poitiers, and died in France the 24th January 1380.

130. On his landing at la Hogue (on the 11th of July) he is said to have fallen, and to have imitated Cæsar and the Conqueror in turning the accident to a good omen, saying that « the land was desirous of him. »

131. Lord John Beauchamp, brother of Thomas, third earl of Warwick, one of the founders of the Garter, was in Flanders 1338, with the King. At Crécy he carried the royal standard, was made captain of Calais, after its surrender, admiral of the fleet and warden of the Cinque Ports; he died the 2nd December 1360.

132. This is apparently an error for Reginald de Cobham, who was first baron Cobham of Sterborough, son of Reginald Lord Cobham of Orkesden. He was made knight of the Garter in 1352, captain of Calais castle in 1353, (Fr. Rot. 27 Edward III.) and died of the plague the 5th of October 1361. Ralph de Cobham was the son of Henry, half brother to Reginald above mentioned.

133. Bartholomew, second son and heir of Bartholomew, second Lord Burghersh, was in Flanders with his father in 1339, at Crécy, Calais and Poitiers; and is reckoned among the founders of the Garter. In the Issue Rolls, 9 Edward III. (Devon, p. 141) is a note of L80. paid him in advance on his account as receiver of Ponthieu. He died the 5th of April 1369.

135. Guy, Lord Bryan, son and heir of Sir Guy Bryan, succeeded his father in 1349. He served in Scotland and in Flanders, and was rewarded for his conduct in the night defence of Calais, with 200 marks (Liberat. 24 Edward III. membr. 5.— Rymer, vol. iii, p. 195); he was admiral of the Western Fleet in 1356, (Rot. Franciæ de anno 30 Edw. III., membr. 16.— Rymer, t. iii. p. 328. Also Exchequer. A. R. Navy 604/10, 44 Edward III.) and elected into the Garter on

the death of Chandos in 1369, being called *Guido de Bryan, chivaler*, in an entry relating to his appointment as commissionner *re Ivo Beaustan*, a Breton esquire. (Rymer's *Fœdera*, vol. iii, pars ii, p. 1030, col. i. A. D. 1375.) He died the 17th of August 1390. See also *Issue Roll of Thomas de Brantingham*, etc. (London, 1835, 8vo.) 44 Edward III. p. 461, where is an entry of *L* 200. paid him for wages, and as a reward, for 99 men-at-arms and 200 archers. In the Exchequer Rolls in the Augmentation Office, 27 Edward III. is one, containing the particulars of the expenses of Sir Guy de Bryan, knight, and family to Calais, on the 17th of February, and returning the 20th of March. (Exch. A. R. ancient Miscellanea. Nuncii 628/11.) Cf. Luce's Froissart, t. vi, p. XIV.

136. Of Sir Richard de la Vache, or his family, presumed to be of Gascon origin, but little appears to be known. Beltz (*Memorials of the Order of the Garter*, etc., p. 106, ch. XXXI) tells us that he was elected into the Order of the Garter on the death of Lord Lisle in 1355. In 1361, he was appointed constable of the Tower for life, and died in January 1366.

137. Richard, Lord Talbot, succeeded his father Gilbert, Lord Talbot, in 20 Edward III. He served in the wars of France in that year and in 29 Edward III. He died the 30th of October 1356.

139. John, son of Sir Edward Chandos, in the words of Du Guesclin "the most illustrious knight in the world," served in the campaigns of 1339, was present at Crécy, Poitiers, Nájera, and fell at the bridge of Lussac, 31 December 1369; he was also good musician, being invited by the King to sing with the royal minstrels. Being already the knight of some fair lady, he was one of the founders of the Garter, and his plate is still remaining in the stall he formerly occupied in St. George's Chapel [1].

---

[1] See Luce's Froissart, t. iv, p. 91, § 324, and p. 322; and t. v, p. 28, § 381. In Rymer's *Fœdera*, vol. iii, p. 343, is a deed of gift of two parts of the manor of Kirkeld in Lindsay to Sir John Chandos, for his good service at the battle of Poitiers.

There is a paper by Sir Samuel Rush Meyrick in the *Archæologia*, vol. xv, p. 484-495, and a more valuable one by Benjamin Fillon (Londres et Fontenay, 1856, 8vo. magno, 35 pages), which is illustrated by the signature and handwritting of Chandos, the signet of the Black Prince and James Audley, the seals of John de Creswell, Hugh de Calvlley

Sir James, son of James de Audeley of Stratton Audley, Oxfordshire, the friend and companion of the Prince and Chandos, shared in their glory in the French wars, was appointed seneschal of Aquitaine in 1345 (Rot. Vasc. 19 Edward III., memb. 8; Rymer, t. iii, fol. 32), King's lieutenant seven years afterwards (*ibid.* 26 Edward III. membr. 7, Rymer, vol. iii, p. 239), great seneschal of Poitou in 1369, and died the same year at Fontenay-le-Comte, " to the great sorrow of the Prince and Princess of Wales, as well as of all the barons and knights of Poitou, " for he was « uns moult sage et vaillans chevaliers. » (Luce's Froissart, t. vii, p. 137.)

141. Thomas de Holland, earl of Kent, son of Sir Robert de Holland; served in Flanders in 1340, was at Crécy and Calais, and died in Normandy the 28th December 1360. He married Joan Plantagenet, grand-daughter of Edward I., afterwards princess of Wales, and in her right assumed the title of earl of Kent in 1358. He was one of the founders of the Order of the Garter.

145. The King's charter upon this occasion demanding the usual aid, printed in Rymer's *Fœdera*, last edit., vol. iii, p. 90, is dated Calais, the nativity of the Virgin, 8th of September, 1346.

149. Roger Mortimer, second earl of March, at this time only 17 years of age, was at the battle of Crécy, in 1354 assumed the title, in the following year was appointed warden of the Cinque Ports and died at Rouvray in Burgundy in 1360. He was one of the founders of the Garter.

151. John of Montagu, nephew, says Froissart (vol. vii, p. 219. Cf. p. 362), of William of Montagu, earl of Salisbury, whom later he was to succeed with the title, was at the battle of Crécy. In 31 Edward III. he was retained to serve the King with six horses. He

---

Hugh and Geffrey Worresley, Robert Knolles and Thomas Percy, whose signature is given as that of John de Harpeden.

At the beginning of this century, the name of *Chandos* was recalled on the occasion of a law suit, which made a great noise and gave rise to Sir Egerton Brydges's papers (1822, fol.), and *Chandos Family* (30 pages, 4to., no title. Reprinted from the Introduction to Sudeley Castle); to George Frederick Beltz's *Chandos Peerage Case* (London, 1834, 8vo.); and to *A Letter in a statement relative to the Barony of Chandos*, in the *Synopsis of the Peerage of England* by Sir Nicholas Harris Nicolas. London, 1841, pp. 14, 12mo.

married Margaret, daughter of Thomas de Monthermer. In 11 June 1369, Edward III. caused safe-conducts to be delivered to John " Montagu, chivaler, " and to William " Montagu, " esquire, who were on the eve of crossing over to join the expedition of John, Duke of Lancaster. (Rymer's *Fœdera*, vol. iii, p. 870.) John of Montagu was summoned to parliament amongst the other barons from the 31 Edward III. to 13 Richard II. in which year (1390) he died.

155. Robert Bertrand, Baron de Bricquebec, was appointed Marshal of France in 1325, and died in 1348. (Anselme, *Histoire généalogique de la Maison royale de France*, t. vi, p. 688, § XXIX.)

160. Did we suppose our author to be an eye-witness of what he here relates, his confirmation of the account of the landing, as it has been reported by Walsingham [1], although evidently from a different source, would present us with a very remarkable difficulty; but as it is clear that in the early part of his chronicle he speaks from hearsay and not from actual observation, we may safely believe from the silence of the King himself and Northbury, as indeed from the prior statement respecting the creation of the knights, and the uncertainty as to the place where the English host would land, unknown until a few days before even to themselves, that the landing at la Hogue was unopposed. At the same time this mention of the Marshal Bertrand, occurring in no other writer, is worthy of attention.

There is a proverbial similitude, « as bold as Beauchamp, » which will detain us an instant. Of this surname there were many earls of Warwick, amongst whom we may conceive, with Dr Fuller, that Thomas, the first of that name, gave chief occasion to this proverb. In the year 1346, with one squire and six archers, he fought against a hundred men, at la Hogue and defeated them, slaying sixty Normans, and giving the whole fleet means to land.

174. Northbury says that a gallant defence was made at the bridge, « et les Fraunceys defenderent ledit pount fortment. » (Robert de Avesbury, p. 126.) See also the preceding letter.

176. Jean, vicomte de Melun, comte de Tancarville, eldest son of Jean, the first viscount de Melun, great chamberlain of France in

[1] *Historia Anglicana*, edited by Henry Thomas Ryley, vol. i, London, 1863, 8vo. p. 267.

1347, governor of Burgundy, Champagne and Brie, was taken prisoner at Poitiers, with the archbishop of Sens, his brother, and died in 1382 [1]. See Anselme, *Histoire généalogique et chronologique de la maison royale de France*, t. viii, p. 314. Cf. *Histoire du château et des sires de Tancarville*, par A. Deville. Rouen, 1834, in-8º. (Maison de Melun, p. 154-161); and Luce's Froissart, sommaire du premier livre, t. vi, p. xxvi, note. (Jean de Melun, 1362.) Holinshed says that at Caen he was taken by one named *Legh*, ancestor to Sir Peter Legh, then living, and that for his service the king had given him the lordship of Hanley in Cheshire, then occupied by the said Sir Peter.

177. Raoul [2], son of Raoul de Brienne, comte d'Eu and de Guines, succeeded his father as constable of France in 1344. On his return from this imprisonment he was accused of " felonie " and lost his head at Paris on the 19th of November 1350. See Anselme, *Histoire généalogique et chronologique de la maison royale de France*, t. vi, p. 161, § XXI.

180. This should be " not seventeen years of age, " but it is so clear from subsequent passages (l. 372, 426), confirmed by Avesbury and Froissart, that by *oept* eight is intended, that we cannot honestly avoid the dilemma.

181. We cannot better illustrate the progress of the army to Caen and the subsequent battle at Crécy, than by the following letter of Edward himself addressed to Thomas de Lucy, giving an account of his proceedings from the landing at La Hogue; the first part indeed agrees with that addressed to the archbishop of York, printed in the *Retrospective Review*, New Series, vol. i, p. 120, whilst the rest agreeing much in substance with Northbury, p. 136, as is necessarily the case in relations of the same events, has yet many variations and is dated on the previous day, it ought not therefore I think to be here omitted [3].

---

[1] Barnes and Collins have confounded this nobleman with Charles of Artois, comte de Longueville, who, with his brother comte d'Eu, was also taken at Poitiers.

[2] In the Close Rolls, 21 Edward III., is an order for the closest imprisonment of the Lord of Tankervill, and a similar writ for the comte d'Eu. (Rymer, vol. iii, part 2, p. 116.)

[3] Minot has a poem upon the progress of the army from their landing at la Hogue to their appearing before Calais, intitled :

« How Edward at Hogges unto land wan,
And rade thurgh France or ever he blan. »

Minot's *Poems*, p. 26-33. Cf. Robert de Avesbury, p. 123-140.

« Edward, par la grace de Dieu roy d'Angleterre et de France [1] et seigneur d'Irland, à son chier et feal chevalier Thomas Lucy, saluz. Pour ceo que nous savoms bien que vous orretz volunters bones novelles de nous, nous fesons savoir que nous arrivames à la Hoge prez Harfluz le dozisme jour de juyllet darreyn passé, avec toutz noz gentz seyns et saufs, Ioué en soit Dieux ! et illeoques demurasmes sur le deskippere de noz gentz et chivaulx, et le vitailler de noz gentz, tant que le marsdi prochein ensuant, euquel jour nous movasmes avec notre host devers Valongnes, et preimes le chastel et la ville; et puys sur notre chymyn fesoms faire le pount de Ove, qu'estoit debrisé per noz enemys; et le passames, et preimes le chastel et la ville de Carentyne. Et de illeokes nous tenismes le droit chemyn devers la ville de Saint-Leo, et trovasmes le pount Herbert, prez cele ville, rumpu pour avoir desturbé notre passage; et nous le feismes maintenant refaire. Et lendemayn preismes la ville; et nous adresceasmes droitment à Caen, sanz nulle jour sojourner del houre que nous departismes del Hoge, tant que à notre venu illeoqes, et mayntenaunt sur nostre herbergere à Caen, nos gentz comencerent de doner assault à la ville, qu'estoit moult afforce et estuffé dez gentz d'armes, environ mill et sis centz, et comunes armés et defensables, et maisme trent mill, que se defenderent moult bien et apertement, si que le mellé fut trefort et longe durant; mès loué soit Dieux ! la ville estoit prigns force au derreine, saunz perdre de nos gentz. Et y furent pris le count de Ewe, conestable de Fraunce; le chamberleyne de Tankerville, qu'estoit à la journé escriez mareschal de Fraunce, et des aultres banerettes et chivalers environ cent et qaraunt, et des esquiers et riches burgesses grant foison; et sont mortz tout pleyn de nobles chivalers et gentilshommes, et des communes grant noumbre. Et notre navie, qu'est demurré devers nous, a ars et destruit tout la cost de la mer de

---

[1] That assomption of the title of king of France occurs in several letters addressed to the duke of Brabant, appointing him Edward III.'s lieutenant and vicar-general in that kingdom and others, all dated on the 7th of October 1337 (Rymer, 3d ed., t. ii, pars iii, p. 191, col. 1 sqq.) It is remarkable that the title above mentioned is not to be found in any other instrument in the Fœdera until after the 25th of January, 1340. Edward III. did not, it is supposed, assume the arms of France (l'ècu d'azur aux trois fleurs de lys d'or) until that year. In *L'Art de vérifier les dates*, vol. I, p. 811, Edward is said to have first dated his instruments with the year of his reign over France in 1339. This must, however, be understood to be 1339-40. Cf. above, p. 300, note to l. 113.

Harflue jousquez à la fosse de Colville prez Caen; et si y ount ars la ville de Shirburgh et lez niefz en la haven, et sount ars des grant neefs et aultres vesseals des enemys, que par nous gentz c. ou plus. Et puis demorasmes quatre jours à Caen pour vitailler et frecsher notre host; et de illeoques, pur ce que nous esteims certifiez que notre adversaire fut venu à Roen, que nous ne y poyms passer. Et en le mesme temps nous encounterent deux cardinalx à la cité de Lyseux, et s'afforcerount de nous tenir per coleur de traitié pour nous desturber de notre voiage; mez nous lez rendismes briefment que nous ne lerroms nulle journé pour tiel cause, mez quel hour que raison noz serroit offert, nous ferioms responce covenable. Et, quant noz estoms enformez que ledit pount de Roen fut rumpu, nous nous logames sur la river, devers partz de Sayn bien prez ledicte ville, et ainsi tenismes notre chemyn avant sur ladicte river, et trovames touz les pounts rumpuz ou afforcés et defenduz, si que en nulle maner ne povames passer devers notredit adversaire; ne il, que nous costea de jour en aultre de l'autre parte de l'eau, ne vouloit vers nous approchier, dount il nous peisa moult; et quaunt noz venismes à Poscy prez de Parys, nous trovames le pount rumpu, et adonque notredicte adversaire estoiet plantez ou tout son host et povaire en la cité de Paris, et sy fist baser le pount de Saint-Leo, que nous ne povems passer à Paris de celui part de l'eawe où nous estoims : pour quoy nous demourames à Poscy treiz jours, taunt pour attendre notredit adversaire en caas qu'il vouloit à nous doner bataille, come pour refaire ledict pount. Et endeintres que ledit pount fut en reparaillant, veint ung graunt povair dez ennemiz de l'autre part l'eawe pour disturber le reparailler dudict pount; mez devant que ledict pount fuist refait, achuns dez noz gentz y passerent au poser ung plaunke, et les disconfirent et occirent graunt nombre. Et quaunt nous veismes que notre ennemiz ne vouloit venir pour doner bataille, sy fismes arder et gaster le païz environ. Et chacun jour nous gentz affair avec les ennemiz et tout fois aiant le victoire, louez en soit Dieu ! et passames le pount avec notre host; et pour plus attraire notre ennemi à la bataille, nous nous traiames devers Picardie, où noz gentz orent plusors belles journés sour nos ennemis. Et quaunt nous venismes à la river de Some, nous y trovasmes lez pountz rumpuz, per quoi nous nous traiames devers Saynt-Walleri pour passer à ung gué, où la mer foule et refoule ; et à notre venue illeoques, graunt nombre dez gentz

des armés et des communes nous vindrent à l'encontre pour nous defendre le passage ; mez nous preignons maintenant le passage sur euz à force, et parmi la grace de Dieu si passerent bien mille persons à frount où, avant cez houres, à payn souloient passer trois ou quatre, sy que nous et tout notre host passarems savement et en ung hour de jour, et nos ennemis y furent discomfiz et plusieurs pris, et sy avoit-il graunt nombre dez ennemiz occis à la journée, saunz perdre de nous gentz ; et mesme le jour bientost aprez ce que nous estoms passés, le eawe se monstra del autre part l'eau notredict adversaire ou graunt povair dez gentz si soudainement, que nous n'estoms de rien grevez : pour quoy nous y demouraims et preins notre place, et attendans tout le jour et lendemain tant que al hour de vespre. Et au darain, quant nous voiames qu'il ne vouloit illoeques passer, mez se tourna devers Abbevill, nous nous traiames devers Crescy pour lui encontrer de l'autre part de la fforest. Et le samady, le xxvj. jour d'August, à notre venue à Cresci, notre ennemi se monstra bien près de nous à hour de tierce ou grant nombre de gentz ; car il avoit plus de xij. mille dez hommes-d'armes, desquelx viij. mille furent de gentil gentz, chevaliers et esquiers ; et maintenaunt nous arraimez nos batailles, et ensi attendimes au pee, tant que un pou devant hour de vespere, à quel hour lez batailles se assemblerent en plain champ. Et estoient le bataillez trop fort et longement duraunt, quar il dura de devant hour de vespre tant que à soir, et lez ennemiz se porterount moult noblement, et moult sovent se ralierent ; ainz, loez en soit Dieux ! ilz furent discomfiz, et notre adversaire se mist en fuite, et y furent mortz le roy de Beame, le roy de Maylocre, le duc de Loraigne, l'archevesque de Saunz, l'evesque de Noion, le hault priour del Hospital de Fraunce, l'abbé de Corbell, le counte de Aleunzone, le counte de Flaundres, le counte de Bloys, le counte de Harcourt et son ffitz, le counte de Saumes, le counte d'Auser, le count de Muntbiliart, le counte de Grauntprée, le viscounte de Meloigne, le viscounte de Coarci, le sieur de Risenbergh, le sieur de Morel, le sieur de Kayeu, le sieur de St.-Venant, et tut playn dez aultres countes et barons et aultrez graunt sieurs, dont homme ne puest savoir lez nomes encore. Et moururent en ung petit place où la primer assemblée estoiet, plus de mille et v^c. chivalers et esquiers, estre tout plain dez aultres, si que moururent après de tout pars du champ. Et après la discomfiture nous y demourames tout le nut joien saunz boire et

Bellum de Crescy.

mangier, et le demain matin fut la chace faite, en quel furent occiz bien iiij. mille que de gentz-d'armes que de Geneveiz et aultres gentz-d'armes. Et notredit adversaire après la discomfiture se trait devers Amyas [1], où il fait tuer grant nombre de sez Genevois, et dit qu'ilz lui traieront à sa besoigne. Et homme dit qu'il a fait assembler son povair de novel pour nous doner autre foiz bataille, et si fioms bien en Dieu qu'il continuera devers noz sa grace en maner comme il a fait tant que ençà. Et si soums ore trait devers la mer pour estre refresshé hors d'Angleterre, aussi bien de gentz-d'armes comme d'artillery et aultres choses besoignables, car le journée que noz avons faite a esté bien loigne et continuel ; mez toutefoiz nous ne pensoms à departir du royaume de Fraunce tant que eyoms fait fyne de notre guerre ou l'aide de Dieu. Donné soubz notre privé seel devant Calais, le iij. jour de Septembre, l'an de notre reigne d'Engletiere vintisme, » etc.

193. Every one knows the meaning of *banneret*. (See above, p. 301, note to l. 120.) There is a little poem called *l'Ordre des Bannerets de Bretagne et leur origine*, etc., first published at Caen in 1672, small 12mo, and reprinted in the same place, 1827, 4to. For a long time that piece of wretched poetry was considered as an historical document, even by Moréri (*Le grand Dictionnaire historique*, t. i', p. 53), though at first glance it was easy to find out that it was one of those spurious poems forged with a view of illustrating the antiquity of certain aristocratic families. See *Extrait abrégé des vieux Mémoriaux de l'abbaye de Saint-Aubin-des-Bois en Bretagne*. Paris, 1853, 12mo., preface.

195. John, King of Bohemia, and his son Charles the Fourth, elected King of the Romans the 19th of July 1346. He was crowned Emperor of Rome on Easter Day, April 5th 1355. The crest of the King, three ostrich feathers, with the motto " *Ich Dien*," was adopted by the Prince, and has been since always borne by his successors.

---

[1] Amiens. Is it generally known that the name fo that town was taken as that of a saint on account of the head of John the Baptist being preserved there ?

> And when he fond he was yhurt, the Pardoner he gan to threte,
> And swore by St. Amyas that he should abigg
> With stickes hard and sore even upon the rigg.
> Chaucer, Prologue to the Marchantes 2d Tale.

199. Jean de Hainault, seigneur de Beaumont, de Valenciennes et de Condé. He bore also, in right of his wife Marguerite, comtesse de Soissons, the title of comte de Soissons; he died the 11th of March 1356.

246. Godemar du Faÿ, sire of Bouchon, a great baron of Picardy. He had with him five hundred men-at-arms and three thousand armed commoners. See Robert de Avesbury, *Historia de mirabilibus gestis Edvardi III*. Oxonii, 1720, 8vo. p. 13). Cf. Froissart's chronicle, t. i, p. CCXII, note 2, and CCLVI, note 1; p. 184, 2nd part, p. 406; t. ii, p. XVIII, note 5.

260. The name of this man was *Gobin Agace*, a peasant who had been taken prisoner. Having forced the passage, the King, Froissart tells us, gave Gobin and his companions in captivity their freedom without ransom, a hundred nobles of gold and a good horse.

285. Jacmes II., King of Majorca, succeeded his uncle D. Sancho at the age of twelve years, and reigned from 1324 to 1349. Previously Majorca was in good terms with England, as we may judge from entries published in Rymer's *Fœdera* (Record edit., vol. i, pars i, p. 523, 558 — 18 Edw. II., 1323, 1324); but during the Anglo-French Wars, Jacmes being vassal of Charles V. as lord of Montpellier, was bound to side with him. He was killed three years after the battle of Crécy in an engagement with D. Pedro IV. of Aragon. See D. Vicente Mut, t. ii of the *Historia del Reyno de Mallorca*, en Mallorca, 1650, fol., lib. IV, cap. ii, etc., p. 111-213, etc.; and Colin Campbell, *The ancient and modern History of the Balearic Islands, or of the Kingdom of Majorca*, etc. London, 1716, 8vo., ch. V, p. 178-240. Cf. *L'Art de vérifier les dates*, t. i., p. 753.

334. Raoul, duc de Lorraine and marquis, succeeded his father Ferri IV. in 1329. Champier says of him at the battle of Crécy, that had the rest of the French behaved like him, the English could not have stood before them, « non plus que la perdrix devant l'oiseau de proye. » (*Le Recueil ou croniques des royaulmes d'Austrasie, ou France Orientale, dite à present* Lorrayne, etc. Lugd. sine anno, small folio, liv. ii., ch. ix. *Du duc Raoul, filz du duc Ferry.* sign. f.) Cf. D. Calmet, *Histoire de Lorraine*, liv. XXVI, t. iii., col. 331-352.

336. Louis, the third comte de Flandres, de Nevers and de Rethel. He was only sixteen years of age at the battle of Crécy; he married Marguerite, daughter of John III. duke of Brabant, and died in 1383.

338. Charles de Valois II. comte d'Alençon, de Chartres, etc., surnamed *le Magnanime*, son of Charles de France and Marguerite de Sicile, and grand-son of Philippe the Hardi. He married, I. Jeanne, comtesse de Joigny; II. Mary, daughter of Ferdinand II. of Spain.

340. « For *Joii* it is probable that *Blois* should be the reading, » so says Cox, and sees in him Louis de Châtillon, son of Guy, comte de Blois et de Dunois, and of Marguerite de Valois, sister of Philippe II. King of France. It is true that in Northbury's letter, ap. Rob. de Avesbury, p. 136-140, and in the poem on the battle of Crécy printed by Buchon, the count of Blois is mentioned in juxtaposition with « le counte de Harecourt » as having then fallen; but between the two words there is too much difference.

340. Jean d'Harcourt and Aumale, hostage in England, gave a power of attorney at London, January 12, 1365. (n. st.) to serve his fiefs in France, and especially in the bishopric of Poitiers. (La Roque, *Additions aux preuves de l'Histoire de la maison de Harcourt*, vol. iv, p. 1435.) In 1367, at the request of the Prince of Aquitaine and Wales, and « parmy l'entreprise et pleggerie de nostre cher et feal Loys de Harecourt, vostre oncle, » the count of Harcourt was permitted to cross over to France and to stay there a few months; but on the 1st December of the same year, Edward III. summoned him to return to London and redeem his pledge. The summons was renewed in January of the following year. (Rymer's *Fœdera*, etc. vol. iii, p. 837, 840.) The same year 1368, on the 14 October, Jean VI. married Catherine de Bourbon, one of the younger sisters of the Queen of France. Louis d'Harcourt, uncle of Jean VI., was viscount of Châtellerault, and consequently, as says Froissart, the most powerful lord of Poitou. Before him, Jean IV., first comte d'Harcourt, likewise viscount of Châtellerault, etc., was at the battles of Montcassel, Buirenfosse and Bovines; he married Isabeau de Parthenay, dame de Vibray.

355. On the battle of Crécy, see Froissart, ch. LX, §§ 274-287, t. iii, p. XLVIII. His account gave rise to a paper intitled : *Mémoire sur le manuscrit de la bibliothèque de la ville d'Amiens, et en particulier sur le récit de la bataille de Crécy*, par M. Rigollot, in the *Mémoires de la Société*

des Antiquaires de Picardie, t. iii, Amiens, 1840, 8vo., p. 131-183. Cf. F. C. Louandre, *Mémoire sur la bataille de Crécy*, inserted in the *Revue anglo-française*, Poitiers, 1837, 8vo., t. iii, p. 248; and other dissertations on the same subject by Baron Seymour de Constant (in the same *Revue*, April 1834), reprinted at Abbeville, 1851, 18mo. See also a historical paper by M. de Cayrol, in the *Mémoires de la Société d'émulation d'Abbeville*, 1836, 1837, 8vo., and *Itinéraire au champ de bataille de Crécy*, read at the meeting of the Société des Sciences morales, 2 December 1836, by abbé Caron, and published after his death by Dr. Boucher. Versailles, 1849, 8vo.

On Crécy and Neville's Cross, we will mention also 30 lines published by Th. Wright in his *Political Poems and Songs relating to English History*, etc., vol. i, p. 52, 53; and a poem on the former of those battles, inserted by Gilles li Muisis into his chronicle, and printed first by Buchon (*Collection des Chroniques nationales françaises*, etc., t. xiv, Paris, 1826, 8vo., p. 276-300) and afterwards by J. J. de Smet, t. ii, Bruxelles, 1841, 4to., p. 246-263, of a volume of the *Collection des Chroniques belges inédites*. At the beginning of the poem there is this memorandum : *Notandum igitur quod quidem familiaris domino Johanni de Hannonia, domino de Blaumont, confecit in metro Gallico quemdam rotulum de supradicto bello, et de morte proborum et nobilium virorum, cujus tenorem feci inserere in præsenti opusculo, ad memoriam et solamen futurorum.*

363. The historian of the Bohemian language and literature mentions thus a poem in 142 lines on the death of King John : « Cantio, says Lupacius, quæ eo tempore fuit in ore hominum celeberrima. » (*Geschichte der böhmischen Sprache und ältern Literatur*, von Joseph Dobrosky, etc. Prag, 1818, 8vo., p. 133, 134. Cf. *Wýbor z Literatury ceské*. Prag, 1845, 8vo., p. 1179, 2180 u. ff.)

A rhymer, who knew very well the King of Bohemia, praises him in such terms :

Prend garde au bon roi de Behaigne,
Qui en France et en Alemaigne,
En Savoie et en Lombardie,
En Danemarche et en Hongrie,
En Poulaine, en Prusse, en Cracoe,
En Masauwe, en Russe, en Lestoe,
A la pris et honneur conquerre.
Il donoit ses joiaus et terre ;
Or, argent, rien ne retenoit,
Fors l'honneur : ad ce tenoit,
Et il en avoit plus que nulz, etc.

Confort d'ami. (*Les Œuvres de Guillaume de Machault*, ed. of Prosper Tarbé, p. 103.)

370. Lord Cobham and Lord Stafford were ordered on this business, and their report was that they had found eighty banners, the

bodies of eleven princes, twelve hundred knights, and about thirty thousand common men. Upon which the king ordered the bodies of the principal knights to be carried to the monastery of Montenay, and there interred in consecrated ground. (Froiss.) The particular attention paid to the remains of the king of Bohemia is also noticed by Barnes, from Villani. See libr. XII, cap. LXVI; ap. Murator, *Rer. Ital. Script.*, t. XIII, col. 948-951.

384. The siege of Calais was commenced upon the third of September 1346, and continued until the following August, on the third of which month it surrendered. (Rob. de Avesbury, *Hist. Edw. III.*, p. 140, 141.) The error of the text is unaccountable, unless we attribute it to the carelessness of the transcriber.

419. « The introduction of a third party, if a third person be intended, into the well-known affair of the design upon Calais, is sufficiently perplexing, » so says Coxe, who did not understand the text.

419. Antoine, sire de Beaujeu, son of Edouard II., and of Marie du Thil, killed at the skirmish of Ardres, A. D. 1351, entered Spain via Montpellier, where he was in January 1366. See Froissart, t. vi, p. LXXXII, note 2, as well as t. iv, p. XLVI; Anselme, *Histoire généalogique*, etc., t. vi, p. 724, § XXXV, p. 733, § X ; and Ferd. de La Roche la Carelle, *Histoire du Beaujolais et des sires de Beaujeu*, etc. Lyon, 1853, 8vo. magno, t. i, p. 169-175 (Antoine), 175-191. (Edouard II.)

Froissart, in his *Dit du Florin*, mentions him as being munificent and jolly :

> Il me souvenra souvent
> Coment le sire de Biauju
> Antonnes, qui grans galois fu, etc.

420. Messire Geoffroy de Chargny, who afterwards became porte-oriflamme de France, was made prisoner at the battle of Crécy and received in 1350 a safe-conduct to cross over home. (*Rot. Franc.* 24 Edw. III., membr. 2 ; ap. Rymer, vol. iii, p. 212.) He was killed at the battle of Poitiers, by Lord Reginald Cobham, and buried at the King's expense in the church of the Célestins at Paris.

Like Boucicaut, the little senescal d'Eu, Jean de Saintré, and most of the knights of the time, Geoffroy de Charny was lettered ; he is the author of a tract in prose entitled : « Demandes pour le tournoy que je, Geoffroi de Charni, fais à haut et puissant prince des chevaliers de

Nostre-Dame de la Noble maison, » (Galland, *Mémoires de l'Académie des Inscriptions*, etc., t. ii, p. 739) and of verses which are to be found in the Ms. 25447, fonds français, of the National Library, Paris.

421. Almeric, or Amerigo de Pavia, was afterwards appointed commander of the galleys by the King, by letters dated Westminster, 24th of April 1348. (Rymer's *Fœdera*, vol. iii, p. 159. Cf. Chron. de Froissart, t. iv, p. XXVIII, XL ; p. 66, § 304 sqq.)

452. Froissart mentions that the King was struck twice to the earth by Eustace de Ribaumont, but has nothing of his rescue by the Prince. Walsingham has recorded another anecdote, that the French King in the heat of the action was twice unhorsed by the King of England : « Philippus vero rex Franciæ... dum multos prosternit et perimit, et gutture et femore vulneratus, et bina vice per regem Angliæ equo suo dejicitur. » (*Hist. Angl.*, vol. i, p. 269. A. D. 1346.)

480. The Spaniards under Don Carlos de la Cerda had with forty-four men of war beset the British seas, and shortly before this engagement had taken and sunk ten English merchantmen laden with wine from Gascony. Likely such an act of piracy was the occasion of the naval engagement off Sluys, but it is very easy to understand that the Spanish rovers were very much enclined to scour the British seas, which oftentimes gave rise to very severe retaliation. About 1339, a ship laden with woollen cloth and other goods intended for Bordeaux, having been plundered, Edward III. ordered the seneschal of Gascony to bind all the Spaniards there to repay the loss or go to gaol. (*Rot. Vasc.*, 13 Edw. III., membr. 3. *Pro Petro Garcye*.)

The sea-fight off Rye took place on the 29th of August. Minot has a poem upon it intitled :

> How King Edward and his menze
> Met with the Spaniardes in the see.
>
> *Poems on interesting Events in the reign of King Edward III*, London, 1795, crown 8vo., p. 45-47.

There was also a gold medal struck in commemoration of this victory, representing the King seated in a ship, holding a sword in his hand [1].

---

[1] All the historians of the time expatiate more or less on the famous sea-fight of « L'Espagnol sur mer, » in which the naval pride of Spain was first humbled by an English fleet, and which vindicated for Edward III. his proudest and best deserved title of the

497. The number of the ships taken from the Spaniards are variously reported at fourteen, seventeen, twenty-two, and twenty-six; Froissart and Walsingham being the authorities for the two extremes.

509. Edward III. sent to his son this account of the naval battle of Sluys, June 24, 1340 :

« Très-cher filz, nous pensoms bien que vous estes desirous assavoir bones novelles de nous et coment il nous est avenuz puys nostre aler d'Engleterre : si vous fesom savoir que le joedi après ceo que nous departimes du port d'Orewell, nous siglames tut le jour et la nuyt suaunte, et le vendredi, entour hour de nonne, nous venismes sur la costere de Flaundres, devant Glankebergh, où nous avions la vewe de la flote de nos enemys, qui estoyent tut amassez ensemble eu port del Swyne ; et pur ceo que la tyde n'estoit mie adonques pur assembler à eux, nous y hebergeasmes tut cel noet. Le samady, le jour de Saint-Johan, bien après houre de nonne, à la tyde, nous, eu noun de Dieu et en espoir de nostre droite querelle, entrames eudit port sur nosditz ennemys qui avoyent assemblé lours niefs en moult fort array, et lesqueux fesoient mult noble defense tut cel jour et la noet après ; mès Dieu, par sa puissaunce et miracle, nous octroya la victoire.... Et si vous fesoms sevoir que le nombre des gents-d'armes et autres gents armez amounta à xxx. milles, dequele nombre par eswe cink milles sont eschapées, et le remanant, ensi come nous est doné à entendre par ascuns gentz qui sont pris en vie, si gisent les corps mortz en tut pleyn de lieux sur la costere de Flaundres. D'autre part, totes nos niefs, c'est assavoir *Cristofre* et les autres, qui estoient perdues à Middelburgh, sont ore regaignez, et il y ount gaignez en ceste navie trois ou quatre aussi grandes come la *Cristofre*. Les Flemengs estoient de bone volenté d'avoir venuz à la bataille du commencement, tant que à la fin, issint Dieu, nostre Seignour, ad assez de grace monstré de quei nous et toutz noz amys sumes tutdiz tenutz de lui rendre graces et merciz. Nostre entent est à demorer en pees en le ewe tant que nous eoms pris certeyn point oue nos alliez et autres noz amys de Flandres de ceo que seit affaire. Très-cher filz, Dieu soit gardeyn de vous.

King of the sea. We will limit ourselves to referring to the last book on this prince ably compiled by the Rev. W. Warburton, London, 1876, 12mo. See first decade, A. D. 1347-1357, ch. II, p. 149-151.

« Doné sous nostre secree seal, en nostre nief-cogg *Thomas*, le mescredy en la veille saint Piere et saint Poul. » (Jules Delpit, *Collection générale des documents français qui se trouvent en Angleterre*, etc., t. i, p. 67, 68.)

520. Thomas Plantagenet, surnamed *of Woodstock*, youngest son of Edward III., earl of Buckingham and Essex, by right of his wife Eleanor Bohun, duke of Gloucester, succeeded in the order of the Garter, Guichard d'Angle, earl of Huntingdon, in 1380. He was murdered in Calais prison in 1397.

524. Jean de Grailly, captal de Buch [1], son of Jean de Grailly and Blanche de Foix. He distinguished himself nobly at Poitiers and took prisoner Jacques de Bourbon, count de la Marche and of Ponthieu, whose ransom we find fixed at twenty-three thousand florins. (Compare Rymer's *Fœdera*, vol. iii, part. ii, p. 635, A. D. 1362, with G. Fr. Beltz, p. 30, note, and Devon, *Issues of the Exchequer*, Introd. p. xl.) He was one of the founders of the Garter, and died a prisoner at Paris in 1377. He had married in 1350 Rose, daughter of Bernard, sire d'Albret, but had no issue.

538. The leaders of the English party in Gascony in 1347, are enumerated in a letter from Edward III. *Ad nobiles Vasconiæ, de ipsorum constancia, laudatoria :* « Domino de la Bret, archidiacono de Durford, domino de la Sparre, Arnaldo de Durford, domino de Thouars, domino de Chastileoun, Lespesio de Bearn, vicecomiti de Frounsak, vicecomiti de Benauges, domino de Pomers, domino de Lescun, Johanni Columb de Burdegala, Petro Beger, Johanni Mauleoun. » (*Rot. Vascon.*, 21 Edw. III., membr. 12 ; ap. Rymer, vol. iii, p. 123.)

---

[1] There are many explanations of that word, upon which Du Cange, v° *Capitalis*, t. ii, p. 142, col. 2, has said all that was requisite. Philippe Moreau (*Le Tableau des Armoiries de France*, etc. Paris, 1609, 8vo., p. 245, 246,) contends that *captal* is translated into latin by *princeps*, and hints that perhaps the dukes of Epernon, having become captaux de Buch, availed themselves of this title to assume that of Princes de Buch ; but in many instruments of the XIIIth and XIVth centuries, occurs the word *captal*, which belonged also to the family of Bouglon, lords of Latrêne. (*Rot. Vasc.*, ann. 17 Edw. I., membr. 16, pars 2.)

Another word, no less extraordinary, is also to be met with in the Anglo-French records of Aquitaine and left unexplained, the word *soudan* or *souldich*, borne by the lords of Latrau, or Latrave. Likely enough it is an alteration of *syndic*.

There is, at the British Museum, a muster roll without date, but of the XIVᵉ century : « *Ensuent les barons et gentils de Burdegales.*

« Le seigneur de Duras et son frere, le seigneur de la Sparre, le seigneur de Montferand, le seigneur de Mussydan et monseigneur Amaneu de Mussydan; le seigneur de Castelleon; le nommé de la Mote; le seigneur de la Barde; Ramonet de Sore; le seigneur de Corton; Perot le Bearnès; monseigneur Jehan de Grely; le viscounte d'Uzac; le capitayne de Achille (Rochelle?), le bort de Caumont. » (*Œuvres de Froissart,* publiées par M. le baron Kervyn de Lettenhove, t. xxi, p. 121, 122.)

550. The Prince's appointment took place in 1362. (Rymer, vol. iii, p. 667.) The charter is curiously illuminated. In the upper corner on the left hand are the Prince's arms supported by two angels, and on the right a man is represented in a stooping posture holding over his head a sable shield charged with three ostrich feathers, each having a label, but no motto. The sides of the shield are also supported by angels. Below this drawing is the effigy of another angel, who holds a long scroll in his hand, which occupies the greater part of the right margin, and contains the motto *Honny soit quy mal y pense.*

565. Edward, son and heir of Edward le Despenser, second son of Hugh, earl of Gloucester. He was with Sir Bartholomew Burghersh, in the skirmish, near Romorantin; summoned to Parliament in 1357, as baron le Despencer, in 1359 on the King's staff in France; knight of the Garter in 1360, on the death of Henry, duke of Lancaster; was defeated when commanding the rear-guard of the army at Ribemont in 1373, and died at Cardiff Castle, 11th November 1375. He married Elizabeth, daughter and heir of Bartholomew, Lord Burghersh, and may be reckoned among the benefactors of Froissart, who speaks thus in his *Buisson de Jonece* :

> Le grant seigneur Espensier,
> Qui de largheee est despensier,
> Que t'a-t-il fait?—Quoi? di-je, assés;
> Car il ne fut onques lassés
>
> De moy donner, quel part qu'il fust.
> Ce n'estoient cailluel, ne fust,
> Mès chevaux et florins sans compte.
> Entre mes mestres je lo compte
> Pour seingnour, et c'en est-il un.

566. Ralph, Lord Basset, grandson of Ralph Basset, of Drayton. He served in the French war in 33 and 34 Edward III., and in the 3

Ric. II. under Thomas of Woodstock, was made knight of the Garter in 1368, on the death of Lionel, duke of Clarence. He died the 10th of May 1389.

567. There is in Rymer's *Fœdera*, third edition, t. iii, pars iv, p. 90, col. 2, a grant of arms to Oton de Maundell, knt. (22 Oct. 1390), and elsewhere a Nicholas lord Meinill, Meinel, Maisnil. (Dugdale's *Baronage*, t. i, p. 735, col. 2 ; t. ii, p. 111, col. 2.)

570. « Là estoient dalès le Prince et à son frain messires Jehans Chandos et messires Pieres d'Audelé, freres à monseigneur James d'Audelée, » etc. (Froissart, vol. v, ann. 1356. p. 46. § 389.)

579. The men-at-arms, in France as in England, were essentially horsemen, although during some reigns they fought usually on foot. Nevertheless in a manuscript of 1442, the English being still masters of a great part of France, there is a mention of 50 men-at-arms horse and 20 foot for the garrison of the town of Mantes. (Daniel, *Histoire de la Milice françoise*, etc. 1721, 4to., liv. iv, c. II, t. ii, p. 226.)

In the poetical works of Eustache Deschamps, one may see personified Vaillance complaining of being neglected nowadays :

Les jeunes gens poursuioient,
Lances, baclnez portoient
Des anciens chevaliers,
Et la coustume aprenoient
De chevauchier, et veoient
Des armes les trois mestiers.
Puis devenoient archiers,
A table et partout servoient
Et les malectes troussoient

Derriere eulx moult volontiers :
Ainsi adonc le faisoient
Et en cuisine s'offroient
A ce temps les escuyers.
Puis gens d'armes devenoient
Et leurs vertus esprouvoient
Huit ou dix ans tous entiers ;
Es grans voyages aloient,
Puis chevaliers devenoient, etc.

La Curne de Sainte-Palaye, *Mémoires sur l'ancienne chevalerie*, 1st edit., t. i, p. 54.

580. In Rymer's *Fœdera*, vol. iii, part ii, p. 302, is a writ from the Gascon Rolls, A. D. 1355, membr. 11, *de marinariis pro passagio principis Walliæ eligendis*, for manning the ship *La Juliane*, commanded by William Baret, appointed to convey the Prince into Gascony.

603. The Black Prince's treasure was very rich if his purse in certain circumstances was light. His council said to him on one occasion : « Rompez la greigneur partie de votre vaisselle d'or et d'argent et tresor pour en faire monnoie. » Under the year 1313,

Rymer has printed the catalogue of Peter of Gaveston's jewels; they are numberless [1].

In Froissart's chronicles, there are, at every step, mentions of jewels which shew how plate and jewellery were usual in the XIVth century, even among inferior classes. In 1330, James Douglas, on his way to Jerusalem, « avoit tout vaisselement d'or et d'argent, pos, bachins, escuielles, hanaps, bouteilles, barilz et aultres si faites choses. » In the account of a succesful expedition in Gascony, the great chronicler says that the invaders had won a great spoil in gold and silver plate, in girdles and jewels [2], etc.

Knowing the Black Prince's taste for articles of virtu, D. Pedro had presented his confederate with a golden table richly ornamented, the description of which, real or not, occurs in Cuvelier's poem [3].

In the last volume of his 4to edition of Froissart, p. 279-282, Buchon has published a document of the year 1392, which gives curious details on the state of silversmith-ware in the XIth century and on the value of gold and silver articles. Like most of the princes of the time, the wisest of the contemporaries of the greatest of the Plantagenets was not less fond of jewellery : in proof of which one may refer to a book published a few years ago [4].

605. The Black Prince did not require to export to Gascony from England such a stock of arms [5], Bordeaux being, at the time, noted

---

[1] *Fœdera*, record edit., vol. II, part. 1, p. 203-205, A. D. 1313, etc.

[2] Froissart, t. i, p. 148, § 70 ; t. vii, p. 383, § 637. Cf. p. 36, § 19 ; p. 251, § 1326, etc.; and Luce's *Histoire de Bertrand du Guesclin*, etc., t. i, Paris, 1876, 8vo., ch. III, p. 60.

In an interesting paper on the home life of a Norman country gentleman in the XVIth century, M. Baudrillart ascribes to a later time the spreading of the use of plate in France. (*Revue des Deux Mondes*, t. xxvii, 1878, p. 165.) It is obvious that such a statement cannot be correct.

[3] *Chronique de B. du Guesclin*, t. i, Paris, 1839, 4to., p. 324, l. 9086. At a later period we see Jacques de Langua, « marchand et bourgeois de Bordeaux, » lending to « Pierre Dagorrondo, marchand de Mauléon de Soule, 5 écus sol, valant 15 fr. 5 s. tournois, sur un carreau d'or contenant 44 pièces. » (Minutes of Donzeau, public notary, 12 juillet 1550.)

[4] *Inventaire du mobilier de Charles V, roi de France*, publié par Jules Labarte. Paris, 1879, 4to.

[5] The exportation of armour was not permitted but by the King's special licence. For the duel between William Douglas and Robert Erskine in 1368, both champions obtained licence to send armour from London to Scotland. The instruments are preserved in Rymer's *Fœdera*, vol. iii, p. 838, 840.

The works on ancient armour are numerous. After Grose and Sir Samuel Rush Meyrick,

for its armour of all description. See our *Histoire du commerce et de la navigation à Bordeaux*, etc., t. i, ch. xiii, p. 315, 316; and Luce's *Histoire de Bertrand du Guesclin*, t. i, p. 452, note 1, where is a mention of a « fer de lance de factura Burdegalis. » (Arch. Nat., sect. jud. XI^a 19, fol. 300.) In 1867, M. Ernest Gaullieur, the keeper of the city records of Bordeaux, has printed for private circulation an interesting paper on *l'Armurerie milanaise à Bordeaux au quinzième siècle*, which was reissued in 1875 at the end of a pamphlet, 8vo., intitled : *Les Gascons et l'artillerie bordelaise au siège de Fontarabie* (1521 à 1524).

Neither Chandos Herald nor Froissart mention the intervention of ordnance in the wars of Edward III. and of the Black Prince. One historian only (Villani,) and he an Italian, wishing to account for the defeat of the Genoese, lays stress upon the fact of the employment of cannon at Crécy.

There are very interesting notices of the early use of guns and gunpowder (c. 1353) in the English army, by the Rev. Joseph Hunter in the *Archæologia*, vol. xxxii, p. 380-387, and by Joseph Burtt, in the *Archæological Journal*, etc., vol. xix, London, 1862, p. 68-75. One of those scholars has found in a book of accounts of money paid out of the King's chamber, from December 25, 18 Edward III., 1344, to the 18th of October, 1347, sundry payments for things provided for the King's use, as « huces » for the *balistæ*, leathern cases for bows and arrows, a tent for the King's own use, and other things connected with affairs of war, and in the midst of them occurs the following pertinent entry : « Eidem Thomæ (Roldeston) super facturam pulveris pro ingeniis, et emendationem diversarum armaturarum, xl. sol. » *Pulvis pro ingeniis*, when instruments of war are the subject, can scarcely be any thing but gunpowder; and, when we find that there was money paid for a tent which was intended especially for the King's own use, we cannot hardly doubt, though the account extends over three years, 1344 to 1347, that these payments were made before the departure of the expedition of 1346, and in contemplation of it.

The Rev. Joseph Hunter ends his communication to the Society of

---

John Hewitt has published in the *Gentleman's Magazine* (July to December 1858, p. 319-99-211-323-436-548; and January to June inclusive, p. 3-123-235-247, 459-575-592) an elaborate treatise, reprinted in three vols. 8vo. at Oxford, 1855-60.

Antiquaries of London with an entry concerning the ammunitions of the castle of Carisbrook in 1379, forgetting that there is an earlier item in the reign of Richard II. dated 16 March 1377-81: « *De Ingeniis vocatis* canons, *et aliis providendis pro castro de Brest.* » (French Rolls, 1 Rich. II. part 2, membr. 15.) To the above references we should add a capital paper by the late Léon Lacabane : *De la Poudre à canon et de son introduction en France*, in the *Bibliothèque de l'Ecole des Chartes*, t. 1st, 2nd series, p. 45-47.

623. Bernard-Ezy, sire d'Albret and viscount of Tartas, who died in 1358. He was left by the Prince his lieutenant in Gascony, upon his first expedition into Quercy and Auvergne.

624. Aimery de Biron, seigneur de Montferrant, swore fealty to the Black Prince, 24th February 1355. In 1373, he was appointed the King's lieutenant in Aquitaine, and in 1375 with the sire de Mussidan, one of the guardians of the treaty between France and England in Périgord. His will is dated 13th December 1384. (Anselme, *Hist. gén.*, etc., t. vii, p. 353.) This and the following Gascon knights are mentioned again below at the battle of Poitiers.

624. Raimond de Montaut, seigneur de Mussidan, de Montendre, etc., one of the forty-one esquires of the company of Bertrand de Terride (See Anselme, t. vii, p. 603); whose daughter Rosine is mentioned by the same compiler, t. iv, p. 448, as the wife of Guy de la Rochefoucauld. He married Marguerite, daughter of Bérard d'Albret, seigneur de Verteuil, and retained still at the end of 1369 the castellany of Aubeterre (Charente, arrond. de Barbezieux). By a deed dated Toulouse, November of that year, Louis, duke of Anjou, gave to Hélie de Labatut, son and heir of master Pierre de Labatut, the King's secretary, 200 pounds torneses out of the revenues of certain parishes of the castellany of Aubeterre, forfeited *per ipsius Edouardi et domini de Muscidano et aliorum sibi adherencium rebellionem*. (Arch. Nat., jj. 100, n⁰ 764.) The Lords de Mussidan, Langoiran, Duras and Rauzan, are mentioned by Froissart amongst the Gascon lords joining Sir Thomas Felton for the relief of Thouars; afterwards they were taken prisoners before Bergerac in company with their leaders. The two former then joined the party of the duke of Anjou, and are mentioned by Froissart as distinguishing themselves at the assault on Duras.

626. The family name of the barons de Rauzan and du Thil was *Angevin*, which may be a clue to their origin. See among the land-registers of Guienne preserved with those of the department of Gironde at Bordeaux, that of the seigneurie du Thil, E. n° 133.

The daughter of a Jacques Angevin, sieur de Rauzan, is mentioned by Father Anselme (*Hist. gén.*, etc., t. v, p. 734) as the wife of Jean de Beaufort, in 1480.

626. He is called by Froissart *Curton*, and afterwards Sir *Petiton de Courton*. He was, with Sir W. Hewet and Faringdon, defeated before Soubise by Evan of Wales, and with difficulty escaped into the town. In Rymer's *Fœdera*, t. iii, p. 1061, A. D. 1376, is a charter addressed to Arnald sire de Curton, and other Gascon lords.

627. Amanieu de Faussat is mentioned on the side of England in the truce of Calais, 1350. (Rymer's *Fœdera*, vol. iii, p. 197.) Fossard is again recorded at Poitiers. See vers. 1325.

628. Probably the same with Guilhem-Sans, the lord de Pommier, or Pommiers, to whom a writ is addressed by Edward as a knight of Poitou, respecting the marshal Boucicault, and also mentioned as one of the parties on the Prince's behalf in the peace of Bordeaux, 1357, ap. Rymer, vol. iii, p. 348. In 1358, Don Pedro IV. King of Aragon, being at Girona, engaged to his service « Aymerique, vizconde de Narbona, y á Juan de Grilli, capdal de Buyg, y á Arnaldo, y á Beltran de España, y á 'N Ayquen Guillen de la Esparra, á Guillen de Pomer, y Arnaldo de Rocatull, y el vizconde de Orta[1], » etc. (Zurita, *Libro IX de los Anales de la corona de Aragon*, cap. XVI; t. ii, p. 289, col. 1.) At the time Cuilhem-Sans seems to have been in favour with Edward III. (Carte, *Catal. des Rolles gascons*, t. i, p. 140.) There was also a Lord Pomiers, according to Froissart, beheaded for treason at Bordeaux. See also the Gascon Roll of Richard II. membr. 16-19. (*Processus judicii redditi contra Willelmum Sans, dominum de Pomers, pro proditione in curia Vasconie, et de castris et terris suis satisfactis ad dominum regem.*)

630. Amongst so many of the same name it is difficult to decide

---

[1] To this list we may add the count of Foix, cousin of the captal de Buch, with whom he had made war in Prussia, and Roger Bernard de Foix, viscount of Castetbon. (*Ibid.*, cap. iii, fol. 272 v°, col. 2, and cap. vii, fol. 276 r°. Cf. Froissart, t. v, p. 102, l. 17.)

as to which may be the individual in question. The most probable, however, appears to be either a Cenebrun de Lesparre [1], married in 1331 to a sister of the captal de Buch, (Anselme, *Hist. gén.*, etc.,t. iii, p. 369 ; see also Rymer, t. iii, p. 26) or a Bernard, seigneur de Lesparre, the uncle of Sybille, wife of Gaston de Gontaut, baron de Biron (*Ibid.*, t. vii, p. 301, § viii). In Rymer's *Fœdera*, vol. iii, pars ii, p. 1028, col. 1, and 1030, col. 1, are two charters addressed to Lord de Lesparre upon the government chiefly of the city of Bordeaux [2], and at p. 1061 is another addressed to Bernard de Lesparre, Arnald, sire de Curton, and other lords of Gascony respecting the payment of ransom for prisoners.

It would seem, from the Gascon Rolls, that Cenebrun IV. had more than one son, since there is in those scrolls a mention of a son of the Lord of Lesparre, named *Ayquem-Guilhem*, who, at the battle of Poitiers, had been taken prisoner by Ives de Kerembars, a Breton esquire. The latter having set him at liberty on parole, and being unable to obtain either answer or ransom, applied to the King of England, who ordered the seneschal of Gascony to interfere and do justice to the Breton, according to the law of war, *juxta legem armorum*. Was this Ayquem-Guilhem an elder son of Cenebrun, who died

---

[1] Cenebrun, *Swarthy complexion*.

[2] Florimond de Lesparre had been elected governor of the city by public poll, *regidor de la ciutat por la eleccion deû poblé*. In 1375, K. Edward III., willing to restore the authority of laws and put a stop to the incredible excesses to which Bordeaux was a prey for a long time, being threatened by anarchy inside and enemy outside, intrusted Florimond with the hard task of restoring both concord and security among the citizens by the reform of its legislation. (Rabanis, *Revue du droit français et étranger*. Paris, 1861, 8vo., p. 490.)

There is in the Cottonian Library, Vespasianus xiii, art. 24, fol. 19, a letter from « Le sire de Lesparre et de Roazan, » governor of Bordeaux, to an anonymous friend, recommending a squire of the writer, Gallyart de Marraben. Bordeaux, Aug. 20. This letter, being origin . has no other claim upon public attention than it is written on paper at a time where notes of that kind, as well as rolls and registers of public accountants, were couched on parchment or vellum. The disquisition of that interesting subject gave rise to a dissertation, which deserves to be pointed out as connected with the history of the domestic annals of Aquitaine under the English rule. After having quoted a number of registers of the *contablie* of Bordeaux, and reproduced the paper marks from 1330, the author offers only two general remarks on this exhibition to shew either that the English received their paper from Bordeaux, or that Aquitaine and England were supplied from the same market. (*Specimens of Marks used by the early Manufactures of Paper*, etc. by Joseph Hunter. — *Archæologia*, vol. xxxvii, p. 447-454.)

before his father, or was he a puisne of Florimont who did not leave offspring? We cannot guess; but there is a conjecture more grounded perhaps than the former: it is that Cenebrun's son was no other than the *bour* (bastard) de Lesparre, whom Froissart speaks of in many places in the years posterior to the battle of Poitiers. The adventurous and disorderly life which this bastard seems to have led might explain why he was so unscrupulous or unable to keep his word. Froissart names the bour de Lesparre among the chiefs of the Great Companies who, the first time in 1366, helped D. Enrique de Trastamare to dethrone Don Pedro el Cruel. He undertook this campaign with the assent of the Black Prince, and hastened to come back to Aquitaine when he was aware that King Edward's son and lieutenant had promised his help to Don Pedro, and that the new plan was to pull down from the throne the sovereign for whom he had just fought. See J. Rabanis, *Notice sur Florimont, sire de Lesparre, suivie d'un précis historique sur cette seigneurie*, etc. Bordeaux, 1843, 8vo., p. 50, 51[1]. — Cf. on Florimont, Devon, *Issues of the Exchequer*, p. 223.

647. Beziers is not mentioned by name either by the Prince or John de Wyngfield in their letters, as given by Robert d'Avesbury (*Hist. Edvardi III.*, p. 213-228); but the latter speaks of having taken many other towns, amongst which Beziers is probably to be included.

678. The Gascon lord mentioned here is enough known to require a memoir of his life. Jean de Grailly, captal de Buch and viscount of Benauges and Castillon, died in 1377, after having made his will, preserved in the XLIst volume of Doat's collection (Nat. Libr.), fol. 197 recto and sqq. By that instrument, he bequeaths many pious legacies, appoints his heir Archambaud de Grailly, and his executors Gaston, comte de Foix, his cousin, Florimont, seigneur de Lesparre, Elie de Pomiers, Amanieu de Balhade, Pierre-Arnaud de Lannemezan, knights, the archbishop of Bordeaux, and others named therein. Date: 6 March 1368.

713. Jean le Meingre, dit Boucicault, écuyer of the duchy of Touraine; he was engaged in the wars of Gascony in 1337, afterwards in Flanders in 1338, 1340, in which year he was at the battle of Bovines; he also served under the sire de Craon, in 1351. In 1357,

---

[1] Extracted from the *Actes de l'académie de Bordeaux*, 1843, p. 96-167.

he obtained a safe-conduct for Santiago de Compostela and for the Holy Land. (*Rot. Franc.*, 28 Edw. III., membr. 9; ap. Rymer, vol. iii, p. 271. Cf. 257 — 31 Edw. III., membr. 15. — and p. 654 Edw. III., membr. 9.) After the death of Jean de Clermont, marshal of France, he was raised to that office. He died at Dijon, 15th March, 1367. In the Issue Roll, 40 Edward III. is an entry of the sum of £285. 14s. 2d. in money lately received by assignment made to him for the ransom of the King of France. (Devon, *Issues of the Exchequer*, etc. London, 1837, 8vo., p. 189.)

The biographer of Jean Boucicaut II. says of the father that he was « moult preud'homme et de grand sçavoir, et toute sa vie et temps employa en la poursuite d'armes, et, à l'exemple des vaillans anciens, qui ainsi le feirent, ne lui chailloit de tresor amasser, ne de quelconques choses fors d'honneur acquerir ; pour lesquels biens faicts et sa vaillance et preud'hommie au temps des grandes guerres en France, au vivant du chevaleureux roy Jehan, fut faict mareschal de France... et toujours sera le vaillant mareschal Boucicaut [1]. »

714. Amaury, sire de Craon, de Sainte-Maure, etc. He had the government of Saintonge, Poitou, Anjou and basse Normandie. He is spoken of in different charters frequently as prisoner between the years 1357-1360, where he became one of the hostages for the preservation of the peace of Brétigny. (Rymer's *Fœdera*, vol. iii, p. 537, etc.) In 36 Edw. III. (*Issues of the Exchequer*, p. 177), is an entry by which it appears that with the comte de Sancerre and the King of France, he had been sold to Edward III. for the sum of twenty thousand pounds. He died 30th May, 1371.

749. Jean de Noyers, son of Miles, comte de Joigny, served under the duke of Normandy in 1346 with four knights and 26 esquires. He died the 10th of May, 1361. In the *Issues of the Exchequer*, 35 Edw. III. p. 174, is notice of a payment of £158. 7s. 6d. to Arnauld-Reymond, viscount d'Anoita, part payment of 15,000 florins, which the Prince had agreed to pay for the count, his prisoner.

750. Froissart calls him « le comte d'Auxerre » (son of Jean de Châlon, comte d'Auxerre, slain at Crécy). There is in the *Issues of the*

---

[1] *Livre des faicts du mareschal de Boucicaut*, ch. III ; in Petitot's *Collection complète des Mémoires relatifs à l'histoire de France*, etc., t. vi, p. 379.

Exchequer, p. 168, 32 Edw. III. an entry of a payment of L562. 10s. paid Lord Suffolk for part of the ransom of the comte « d'Aussore, » taken at Poitiers.

762. In a collection of papers, most of which, still existing, appear to be originals (Cottonian Library, Vespasian, F. XIII., art. 4, fol. 8), there is a letter, on which is written at the right hand in the bottom corner, low down : « De part le cardinal de Pierigeur. » It is dated « Milan, 6 August, » and seems to be directed to King Edward III.

766. The amanuensis of the Worcester College manuscript, like the ape who mistook the Pireus for the name of a man [1], has written twice, in the poem as well as in the rubric, *Brismos* two words in one, believing probably that it was the name of some castle, or house, in the neighbourhood of the fields of Beauvoir and Maupertuis, where the French King was encamped; but Coxe had the luck to shun the blunder and glance at the real meaning.

A briefs mos is one of those common-place expressions so often used by Froissart : « Briefment à parler. » (t. i, p. 128, l. 19, § 59; t. ii, p. 179, § 180.) — « Pourquoi feroi-je lonc sermon, » etc. (*Ibid.*, p. 145, § 145); « Que vous feroi-je loin compte ? plus loing compte ? (*Ibid.*, p. 411, § 65; t. ii, p. 100, § 144, et p. 291. Cf. t. iv, p. 189, § 367 ; t. v, p. 320.) « Que vous feroi-je lonch parlement ? lonch recort ? (*Ibid.*, t. iii, p. 71, § 221 ; t. v, § 431. Cf. t. vi, p. 69, § 495 ; t. vii, p. 319, 363) ; « A brief parole. » (*Ibid.*, t. iv, p. 49.) etc.

767. See Froissart's chronicle, t. v, p. 13, § 375, etc. and p. 255. Talleyrand, son of Elias, count of Périgord, abbot of la Chancelade, was bishop of Auxerre, cardinal-priest of St. Peter *ad Vincula* under the title of *Eudoxia*, then bishop of Albano. He died at Avignon the 17th of January, 1364. Vide François Duchesne, *Histoire de tous les cardinaux françois de naissance*, etc., liv. ii, ch. LXXVI ; t. i, p. 465-470 ; D. Ciaconio, *Vitæ et Res gestæ pontificum Romanorum*, etc. Romæ, 1677, fol., vol. ii, col. 432; and *Gallia christiana*, t. ii, col. 836, B, et 151, D.

In an entry of November 1356, Philippe de Valois, selling to Talleyrand, cardinal of Périgord, the lands of Auberoche and of the Bastide de Bonneval, calls him « dearest. » See Bertrandy, *Etude sur les chroniques de Froissart*, p. 106.

---

[1] La Fontaine, liv. iv, fable 7.

In the *Issues of the Exchequer*, 32 Edw. III. is a notice of L.13. 6s. 8d. paid to an esquire of the cardinal for bringing a charger, a present from that dignitary to the King.

865. The account of the interviews of the cardinal are somewhat differently reported by Froissart and Barnes, (from Villani,) with which the version of our author should be compared.

868. Guillaume V., son of Jean, comte de Tancarville, was elected to the see of Sens in 1346 or 1347, and died in 1376. (*Gallia christiana*, t. xii, col. 74-78.) He was the brother of the comte de Tancarville, taken also at the battle of Poitiers. The archbishop is said to have been the prisoner of the earl of Warwick, who received eight thousand pounds for his ransom. In Rymer's *Fœdera*, vol. iii, p. 644, 647, A. D. 1362, are two extracts from the Patent and French Rolls, entitled: *Pro archiepiscopo de Seintz, de acquietantia*, in which the price of his ransom is stated. — Coxe has confounded that warlike prelate with Jean de Mello, de Merlo, or de Melloto, elected bishop of Chalons in 1354. (*Gallia christiana*, t. ii, col. 289, D.; and t. iv, col. 921, 922.)

869. Jean de Talaru, great *custos*, canon and count, afterwards archbishop, of Lyon. (François Duchesne, *Histoire de tous les cardinaux françois de naissance*, etc., l. ii, ch. CLXXVII, p. 705, 706. Cf. *Gallia christiana*, t. iv, col. 170-172.)

870. Jean de Clermont, seigneur de Chantilly, made marshal of France in 1352, on the death of Guy de Nesle. He was buried in the church of the Dominicans at Poitiers. (Jean Bouchet, *Les Annales d'Aquitaine*, etc. Poictiers, 1634, 4to., p. 204.) Cf. Anselme, *Hist. généal.*, etc., t. vi, p. 56, § IX.

939. Arnould d'Audrehem was made governor of Angoulême in 1343, taken prisoner in Gascony in April, 1351, and on his release, in August in the same year, raised to the dignity of marshal of France. He was taken again at Poitiers, and ransomed in 1360. In 1367, he was again taken at the battle of Nájera, after which and a trial before the victors on accusation of breach of parole [1], he was exchanged for

---

[1] « Como fueron traídos otro día despues de la batalla delante del Rey Don Pedro é del Principe todos los que fueron presos : é como el mariscal de Audenehan se escusó de lo que el Principe le acusaba. » (*Crónica de D. Pero Lopez de Ayala*, año diez é ocho de D. Pedro, cap. xiii, t. i, p. 458. Madrid, 1779, 4to.)

Sir Thomas Felton; being now far advanced in age, he resigned the office of marshal and received that of porte-oriflamme. He died in December 1370. See Luce's Froissart, vol. v, p. 20, note 2; and vi, p. xiv.

942. Gautier, comte de Brienne, duc d'Athènes. He was engaged in the wars of 1339, 1340. In 1341, being summoned to his government of Florence, he refused to return to Italy, and was in 1356 raised by King Jean to the dignity of constable of France. He was buried in the abbey of Beaulieu in Brienne. Anselme has given the inscription on his monument, *Hist. généal.*, t. vi, p. 165, § xxiv.

959. Charles the Dauphin, duke of Normandy, eldest son of Jean, King of France; he acted as regent during his father's imprisonment, and at his death succeeded to the throne as Charles V.

964. Jacques, duc de Bourbon, comte de la Marche and of Ponthieu. He had been wounded at Crécy; was made constable of France in 1354, and was mortally wounded in action against the Tards-Venus, near Lyons, in April, 1361, where he died. It appears from the *Issues of the Exchequer*, 32 Edw. III., p. 168, that he was the prisoner of the captal de Buch. Cf. *Liberate*, 35 Edw. III., membr. 2; ap. Rymer, vol. iii, p. 519, 863, 875.

966. Guillaume de Nesle, sire de Saint-Venant; he married Alice, dame of that barony. With the sires de Bodenay and de Lendas, he was appointed guardian of Charles the Dauphin, and fled with him from the field of battle. His name occurs in Rymer, vol. iii, p. 490, 604, 700, 702, and elsewhere, as one of the hostages for the King of France.

968. Jean, sire de Maignelay, dit *Tristan*, chevalier and échanson de France; he was the prisoner of Thomas de Walkfare (*Rot. Fr.* 31 Edw. III., 1357, membr. 12) and was obliged to mortgage nearly all his lands to pay his ransom. He returned with the King from England in 1363. (Anselme, *Hist. généal.*, etc., t. viii, p. 540, § iii.)

999. Philippe, duc d'Orléans, youngest son of Philippe de Valois and Jeanne de Bourgogne. He died without legitimate issue, the 15th September 1375.

1025. Jean d'Artois, comte d'Eu, received the title in 1350, when it was confiscated under Raoul de Brienne, mentioned by Anselme, t. vi.

p. 126, § xx ; he was the son of Robert d'Artois, comte de Beaumont-le-Roger. He died in 1387. His quittance, with that of his brother, and the rest of the prisoners taken at Poitiers, in 1360, may be seen in Rymer's *Fœdera*, vol. iii, p. 539.

1026. Charles d'Artois, brother of the above. Having incurred the displeasure of King Jean, and having been confined in gaol, he was in favour again, present at the battle of Poitiers and there made prisoner of war. In 1363, his comté of Longueville was given by Charles V. to Bertrand du Guesclin.

1028. There is no mention elsewhere of a Robert d'Artois being at Poitiers. The well known Lord Robert having been wounded at the taking of Vannes, died in 1342, between October 6 and November 20. (Rymer's *Fœdera*, vol. ii, p. 1212 and 1215.) Jean le Bel (*Chron.*, t. ii, p. 13) and Froissart (Luce, t. iii, p. 20 and 224) mistake when they assert that the celebrated outlaw died in England : this error should be corrected by an entry printed in Rymer's collection, vol. ii, p. 1222. Various entries of 1336 and 1337 preserved at Paris in the Trésor des chartes, allude to the residence of Robert d'Artois in Guienne, etc. (*Œuvres de Froissart*, edit. of M. Kervyn de Lettenhove, t. xx, p. 176-179.)

1030. Jean, comte de Sancerre and sire de Saint-Michel-sur-Loire, commanded under the duc de Berry in Flanders in 1383, was at the siege of Turin in 1390, and died in 1402. He is included in the entry in the Issue Rolls before mentioned in the note upon Lord Craon, l. 714. See Devon, p. 177, 36 Edward III.

1032. Charles de Trie, comte de Dammartin. Lord Berners and Johnes, following an erroneous reading, have made Froissart assert that this nobleman was slain at the battle of Poitiers by Reginald de Cobham ; in the edition of Buchon it is rightly read that he was there taken prisoner only, as appears from many entries on the rolls of the Public Record Office. Anselme says that he became the earl of Salisbury's prisoner, and that in 1360 the comte made over his lands of Capy and la Baseque, near Arras, to the constable of Fiennes in exchange for Marrot, assigned by the constable to the earl of Salisbury in diminution of his ransom. Charles de Trie was alive in 1394. (Anselme, *Hist. généal.*, etc., t. vi, p. 671, § x.)

In the close Roll 46 Ed. III., membr. 33 (Rymer, vol. iii, p. 935) there is an entry concerning the liberation from prison of a Jean Danmartyn.

1040. Guichard d'Angle, sire de Pleumartin, and in 1350, seneschal of Saintonge. He was present at the engagement with the English at Saint-Jean-d'Angely in 1346, and was taken before the same town in 1351, and carried to England. After his release at the end of the following year, he was constantly engaged against the English, until his capture at Poitiers. After this he joined the side of England, in 1363 was appointed by the Black Prince marshal of Aquitaine, and in such capacity ordered the following year to levy the revenues in the dukedom. (*Rot. Vasc.*, 38 Ed. III., membr. 4; Rymer, vol. iii, p. 726. Cf. p. 801.) He fought gallantly at Nájera 1367. By an entry dated February 19, 1341 (n. st.), Charles V. gave to Geoffroy de la Celle, knight, 60 pounds torneses of land in Touraine on the estates forfeited of Guichard d'Angle, « chevalier rebelle. » (Archives Nat., JJ. 102, n° 182.) In 1372 he was elected into the order of the Garter, and at the coronation of Richard II. was rewarded with the earldom of Huntingdon and 100 marks per annum for the support of the dignity. He died in the spring of 1380.

1043. Jean, son of Olivier, sire d'Aubigny, and Eustachie du Puy. In the Issue Roll, 32 Edw. III., p. 167, is a notice of L333. 6s. 8d. money paid to Sir John Wynkefield, in part payment of 2500 marks, for Lord « Dauboneye, » his prisoner. Cf. p. 173.

1044. Eustache de Ribemont, the same with him mentioned by Froissart, as rewarded with a chaplet of pearls by Edward for his gallant bearing in the night affray at Calais. He was the third husband of Idoine de l'Isle, comtesse de Soudre, widow of Thibaut de Moreuil.

1076. « Le seigneur de Pommiers, messire Helie et messire Aymenion de Pommieres, » ed. Kervyn, t. xxii, p. 371-375. Amanieu and Elie de Pommiers are frequently mentioned in the English records. In the Issue Roll, 32 Edward III. is notice of a payment to the latter, where he is styled *domino d'Arbenac* [1], of L20 in part of 30,000 florins

---

[1] Arbanats, département de la Gironde, arrondissement de Bordeaux, canton de Podensac. In 1313, Bertrand de Goth, nephew of Pope Clement V., vindicated a right of high and low justice *in villis de Portet et Arbanaz*. (Gascon Rolls, ann. 6 Ed. II., membr. 12.)

due to him for his prisoner, the earl of Eu. Cf. *Rot. Vasc.*, 39 Ed. III., membr. 2 ; ap. Rymer, vol. iii, p. 674, 747.

1094. The following reconnoissance of Eustache de Ribemont to King Jean of the position of the English army will best illustrate this passage, whilst its own merits render an apology for its insertion unnecessary : « Sire, nous avons reconnu de près les ennemis, nous avons remarqué leur nombre, leur poste et considéré l'ordre qu'ils tiennent. Autant que je le puis juger à leurs bannières et pennons, ils ne sont pas en tout plus de deux mille hommes d'armes, six mille archers et peut-estre mille ou douze cens brigands. Ils se sont logez environ à une lieue d'icy, sur une colline qui ne contient guère que deux mille pas de terrain, environnée tout à l'entour de hayes vives et fort épaisses, coupée par le milieu d'un chemin un peu creux et si estroit, que quatre hommes, mesme trois, n'y sçauroient monter de front, et de plus couvert des deux costez de gros buissons tous bordez d'une partie de leurs archers, qui travaillent encore à se retrancher d'un nouveau fossé. Au bout de ces hayes sont leurs gens-d'armes à pied, tenant chacun leur cheval par la bride, sur un haut, entre d'autres buissons et de fortes vignes, couverts du reste de leurs archers rangez en maniere d'une herse. A la gauche, où les hayes et l'avenue ne semblent pas si rudes, les ennemis sont remparez de leurs chariots embarrassez les uns dans les autres. Sur la droite, il y a une autre petite éminence, vers laquelle j'ay veu filer de la cavalerie qui s'y veut placer, comme je croy, pour nous donner dans les flancs, lorsque nous les attaquerons. »

1105. Sir Eustace, a knight from Hainault, although his title was borrowed from Auberchicourt, near Douay, « appert et hardi chevalier durement et bon guerrieur ossi [1], » was son of Sir Sanchet d'Abrichecourt, one of the founders of the Garter. He married on Michaelmas Day, 1360, at Wingham, in Kent, the countess dowager Elizabeth of Kent, daughter of William V. duke of Juliers, niece to Queen Philippa, and relict of John Plantagenet, earl of Kent. (Beltz, *Memorials of the Garter*, p. 91.) Another Aubricicourt, Nicholas, had been knighted by Edward III. in 1331. (Rymer's *Fœdera*, vol. iii, p. 824.)

1155. The following extract from Barnes, p. 506, may serve to

---

[1] Luce's Froissart, liv. i, § 428 ; t. V, p. 352.

explain this passage : « At the beginning of this justing, while marshal d'Endreghan stood still to behold the strength and skill of the young gentlemen of either party, the other marshal, the Lord John Clermont, thinking to enter at the hedge gap and so to come at the back of our van, made haste thither; but the earls of Salisbury and Suffolk, who led the English rear, and beheld his motion and guessed his design, posted to that gap, which they fenced with an hedge of steel, and so the rear came to sustain the first main stress of the battle. »

1166. « Le prince de Galles, attaqué sur ses derrières, fit volte-face ; et ce fut son arrière-garde, placée sous les ordres du comte de Salisbury, qui eut à soutenir le premier choc. Ce qui est certain, c'est qu'aucune chronique française ne mentionne cette particularité d'une importance capitale. » (Luce, *Histoire de Bertrand du Guesclin*, t. i, ch. vi, p. 175.)

1233. Du Cange has expatiated upon the use of that hue and cry in battle. See at the end of his Glossary, t. vii, *Du Cry d'armes*, dissertation xi, p. 46-52 ; and *De l'Usage du Cry d'armes*, diss. xii, p. 53-56.

1280. Compare Froissart, ed. Kervyn, t. v, p. 540, who adds that in heading his men, he was attended by his four squires, whose names are given by Ashmole : Dutton, Delves, Fowlehurst and Hawkestone.

1310. John, Lord Mohun, of Dunster, son of John, the third Lord Mohun, served in the wars with France in the retinue of Sir Bartholomew Burghersh, whose daughter he married. At the battle of Poitiers, he was included in the retinue of the Black Prince. In the 47 Edw. III. he accompanied the expedition into Flanders. The precise time of his death is uncertain, but it happened in 1375 or 1376. He was one of the founders of the order of the Garter.

The Moion family was very ancient and in existence on the continent before the conquest of England, where

> Li viel William de Moion
> Out ovec li maint cumpaignon.
>
> *Le Roman du Rou*, vol. ii, p. 246.

See Dugdale's *Baronage of England*, vol. i, p. 498, col. 1 ; *The Norman People*, etc. London, 1874, 8vo. p. 334, art. Mohan ; the *Domesday Book*, vol. iv, p. 40 ; Sir Henry Ellis's *A general Introduction*, etc., vol. i, p. 214, and vol. ii, p. 365.

1322. He is called by Froissart *Languran*. From Anselme, it appears that the seigneurie of Langoiran, at this time, was in the hands of the family of d'Albret. Amanieu d'Albret, seigneur de Langoiran, is twice mentioned in the English Rolls, 1355, 1360; probably the Arnaud-Amanieu, afterwards, in 1382, great chamberlain of France, but who before had fought on the side of Edward. A sire de Langoiran was killed in single combat by a knight named Bernard Courant, before the walls of Cavillac.

1347. A contemporary French rhymer bestowes a similar praise to King John after the battle of Poitiers :

Là fut pris li bons roys de France,
Qui ot tel cuer et tel constance
Qu'onques Judas Machabeus,
Hector, ne Cesar Julius,
Alexandres, ne Charlemainnes,
Qui tint l'empire en son domainne,
Godefroy de Buillons, ne Artus,
Ajaus, Achilles, Troillus,

Gauvains, Tristan, ne Lancelos,
Rolans, ne Ogiers (bien dire l'os),
Guillaumes, Olivier ne Pompée
N'orent si très-bonne journée
Ne ne firent tant comme il fit.
En un jour trop en desconfit ;
Mais soulz ne pooit pas souffire, etc.

Confort d'amy. (*Les Œuvres de Guillaume de Machault*, p. 101.)

1353. King Jean's son, whom he had by his side, was Philippe, his youngest son, afterwards duke of Burgundy, founder of the second line of that house, who here earned for himself the name of « le Hardi, » the Bold.

1362. He is called by Sir Bartholomew Burghersh, *the comte de Salbirys*, and by Froissart, *Saarbruck*. In the lists of prisoners in Rymer he is written *Jean, comte de Salesburce*, and *Salsbruce*, and in the French Rolls, *Salebrugg*. There is also in Rymer, vol. iii, p. 494, a writ for the apprehending certain parties suspected of having attacked and wounded the count of Salesbrigge, a prisoner of the King, at Wallingford. Cf. p. 408, 475, 478, 850, etc.

1365. Bernard, comte de Ventadour, married in 1337 Marguerite de Beaumont. (Anselme, *Hist. généal.*, etc., t. vi, p. 86, § x.) In the *Issues of the Exchequer*, 32 Edw. III., is an entry of 6000 florins paid Sir B. Burghersh, in part of 30,000 florins, in which the King was bound to him for his prisoner the count de Ventadour. In the Liberate Rolls, 37 Edw. III., membr. 3, is an order for the payment of L.200. to Sir B. Burghersh for the same prisoner. The latter is printed in

Rymer, *Fœdera*, vol. iii, p. 706. Frequent mention is made of him in the same collection, namely in company with the comte de Tancarville and the maréchal d'Audrehem (*Rot. Franc.*, 31 Edw. III., membr. 2 — once as marshal of France, p. 348), and of his son Louis.

1379. Jean de Landes was one of the guardians of the duke of Normandy, and conducted him out of the action, but afterwards returned with Bodenay and joined the king's division. By Robert d'Avesbury he is called *Baundos*. He is in the list of dead in the Prince's report to the bishop of Worcester. See the *Chronicle of London*, p. 208.

According to the pedigree of this family as given by de Courcelles, *Histoire généalogique et héraldique des pairs de France*, etc., t. v, Paris, 1825, 4to., p. 15, no XII, it was at this time represented by Robert II. baron de Matas, who was living in 1363. The individual named in the text, however, is in the lists of the dead by Robert d'Avesbury and Burghersh, by the latter of whom he is called *Geoffrey de Matas*.

1380. According to Burghersh, Raynald de Pount. Robert d'Avesbury and the Black Prince call him *Renaud de Pountz* and *Pointz*. After the Black Prince had left Aquitaine, the sire de Pons, a baron of Poitou, accompanied the duke of Lancaster against Montpaon, but immediately afterwards joined the side of France. He was, in 1372, taken by the English before Soubise, but rescued by Evan of Wales. (Froissart, ed. Kervyn, t. xxii, p. 375, 376.)

1409. The following copy of a letter from Sir Bartholomew Burghersh to Sir John Montagu upon the result of the action at Poitiers, from a Ms. written but a very few years after the battle, is valuable as throwing great light on those lists already furnished by the Black Prince himself, printed by Sir Harris Nicolas at the end of the *Chronicle of London*, and Robert d'Avesbury, p. 252-255 : « Fait à remembrer que le Prince se parti de Burdeux lendemayn de Saynt-Johan en Auguste, l'an de nostre Seignur M.CCC.LVI., chivacha par Agenés, Limosyn, Alvern et Beryu et sur la river de Leyre de Nivers, qu'est l'entré de Beryndun [1], parce tanque à la cité de Tours pur passer en Fraunce ; mès toutz les pountz furent rumputz issin qu'il ne pooit passer. Et tut le chymyn il ne trova reste avance, tanque il vient

---

[1] Bourgogne, Burgundy (?).

à une chastelle appelliz *Romorentyne*, qu'est envirun, et deveaunt ceo qu'il vient illoqes si avoit pris vi.xx. hommes d'armes, et deyns ledit chastelle furent le seignoures de Crone, un de graunt seignoures de Fraunce, et mons. Bussigaunde oue l. hommes d'armes, et monsieur le Prince adsege ledit chastel per viij. jours, et li primer jour prit tote le force dudit chastel forspris un grosse tour, et auxi prist xl. hommes d'armes, et ledit seignour de Crone et Bussigaunde se mysterent deyns ledit tour, et per force de feu et de myne et d'engyne il se renderent prisoners. Item le Prince demorra devaunt ledit cité de Tours, où fuist le count de Poyters, filtz à roi de Fraunce, ou la graunt power de gentz par iiij. joures, et nule de ladit cité n'osast isser. Item le samadi procheyn ensuaunt vient ledit Prince à un chastelle appelliz *Chabutorie* [1] en Peytowe, là où le roy de Fraunce avoit cuché le nut devaunt, et là furent pris le count de Assure, le counte de Junye et le marshalle de Burgoyne, que veignent al host le roi de Fraunce ; et là furent mortz et pris cc.xl. hommes d'armes. Item le lundi prochein ensuaunt le xix. jour de Septembre, li assemblerent les batails d'un part et d'autre decost Poiters à un dileu, et là furent pris le roi de Fraunce ; monsieur Philippe, son fitz puisné, count de Poyters ; le count de Pountif ; mons. Jakes de Burbonnie ; le count de Ewe ; le count de Aubeville ; le count de Tankerville ; le count de Ventadourun ; le count de Salbirys ; le count de Vendome et son frere ; le count de Russi ; le count de Vendemende ; le count de Danmartyn ; le count de Nesson ; l'erscevesque de Seyns ; le chastelayne de Compost ; le marshal de Oudenham ; mons. Guichard de Aratz ; mons. Moris Maynet, captayne de Poyters ; le seignour de la Toure ; le seignour d'Erualle ; le seignour de Crew et son frere ; le seignour Vilehernalde ; le seigneur de Maugeler ; mons. Arnald de Mounteuerye ; mons. Johan de Blaunk ; le seigneur d'Aubeney ; le seignour de Sully ; le count d'Ausor ; le viscount de Nerboun ; et outre ceo furent pris ij. mille v.c. persones, desqueux furent ij. mille hommes d'armes, des mortz. Item à mesme le bataille furent mortz le duke de Burboun, mons. Robert Durasce, del saunc de Fraunce ; le duk d'Athenes, conestable de Fraunce ; l'ercevesque de Chalouns ; le marshal de Clermound ; le viscount de Boures ; le viscount de Richohardus ; mons. Raynald de Pount ; mons.

---

[1] La Chaboterie, a farm situated in the commune of Mignaloux, département de la Vienne, canton de Saint-Julien-Lars.

Geffray Charny; mons. Geffrey Matas; et outre ceo furent mortz ij. mille et viij. cent persones, desqueux furent ij. mille hommes d'armes. Item des avantditz mortz et serjentz furent mille chivalers, que porters-baners et poynouns. Item le roy de Fraunce avoit à la journé viij. mille hommes d'armes et iij. mille hommes à pié, et le Prince avoit à ladit journé iij. mille hommes d'armes, ij. mille archers et mille servaunt. Item c'este tote le copie de la letter que mons. Berthilmew Burwas envoia à mons. Johanne Beaucham, par Sir John de Collandesbergh, prison audite Bertilmew. Item ledit Prince ne paroit à la journé de toet maner de gentz, mès lx. persones, desqueus furent iiij. hommes d'armes. »

There is in the *Archæologia*, vol. i, p. 213 a letter from the Black Prince to the bishop of Worcester, dated Bordeaux, 20th October 1356, relating to the battle of Poitiers.

The following letter of the Pope Innocent VI. to the Black Prince after the battle is not noticed by Barnes, who has given us translations of two letters from Innocent, dated Avignon the third and sixth of October, nor has it, that I am aware, been elsewhere printed. The original is in the Cottonian Ms. Galba E.x. fol. 56.

Papa eleganter hortatur Principem Angliæ ad pacem et misericordiam post captionem Regis Franciæ, per multa bona exempla leonis et principis apium.

« INNOCENTIUS episcopus, servus servorum Dei, dilecto filio, nobili viro, E. primogenito, etc. salutem et apostolicam benedictionem. Illa, fili, consuetudino regnancium, ille mos principantium semper fuit, sicut antiquorum scripta fidelia protestantur et usque ad hæc tempora observantur, ut quanto amplius successibus habundarunt felicibus, tanto promptiores ad pacem tantoque fuerunt ad concordiam proniores. Hanc etiam bestiarum fortissimus, et qui inter eos regio nomine fungitur, benignitatem leo sequitur, hanc apium princeps mansuetudinem imitatur; ille, siquidem provocatus, quantumlibet prostratis novit ignoscere, hic inter apes aculeo solus caret. Te igitur, quem inter cæteros mundi principes in ætatis tuæ recentia victoriarum Dominus clarum fecit gloria triumphorum, ad ea quæ pacis et concordiæ sunt, eo promptiorem invenire sperantes, quo tuorum felicitatem successuum, ab eo recognoscis humiliter, et ei solum reputas reverenter, a quo omnem fortitudinem esse constat. Nobilitatem tuam, quo frequencius eo instantius deprecamur, tibi tuæ salutis intuitu

paternis affectibus suadentes, quatinus ad pacem et concordiam cum carissimo filio nostro in Christo, Johanne, rege Francorum illustri, reformandam habilitans animum, cor præparans, disponens et mentem, ad ea quæ venerabilis frater noster Talairandus, episcopus Albanensis, Apostolicæ sedis nuncius, tibi super hiis pro parte nostra retulerit, credas indubie, illaque ad effectum speratæ et votivæ consummationis adducas. Dat. Avinioni, xiij. Kal. Novembr. »

We find in an imperfect book, very little known even in France, another such letter :

« INNOCENTIUS, episcopus.... Quanquam, fili, ex tuorum felicitate successuum cum mundo sentiens ut probabiliter glorieris, tenemus indubie quod sicut Deo devotus et ex devotis parentibus editus triumphorum gloriam et victoriarum honorem ad dictum Creatorem tuum, a quo est omnis victoria omnisque triumphus, cum reverentia refers ; tenemus quod in eis effusionem cruoris humani consideras ; tenemus quod animarum pericula intueris et quod proinde in conspectu ipsius Dei tui eo te humilias amplius quo sicut circumspectus et prudens plane propendis debere te illi pro hiis referre gratias, pro hiis ab eo veniam deprecari. Licet etiam ipse idem Deus, prout vult distribuens dona sua, te victoriarum titulus et triumphorum pompa fecerit gloriosum, detestatur tamen plebis sue stragem, nec regnantium rancorem aut odium, jus vel injuriam compensari vult excidio fidelium et innocentium populorum, quod nos, attenta nobis meditatione pensantes non revocamus in dubium, ymmo verisimiliter certi sumus, quod tu quanto de manu Domini prosperiora te suscepisse cognoscis, tanto ad pacem eris prumptior, tanto ad concordiam favorabilius inclineris, maxime quod ea sit consuetudo potentium imitantium pietatem, ut plus eos ad clementiam quotidie posteritas excitet, plus ad mansuetudinem indefinite inducat.... Hanc igitur occasionem, hanc causam a te exhibere possis exigimus, et pro pace inter carissimum in Christo filium nostrum Johannem, regem Francie illustrem, quem ad carcerem tuum bellatus eventus adduxit adjutore Domino, reformanda, nobilitatem tuam confidenter adimus, illam quanta possimus affectione rogantes, ac viscera misericordie Dei obsecrantes attentius, quatenus reddens gratitudinis vicem domino Deo tuo, pro hiis que tribuit ipse tibi, ad pacem et concordiam habilites animum, cor prepares, dispones et mentem... et no longis sermonibus diffusius extendamus, epistolam precibus nostris adicibus et que venerabilis frater Talirandus, episcopus

Albanensis, et dilectus filius noster Nicolas Triter, Sancti Vitalis presbiter cardinalis apostolice sedis, unum vel alterum eorum tibi super hoc, pro parte nostra, per se vel per alios retulerint vel indicarunt, credas indubie illaque speratis operum fructibus pia velis prosecutione complere. Avenione, v. Nonas Octobris, pontificatus nostri anno quarto. » (J. Delpit, *Collection générale des documents français qui se trouvent en Angleterre*, t. i, p. 79, 80.)

Among the Baluze manuscripts, t. lxxxvii, fol. 183, Nat. Library, there is a letter dated September 27, 1356, directed under shape of a circular, by the officers of the council of the King of France, to the bishop of Alby, (Albano?) concerning the battle fought at Poitiers eight days before, Monday September 19.

1409. We think proper to reprint here a cotemporary *Complainte sur la bataille de Poitiers*, published by Ch. de Beaurepaire in the *Bibliothèque de l'Ecole des Chartes*, t. ii, 3d series, Paris, 1851, 8vo., p. 257-263.

  Grant doulour me contraint de faire ma complainte   1
De l'ost devant Poitiers, là où persone mainte
Fut morte et le roy prins par la fausse gent feinte,
Qui s'enfoy ; dont fut leur traison atteinte.
  Quant virent que nostre ost pooit bien desconfire   5
L'ost des Anglois, si distrent : « Se les alons occirre,
Guerres seront faillies, si sera pour nous pire ;
Car nous perdrons chevauche. Miex est de nous enfuire. »
  Onques cop n'i ferirent d'arme ne de plançon ;
Mais distrent : « Fuions tost ; se ne nous avançon,   10
En fuiant serons mors, pris ou mis à rençon. »
De tels gent ne puent aistre dicte bonne chançon.
  Non contretant leur fuite, fuiant ont esté pris.
Por ce ne sont pas quite que ne soient repris
De leur grant traïson, en quoy ont tant mespris   15
Que leur gentillece a perdu honneur et pris.
  Ils se dient estre nez de noble parenté :
Hé Dieux ! dont leur vient-il si fausse volenté,
Que d'aucun ben fait faire ne sont entalenté ?
C'est de lor grant orgueil dont ainsi sont tenté ;   20
  Car en Dieu renoier chascuns d'euls s'estudie,
Et à le parjurer chascun se glorifie.
Jà n'i aura celui qui le loe ne prie ;
Car il leur est avis qu'autres dieux qu'eulz n'est mie.
  Boubanz et vainegloire, vesture deshoneste,   25
Les ceintures dorées, la plume sur la teste,

La grant barbe de bouc, qui est une ordre beste,
Les vous font estordiz comme fouldre et tempeste.
    Tels gens où reigne orgueil, qui est si vil peché,
Sont de touz mauvais vices et d'ordure entesché ;   30
Tous temps seront traistres, puisqu'il sont aleché,
Car touz les bens de grace sont en euls asseché.
    Or voient comme orguil et leur grant surcuidance
Et leur haute maniere en honeur les avance !
Leur grant orgueil les a tresbuchés en viltance   35
Et leur grant convoitise et leur insuffisance.
    Quant euls aus mareschaus pour passer se montroient
Garçons armez, chevauls l'un de l'autre empruntoient,
Leurs soillars et leur pages pour gens d'armes contoient :
Ainssi un seul pour quatre du roy gages prenoient.   40
    Par leur grant convoitise, non pour honneur conquerre,
Ont fait telle paction avec ceuls d'Engleterre :
« Ne tuons pas l'un l'autre ; faisons durer la guerre ;
Feignons estre prisons, moult y porrons acquerre. »
    Par tele convoitise ont maint grant don receu   45
Des Anglois, par lesquels est revelé et sceu
Et par leur contenance a esté aperceu
Que par traïson ont ainssi le roy deceu.
    La très-grant traïson qu'il ont lonc temps covée,
Fut en l'ost dessus dit très-clerement prouvée,   50
Dont France est à touz temps par euls deshonorée,
Se par autres que euls ne nous est recouvrez.
    De traïson en cuer portoient la baniere ;
Du conseil reveloient aux Englois la matiere.
Quant le roy apperçut leur très-fausse maniere,   55
Si les a du conseil tous fait bouter arriere.
    Les traïstres en ont grant indignation,
Si ont contre le roy fait conspiracion
De li et ses enfans metre à destruction ;
Dont sont venu bien preis de leur extencion.   60
    Quant orent mis le roy où le vouloient rendre
Et virent que ce fut à l'assaillir et prendre,
Ne s'adrecerent pas d'aler le roy deffendre,
Mais s'enfuirent tuit : qu'ancor les puit-on prendre !
    Il n'est cuer qui peust d'euls dire trop laidure ;   65
Fauls, traistres, desloyaus, sont infame et parjure ;
Car par euls est le roy mis à desconfiture,
Qui est li très plus noble de toute creature.
    O poy de gent demore le roy en la bataille ;
Comme très-vaillant prince, fiert d'estoc et de taille,   70
Mors en abat grant nombre, ne les prise une maille,
Dit : « Ferez, chevalers ; ce ne sont que merdaille. »

>   Fierement se combat et de grant vasselage ;
>   Los, pris, honeur emporte sus touz ceuls de parage.
>   Se touz les autres ussent esté de son corage,   75
>   Anglois ussent esté cunquis et mis en grant servage [1].
>   Quant le roy se vit pris, si dist par grant constance :
>   « Ce est Johan de Valois, non pas le roy de France.
>   Maint escu percié et rompu mainte lance
>   Seront que vous aiez du roy françois finance. »   80
>   Dieu veille conforter et garder nostre roy
>   Et son petit enfant qu'est demoré o soy,
>   Et confonde traïstres qui par leur grant effroy
>   Et tray leur seigneur à qui il devoient foy !
>   Endurer aventures paciemment convient,   85
>   Combien que soient dures ; mais quant il en sovient,
>   Grant douleur font au cueur. Se ren en survient
>   Qui met en esperance, quatre foiz miel avient.
>   Dieu done à nostre duc faire tele aliance
>   De gens fermes, entiers et de si grant puissance,   90
>   Que des anemis puissent prandre vengance
>   Si qu'ancore paisson veoir nostre roy en France,
>   S'il est ben conseillé, il n'obliera mie
>   Mener Jaque Bonhome en sa grant compagnie ;
>   Guerres ne s'enfuira pour ne perdre la vie   95
>   . . . . . . du roy. . . . . . .

Let us mention also another piece of poetry *Comment Franc-Vouloir fut subjugué aux batailles de Crecy et de Poitiers par Folie,* inserted into the *Miroir de Mariage*, published by Crapelet. (*Poésies morales et historiques d'Eustache Deschamps*, etc. Paris, 1832, 8vo., p. 233.)

Long afterwards, painting associated itself with poetry to preserve, at least in England, the recollection of the two decisive battles fought by the greatest of the Plantagenets. There is in the throne room of Windsor Castle a large picture executed by command of William III. On a space of 20 or 24 yards is depicted the triumph of the Black Prince presenting King Jean of France and King David of Scotland, his prisoners, to his father.

Page 93, heading. *Clergie* undoubtely means *clergy*, as in the account of the entry of Isabel of Bavaria into Paris in 1389 : « En devant l'eglise Nostre-Dame, l'evesque de Paris estoit revestu des

---

[1] Froissart says : « Et le roy de son costé, fut très-bon chevalier ; et si la quarte partie de ses gens luy essent ressemblé, la journée eust esté pour eux. »

armes Nostre-Seigneur, et tout le college aussi, où moult avoit grant clergie; » but it was more comprehensive than now.

We have no occasion to examine the various meanings of *clergie* and *clerc*, the commonest, as to the latter being *clerk, amanuensis, actuary* [1]; but it is by no means idle to state that at Bordeaux the individuals of that class of society, even in orders (shavelings), could carry on a trade and keep a wife [2].

---

[1] A Nonneguin le fil Martin
Le Singe, qui bien sot latin,
Et qui estoit clercs couronnez,
D'escrire à court et de conter
Que li frais pooient monter.

Jean de Condé, ap. du Cange, *Gloss. med. et inf. Latin.*, t. ii, p. 394, col. 1, v° *Clerici*.

[2] *Pro Guillelmo Fitz Piers-Ayquem et aliis.* (Rot. Vasc., 29 Edw. III., membr. 9.) R. senescallo suo Vasconie et constabulario suo Burdegale... salutem. Ex parte dilectorum nobis Guillelmi Fitz-Piers Ayquem, Johannis Ayquem, Johannis de la Taste et Guillelmi Fitz Arnaude-Ayquem, clericorum, burgensium et mercatorum de Burdegala, nobis est graviter conquerendo monstratum quod licet ipsi totis temporibus retroactis custumas de bonis et mercandisis suis in dicta civitate juxta libertates et consuetudines ejusdem civitatis, prout alii burgenses civitatis illius solvunt, hocusque solvere consuevissent, absque eo quod ipsi custumas aliquas de bonis et mercandisis suis cum forinsecis vel alienigenis solvere compellebantur, vos tamen, pro eo quod predicti Guillelmus, Johannes Johannes (sic) et Guillelmus clerici sunt, pretendentes ipsos cum forinsecis et alienigenis pro bonis et mercandisis suis solvere debere, ipsos ad custumas de bonis et mercandisis suis cum forinsecis solvendas compellere nitimini, ut asserunt, minus juste et contra libertates et privilegia burgensibus civitatis predicte per nos et progenitores nostros concessa. Super quo supplicarunt sibi per nos de remedio provideri. Nos volentes, etc. — Concessum.

Pro clericis de civitate Burdegale tonsuratis et uxoratis, de non inquirendo. (Rot. Vasc. 29 Edw. III., membr. 3 et 5. — Rymer, vol. iii, p. 310.) R. senescallo suo Vasconie et constabulario suo Burdegale... salutem. Gravem querelam dilectorum et fidelium nostrorum majoris, juratorum et aliorum de communitate civitatis nostre Burdegale, recepimus, continentem quod, licet ipsi omnes et singuli tam clerici tonsurati et alii qui in civitate predicta de redditibus, mercandisis, artificiis et laboribus suis vivunt et onera ejusdem civitatis supportant, quieti sint et esse debeant, ipsique et eorum antecessores a tempore cujus contrarii memoria non existit, semper hactenus quieti esse consueverunt de custuma propriorum vinorum suorum in propriis vineis suis crescencium apud castrum nostrum Burdegale solvendis, vos tamen, prefate constabularie, pro eo quod invenistis per privilegia regia esse concessum quod clerici filii burgensium civitatis predicte de custuma vinorum suorum propriorum in eorum vineis propriis crescensium liberi esse debent, asserentes alios clericos de civitate predicta, qui non sunt filii burgensium, a libertate predicta fore exclusos, quamquam dicta concessio ad filios burgensium beneficiatos et in servicio ecclesiastico in dies occupatos, qui coram nobis, vel officialibus aut ministris nostris, non sunt justiciabiles, nec ad onera eidem civitati incumbencia supportanda contribuunt, et non ad clericos filios burgensium, etc.

According to the doctrine of the decretals, confirmed by the council of Trent, the clerks, under the subdeaconship, could marry and keep the benefit of clergy, on certain conditions : 1st not to be bigamist, viz. in the canonical language, not to have contracted a second matrimony ; 2d not to have wedded a widow ; 3ly to continue to wear the clerical crown and the costume imposed on clerks [1]. Originally commerce was forbidden to clerks; but in the decretals there is no such prohibition except against the clerks who make themselves jesters, buffoons, butchers or bakers [2].

In fact, a multitude of clerks drove a trade ; the proof of which frequently occurs in the decisions of the Parliament of Paris. They are to be compared with the regulations promulgated in 1317 *Pro custumis a clericis conjugatis exigendis.* (Gascon Rolls, 11 Ed. II., membr. 17, dorso. — Rymer, vol. ii, p. 135, col. 2.)

At the end of the XIIth century, Pope Innocent III. having anew forbidden the marriage of clergymen, Walter Mapes composed a bitter satire, which has been printed by William Camden in his *Remains concerning Britaine*, etc. London, 1614, 4to., p. 338, 340. Cf. Robert Henry, *The History of Great Britain*, vol. iii, London, 1777, 4to., ch. v, § 2, p. 498; and Boulard's French translation, t. iii, Paris, 1792, 4to., p. 500.

1453. Compare that account with Gower's description of a procession on Queen Olympia's birth day :

> There was great merth on all side,
> Where as she passethe by the strete,
> There was ful many a timbre bete,
> And many a maid carolende.

Confessio Amant., lib. vi, fol. 137 a. b. edit. Berthel. 154. — Pauli's ed. London, 1867, 8vo., vol. iii, p. 63, l. 12. — Warton's *History of English Poetry*, vol. ii, p. 9, col. 1, notes.

1484. He was engaged there in deciding differences respecting the purchase of the French prisoners, amongst which were the pretensions

---

[1] Constitution or decretal of Pope Boniface VIII., 1298; 3d part of the *Corpus juris canonici*, lib. iii, tit. 2. — Decretal of Clement V., 1312, in the Clementines ; 4th part of the same, lib. iii, tit. 1. — Conc. Trid., Sess. 23. (*De reform.* C. G.) Cf. Cangii Gloss., t. ii, p. 393, col. 1, V⁰. *Clerici conjugati*.

[2] See a constitution unique in VI⁰. III. 1, and the text of the Clementines as above.

concerning the taking of the French King, in the respective claims of Sir Denis Morbeque and Bernard de Troye. Compare Collins, p. 108, with Issue Roll, 37 Edw. III., p. 180; Rymer's *Fœdera*, vol. iii, p. 467; and the *Chronicle of London*, A. D. 1360, p. 209.

1499. In Rymer, vol. iii, p. 348, is the King's writ dated the 20th of March to the sheriff of Devonshire, John Dabernoun [1], ordering him to provide the necessary supplies and carriage for the Prince and the King of France, intending to land at Plymouth.

1501. Barnes, p. 526, has a very spirited account of the entry into London of the Prince with his noble prisoner. The latter was in civilian dress, his coat of arms and helmet having been dispatched to England by a special messenger, bearer of news from the battle of Poitiers. (Poll Exit. 30 Edw. III.; ap. Rymer, vol. iii, p. 343.)

1509. It would seem clear from this passage that the confinement of Isabella at Rising Castle in Norforlk was not a very close one, and that, independently of the King's annual visit, a greater degree of liberty was allowed her than has been generally supposed. At the same time, we have evidence from letters of safe-conduct to William de Leth, dated the 4th of April, that she was at Rising in the previous month; in which she is called « Carissimam matrem nostram, Isabellam, reginam Angliæ. » (Rymer's *Fœdera*, vol. iii, p. 352.)

We avail ourselves of this opportunity to venture a hint concerning the King's messenger to his mother: was he not the William Delict, a citizen of London, in whose house in Fenchurch Street Sir William Wallace was lodged before he was brought to his trial in the great hall at Westminster? Very likely, this Delict was a Scotchman from Leith, who had betrayed and left his country to side with Edward III [2].

1512. This kind of sport generally prevailed among ladies, chiefly in England, from the earliest times, as illustrated by the vouchers

---

[1] That name ought to be spelt *d'Abernon* from Abernon, near Orbec, in the old province of Normandy, which was the original seat of the family. Reginald of Abernon having had a grant of Addington (Surrey) in the time of Henry II., bore the name, as well as his descendants, who nevertheless preserved the arms of Abernon, with different tinctures, as they still do.

[2] Stow's *Annals or a generall Chronicle of England*, reign of Edward III., p. 209.

collected by Strutt.[1]. It is alluded to in a tract of the XVth century [2]. Still in *Love's labour's lost*, act. IV, sc. 1, the princess says to a gamekeeper :

> Then, forester, my friend, where is the bush
> That we must stand and play the murderer in ?

1573. This treaty is printed at length in Rymer, vol. iii, p. 487. The swearing of the kings took place in the church of Saint-Nicolas, Calais, whereas Barnes says, refusing the offered Pax : « they kissed each other with hearty demonstrations of a mutual friendship. »

1588. Joan, countess of Kent, daughter of Edmund of Woodstock, earl of Kent, second son of Edward the First ; she was first married to Sir Thomas Holland, and on his going abroad, was contracted to William Montagu, earl of Salisbury, from whom she was divorced on the petition of Sir Thomas by a bull of Pope Clement the Sixth. Her husband died on the 28th of December 1260, and she became the wife of the Black Prince on the 10th of October in the year following. Compare Rymer's *Fœdera*, vol. iii, p. 626, 632. A. D. 1361.

1656. Charles, son of Guy de Châtillon, count of Blois ; he was killed at the battle of Auray, to which allusion is here made, contending for the dukedom of Britanny, which he claimed in right of his wife, Joan, daughter of Guy, brother of John III. duke of Britanny. The particulars of the battle of Auray are given at length by Froissart, ed. Kervyn, t. xvii, p. 408-410.

1685. Bertrand du Guesclin, the hero of the French at this period, was born about 1314, and died in July 1380. A life of him by Claude Menard was issued at Paris, 1618, an another (*Anciens Mémoires du quatorzieme siecle, depuis peu découverts*, etc.), by Le Febvre, printed at

---

[1] *The Sports and the Pastimes of England*. London, 1834, 8vo., p. 11-14 and 50, 51.
[2] *Le Débat des hérauts d'armes de France et d'Angleterre*, etc. Paris, 1870, 8vo., p. 3, § 7, and p. 129.

Among the pleasures offered to a lady in the Squyr of Lowe Degre, a father says to his daughter :

> « To-morowe ye shall on hunting fare,
> And ryde, my doughter, in a chare....
> Homward thus shall ye ryde,
> On haukyng by the ryvers syde, etc., »

Ritson's *Ancient Engleish metrical Romanceës*, vol. i, l. 739, 773, p. 176, 177.

Douay, 1692, both 4to.; but there is a much better one in the press in Paris by an eminent scholar M. Siméon Luce, of which the first volume has already made its appearance.

1687. Jean de Bourbon, comte de la Marche, son of Jacques de Bourbon, who was taken prisoner at Poitiers; at this time he was only sixteen years of age. He was afterwards at the battles of Comines and Rosebecq in 1382, at the siege of Taillebourg in 1384; followed Charles the Sixth to Gueldres in 1388, and to Languedoc in 1391, and died the 11th of June 1393.

1692. Sir Hugh Calvely, or Calverley, of Lea in Cheshire; was at the battle of the Trente, under Sir Richard Bembrough, in 1350[1]; was afterwards at the battle of Nájera, in 1377 was captain of Calais. In 1378, he took part in the crusade against Clement VII., and was driven from the territory of the earl of Flanders by the French king. In 1386, he founded a monastery at Bunbury in Cheshire, in which church his monument is still to be seen.

1694. He was the fourth son of Thomas Gurnay, one of the murderers of Edward the Second. He was a soldier of fortune, and appears to have been at Crécy, Poitiers and Nájera; and was afterwards appointed seneschal of the Landes. He married 1. Alice, sister of Thomas Beauchamp, earl of Warwick; 2. Philippa, sister of John, lord Talbot. (Gough, *Sepulchral Monuments in Great Britain*, n° 21.) His appointment to the custody of Brest castle, under the Duke of Lancaster, 1357, is in Rymer's *Fœdera*, vol. iii, p. 283. Having died in 1406 at the age of 96 years, Mathew Gurnay was buried at Stoves-under-Hampden. Leland, in his *Itinerary*, vol. ii, p. 63, 64, and vol. iii, p. cxi, has given this inscription engraved on his tomb, where are enumerated the battles in which this « moult vaillans chevaliers, » as Froissart calls him, had taken part : « Icy gist le noble et vaillant chivaler Matheu de Gourney, etc. qui en sa vie fu à la bataille de Benamary, et ala après à la siege d'Algesire sur les Sarrazins, et aussy à la bataille de l'Escluse, de Cressy, de Deygeness, de

---

[1] See le *Combat de trente Bretons contre trente Anglois*, published by G. A Crapelet, 2nd edition, Paris, 1835, 4to. *passim*. Twenty years afterwards we find an item concerning a sum ordered to another champion of the same fight, Morice de Treseguidi, by the King of France for a journey to Spain. See D. Mórice, *Mémoires pour servir de preuves à l'histoire de Bretagne*, t. ii, col. 283, 284.

Peyteres, de Nazare, d'Ozrey et à pluseurs autres batailles et asseges, en lesquelx il gaigna noblement grant los et honour. » It has been supposed that he was the prototype of Chaucer's Knight. See Chaucer's Prologue to the Canterbury Tales, lines 43 to 78.

Cuvelier, a rhymer contemporary with Chandos herald, mentions Mathew Gurnay at least eight times in his Chronicle of Bertrand du Guesclin. See E. Charrière's edition, Paris, 1839, 4to., vol. i, p. 262, 296, 335, 342, 349, 353, 357, 359, 361. See also Camden's *Britannia*, etc. London, 1763, fol., col. 71; and above all Daniel Gurney's *Record of the House of Gournay*, printed for private distribution only. London and King's Lynn, 1848-58, 8vo., p. 743, 655, 670, 685.

1703. The account of Froissart is the same; namely, that they sent to ask a free passage and supplies for some pilgrims, who had undertaken an expedition into the kingdom of Granada to revenge the sufferings of the Saviour, to destroy the infidels and exalt the cross.

1754. We learn from the Spanish historians, that Don Pedro first retired to Portugal, where he offered his daughter Beatrice to the Infant; this being refused, he proceeded to Monterey in Galicia, thence to Santiago, where he murdered the archbishop, and afterwards to Coruña, where finding twenty-two ships, he embarked for Bayonne [1].

1795. Fernando de Castro is supposed to have been the brother of the famed Inez de Castro; his life is said to have been spared after the death of Don Pedro on account of his fidelity to his sovereign. (Dillon, vol. ii, p. 119.)

1902. In the *Ancient Mémoires*, etc. of Le Febvre, p. 196, where the battle of Nájera is described, amongst the ensigns spoken of are « les lys de la France et les léopards d'Angleterre; » the English troops therefore appear to be here signified by their standard, though I do not suppose they had much right to the royal flag.

To the remark of Coxe we will add one of ours. This passage is ambiguous. As it is written, it seems to be an allusion to some romantic tradition, or prediction like the prophecies of Merlin, so widely spread at the time.

[1] Don Pero Lopez de Ayala, año 16 de D. Pedro, cap. x, t. i, p. 414, 415. — Ferreras, *Historia de España*, t. viii, p. 142, 143, n. 6-8. — John Talbot Dillon's *History of the reign of Peter the Cruel*, etc. London, 1788, 8vo. — Mérimée, *Hist. de D. Pedro Ier*, etc., p. 463-465.

As to the leopards, the question of their introduction into the arms of England has been much discussed. Some people, without elucidating it, have asserted that originally the British leopards, before the XIIIth century [1], were lions, and a single one, instead of three [2]. In the latter case, the adoption of the King of animals in early English heraldry might be traced up to the dukes of Normandy. In 1686, the abbé Vertot found among the ruins of a chapel of the abbey of Fécamp a tomb stone bearing an epitaph of a Robert, infant son of a duke Richard, and the image of a lion, with this inscription : ECCE VICIT LEO DE TRIBV IVDA RADIX DAVID [3].

And if we refer to the chronicle of John, monk of Marmoutier, we will see that Geoffroy le Bel, another duke of Normandy, had young lions painted on his shield [4], a decoration which was to be noted on the tomb of William de Valence, earl of Pembroke, 1196 [5].

It is almost idle to state that the seal of the township of Bordeaux during the English dominion was a lion rampant. See *Archives historiques de la Gironde*, t. iii, p. 161, n° LXI, where a fragment of such a seal appended to a charter of 1342 is represented.

On that of the Black Prince, as engraved in the *Fœdera*, 3d edit., t. iii, part. i, p. 132, and on the title-page of Ainslie's *Illustrations of the Anglo-French Coinage*, London. 1830, 4to., the crest of the head piece of the helmet is a lion passant.

On the other hand, there are no lack of scholars who maintain

---

[1] *Heraldry ancient and modern including Bouteli's Heraldry*, by S. T. Aveling. London, Warne and C°, 8vo.

[2] In the Romance of Richard Cœur-de-Lion, the King is said to have borne :
On his schuldre a scheeld of steel,
With three lupardes wrought ful weel.
H. Weber, *Metrical Romances*, etc., vol. i, p. 222.
Another rhymer at a less remote date called King Richard II. « le roy qui les liepars porte en blason. » (*Archæologia*, vol. xx, p. 99.)

[3] *Histoire de l'Académie royale des inscriptions et belles-lettres*, t. iii, p. 276, hist.

[4] *Recherches sur le commerce, la fabrication et l'usage des étoffes de soie*, etc., vol. i, p. 226, note. Cf. vol. ii, p. 128.

[5] « The fascia of the chest is an enamelled plate, as is the cushion under the head, which is richly ornamented with rows of quatrefoils and escutcheons alternatively, charged with the singte coats of England, G. 3 lions passant guardant Or. » (Richard Gough, *Sepulchral Monuments in Great Britain*, vol. i. London, 1786, large fol., p. 76, pl. 27. Cf. p. cxviii, and plate to face p. cxlvii.)

that prior to Henry II. there were only two lions or leopards on the Royal shield, and that this monarch, in right of his wife, Eleanor of Aquitaine, added a third, A. D. 1154, to the two he already emblazoned, and from that period three lions or leopards have been the National arms of England.

This question of lions *versus* leopards may be farther elucidated by a reference to a collection of Dutch historical medals and among which is one that has evidently been struck to comemorate the grant of the Duchy of Guienne by Louis XI. to his brother Charles, who is thereon represented on horseback, fully armed, with a drawn sword in his hand, his visor up, his tunic studded with the *fleurs de lys* of France and the leopards of Guienne. His horse is adorned in a similar manner. The motto is : « DEUS (undoubtedly for DIVUS) KAROLUS MAXIMUS AQUITANORUM DUX ET FRANCORUM FILIUS. » The other side represents a Duke of Aquitaine seated under an open canopy supported by two angels on which are the arms of France and of Guienne and the verse of the Psalms, *Deus judicium tuum Regi da, et justiciam tuam filio Regis* [1].

1988. Sir John, afterwards John second Lord Devereux, was son of Sir Walter Devereux, He does not appear, probably on account of his youth, to have taken any part in the previous wars. He became afterwards one of the heroes of Froissart. In 1370, he was governor of Limousin, in the same year was with the Prince at Limoges, seneschal of la Rochelle in 1372, was taken prisoner at Chisey in March 1373, governor of Calais in 1380, warden of the Cinq Ports in 1387, knight of the Garter in the year following, and died in February 1393.

1988. By *Briquet* and *Cressewell* are probably intended the Sir Robert Briquet and Sir John Trevelle, mentioned by Froissart ; the latter is by Barnes called Sir John Charnelle (Charuel ?). In Kervyn's edition of Froissart, the Sir John Treuelle is read *Jean Carsuelle*, which would very nearly agree with the text. Sir Robert Briquet and John Creswell are mentioned at Nájera as fighting under Sir J. Chandos (Kervyn's edit., t. vii, p. 204, 212). John Creswell is also mentioned

---

[1] Van Mieris, *Historie der Nederlandsche Vorsten*, etc., vol. i, The Hague, 1732, fol., p. 466. The Cabinet des médailles et antiques de la Bibliothèque Nationale possesses a fine golden specimen of this valuable medallion.

by Froissart in 1371 as having the castle of Moncontour given into his custody, conjointly with Hewet and Holgrave, to keep the frontier against Anjou and le Maine, and in 1373 as having been taken prisoner at the battle of Chisey. (*Ibid.*, t. viii, p. 88-90, etc.)

1992. Bernard de la Salle. He is mentioned by Froissart and Barnes as passing the Pyrenees on the Wednesday in the company of the King of Majorca. Barnes adds Lortingo (Lartigo?) de la Salle, but is not borne out by Froissart.

2034. There is a valuable essay on those adventurers published under the title of *Des grandes Compagnies au quatorzième siècle*, by E. de Fréville, in the *Bibliothèque de l'Ecole des Chartes*, t. iii, 1st. series, p. 258, and t. v, p. 232.

Those *condottieri* had been driven out of France by Bertrand du Guesclin; but the negociations between their leaders and Don Enrique de Trastamare were managed by marshal Arnoul d'Audrehem and Charles V. The treaties are of date July 22, and August 13, 1362. (D. Vaissete, *Histoire générale de Languedoc*, t. iv, p 316, 317; Pr. Mérimée, *Histoire de don Pedro Ier, roi de Castille*, p. 368, note 2.)

2096. The birth of Richard II. at Bordeaux is recorded by Froissart 6th January 1367. See t. vii, p. 111, note, and b. iv.

2096. The history of the life and fate of Richard II., son of the Black Prince and successor to Edward III., his grand-father, (1377-1399) is too well known to give matter for a note; but it is not unseasonable to mention a poem which might be considered as a sequel to that of Chandos Herald. The twentieth volume of the *Archæologia* contains (p. 295-723) another metrical chronicle in French, written by a contemporaneous rhymer and translated into English by John Webb.

2124. Jean de Montfort, duke of Britanny, count of Montfort and earl of Richmont; was proclaimed duke of Britanny on the defeat of Charles of Blois at Auray in 1364; but upon concluding a treaty with Edward in 1372, he was driven thence and obliged to retire to England in the following year. He was elected into the order of the Garter in 1375, reinstated in his dominions in 1381, and died in November, 1399. A very excellent summary of his life and

especially of his conduct with regard to Olivier de Clisson, is given by G. Fr. Beltz, *Memorials*, etc., p. 195.

2128. Olivier, sire de Clisson, comte de Perhoet, etc., served at the battle of Auray in 1364, and continued in active service, for some years in company with Bertrand du Guesclin, until 1380, when he was made constable of France, in which capacity he commanded the vanguard at the batle of Rosebecq in 1382. In 1387 he was imprisoned by order of the duke of Britanny, and obtained his liberty only by the payment of an enormous ransom. He died the 5th of February 1407.

2128. Sir Robert Knolles, whom Froissart always calls *Canolle*, and who had, in company with Clisson, distinguished himself in the wars of Brittany, chiefly at the battle of Auray, is probably here intended. See farther on, note to l. 2329.

2156. Gaston de Foix was born in 1331, and died in 1391. Froissart has delineated his character in detail, but seems to have had no notion of the noble and gallant troubadour being also a brother in poetry. His surname *Phébus* is not accounted for; some say it was given from his fondness for the chase, others from his fair complexion, or auburn hair, a rarity in the Pyrenean countries, and others from his adoption of the sun as his armorial bearings.

In his *Dit du Florin*, Froissart confirms thus his praise of this prince in his chronicles:

> Vraiement il n'y fault riens
> Que largheces et courtoisies,
> Honnour, sens et toutes prisies
> Qu'on peut recorder de noble homme
> Ne soyent en celui qu'on nomme
> Gaston, le bon comte de Fois.

He was renowned then « pour le plus able et soubtil homme d'armes qui fust en toutes les routes, et le mieulx amés de tous povres compagnons [1]. »

2156. Gaston Phébus III., son of Gaston, comte de Foix, and Eleanor, daughter of Bernard, comte de Cominges; he was very fond

---

[1] Luce's Froissart, t. iv, p. 184, l. 24. Cf. t. v, p. xxvi, xli, xlvii, lv. As a true knight, *cavallero determinado*, he had a motto in two lines of French ryme.

of cynegetics, and at first adhered to the English party [1], contrary to his father [2]. Having been appointed by Charles V. governor of Guienne and Languedoc, which government he held until 1381, he gave a power of attorney for the liberation of Sir Thomas de Felton, seneschal of Aquitaine [3], and died in 1391 at the advanced age of eighty years.

2176. Dax, the Roman *Aquæ Tarbellicæ*, now a seat of sous-préfecture in the département des Landes, was particularly noted for its warm springs, and its remarkable mural fortification doomed to fall, some years ago, by order of its town council, in spite of Léo Drouyn and the late M. de Caumont; here are also the remains of an amphitheatre, of a very humble kind, still used at times for bull, or rather cow fights.

The gallant author of the *Illustrations of the Anglo-French Coinage*, whom we have had already occasion to quote and who may be consulted with advantage (see p. 86, 87, 96, 97, 145-157 [4]), is bold enough to state, p. 147, note, that the Black Prince, previous to entering Spain, held his court for three or four months at Dax, where his house « is still pointed out; » adding that he coined money there, and that the supporter of Don Pedro el Cruel did the same at Tarbes, on his way across the Pyrenees. We never heard of those circumstances; but it is never too late to learn.

---

[1] See a letter of Gaston-Phébus to the Black Prince to inform him of his visit at Angoulême, or Périgueux, and to hunt with Chandos's dogs. (*Archives historiques du département de la Gironde*, t. iv, p. 111, n° LXXXVIII. 3 August 1360.)
Four years afterwards we find the Black Prince dating an act of confirmation of the marriage settlement between the Earl of Cambridge and the Duchess of Burgundy : *Donné à nostre chastel d'Engolesme*. (Rymer, vol. iii, p. 761. Feb. 20, 1364.) There is another charter dated from the castle of Angoulême by the same 26 Jan. 1367. (Louvet's *Traité en forme d'abrégé de l'Histoire d'Aquitaine*, etc. Bordeaux, 1659, 4to., vol. ii, p. 83-89.) If we are well informed, there was in that castle, which no longer exists, a room known by the name of *la chambre du Prince Noir*.

[2] A letter from Galois de la Baume, master of the cross-bowmen of the King of France, informs us that the count de Foix had entered Paris with the most part of his company, 1st September 1338. (*Archives de la Gironde*, p. 162. Cf. p. 100.)

[3] *Ibid.*, t. viii, p. 197, n° LXX.

[4] Among the *desiderata*, we will limit ourselves to one. In 1344, Edward III. having ordered two different sorts of gold coins to be struck in the Tower of London, one with two leopards, the other with a single one, bespoke a similar work to be executed at Bordeaux. (*Rot. Vascon.*, 18 Edw. III., membr. 3.) .

2189. No doubt the Black Prince felt inclined to enter Spain through the defile of Roncesvalles, a place of pilgrimage very well known in England, as we may judge by names. An hospital *Beatæ Mariæ de Rouncyvalle* in Charing, London, is mentioned in the *Monasticon Anglicanum*, vol. ii, p. 443, and there was a Runceval-Hall in Oxford.

The hospital or chapel of St. Mary Rounceval, in the parish of St. Martin in the Fields, was undoubtedly a cell to the priory of Roncevaux (Span. *Roncesvalles* in Navarre), and was endowed with lands.

2194. Now Miranda de Arga, province of Navarre, diocese of Pampeluna, on the Arga, not to be confounded with Miranda de Ebro, a town situated on that river and in the diocese of Burgos.

2202. Mosen Martin Enriquez, seigneur de Lacarre. In the convention between Pedro, King of Navarre, and the Prince of Wales, 23rd of September 1366, he is appointed as one of the plenipotentiary agents of the same King, and is styled « mesire Martin Henrriquiz, sire de Lacarre; » and also *consanguineus noster et vexillarius regni nostri Caroli, regis Navarræ*. (Rymer's *Fœdera*, vol. iii, p. 800, 802. A. D. 1366.) Upon the capture of the King of Navarre we find him governor of that country. See Yanguas y Miranda, *Diccionario de Antigüedades del Reino de Navarra*, t. ii, Pamplona, 1840, 4to., p. 157-164. Cf. Rymer's *Fœdera*, 1st ed., vol. viii, p. 755, and 3d ed., t. iii, pars iv, p. 90, col. i. (*De Conductu, marescallo Navarræ.* West., 15th Oct. 1393.)

2221. Froissart also speaks of the confirmation of the treaty between the three Princes at Peyrehorade; ed. Luce, t. vii, p. v.

2247. Hugh de Hastings served in Flanders 14 Edw. III., in the 16 Edw. III. was summoned to Parliament as a baron. In 1346, as « *consanguineus regis* » he was appointed the king's lieutenant in Flanders and commander of his forces there, and in the following year took part in the expedition into Britanny in the retinue of John, Duke of Lancaster; in 33 Edw. III. he was in the wars of Gascony, and in 43 Edw. III. served again in France under the same duke.

We do not know whether Hugh was the founder of the *bastide* of his name in the Landes of Gascony; but we are aware that it was in existence as early as 1341. See *Rot. Vasc.*, 15 Edw. III., membr. 15;

ap. Rymer, vol. ii, pars ii, p. 1169. *De Portu apud bastidam de Hastyngs habendo.*

2248. Sir William Beauchamp, of Bergavenny, fourth son of Thomas, earl of Warwick. The present occasion appears to have been his introduction to active service; he was afterwards at Limoges and Montpaon, and in 1373 in the campaign in France under the Dukes of Lancaster and Brittany. In 1376, he was elected into the order of the Garter; in 1380 and afterwards he served in Brittany and Spain, and was appointed in 1383 captain of Calais, which appointment he held until 1389. In 1392, he was summoned to Parliament as baron of Bergavenny; and on the accession of Henry IV. appointed justiciary of South Wales, and governor of the castle and county of Pembroke. He died on the 8th of May 1411.

2251. John, son to Ralph, lord Nevil of Raby. In 1360, he was knighted; in 1369, invested with the Garter, and in the following year appointed admiral of the Fleet Northward. In 1376, he was impeached upon his conduct in Brittany, but acquitted. In 1378, he was appointed lieutenant of Aquitaine, and in the same year with the Earl of Northumberland retook Berwick, after which he departed for his government. He died in October 1388. In Rymer's *Fœdera* may be seen, from the Gascon and other rolls, notices of his prisoners, with the negociations for their respective ransoms.

The Nevilles were so widely spread in England that we are unable to tie to any branch « Bernard de Neufville, » esquire, captain of Caudrot in 1342. See Bertrandy's *Etude sur Froissart*, p. 87. Later occur a Jean de Neuville (Luce's Froissart, t. vi, p. LXXXII), and another whom we cannot identify.

A petition directed to King Henry IV. by Monot de Cantalop, a Gascon esquire, and two brothers of his, mentions a lord of Nevill as having been a lieutenant of Richard II. in their country. « Et soit ensi, says the applicant, qu'ils aient .j. houstiel appellé *Camarsac* près de vostre ville de Bourdeux, lequiel ja grant temps fut amblé et tolu par les Franceois à l'escuer de qui estoit; vient après le seignur de Nevill', lequel estoit lieutenant de vostre predecesseur, cui Dieu absoille! » etc. (Cottonian Library, Vespasian, F. xiii, fol. 25 recto, n° 31.) — The remainder of the document, which may be interesting

for an antiquarian lawyer or a historian of Bordeaux, would be out of place here.

2259. Froissart says that he served under Chandos with 30 lancers at Auray; but a sire de Rais, had fought there on the side of Charles de Blois, and had been taken prisoner by Chandos. (Lobineau, *Hist. de Bretagne*, t. i, p. 294, 336.) In 1370 he again served under Bertrand du Guesclin, but with the Duke of Brittany in 1372, and was one of the 200 lances under Olivier de Clisson in 1377. On the 17th of August, 1381, the barony of Rais was ceded to the Duke of Brittany by Jeanne, dame de Rais, daughter of the late Giraud de Rais, probably the individual of the text.

2262. In Anselme, *Hist. généal.*, etc., t. vii, p. 512, we find a daughter of Louis Bouchard, sire d'Aubeterre, married in 1379 to Péan de Maillé, seigneur de Brezé, and, and at p. 17 mention is made of a Savary Bouchard, sire d'Aubeterre, marrying in 1418 a Marguerite de Montbazon.

2263. Garcia du Castel, as clearly shown by his name, was a native of the Pyrenean region. In the third book of Froissart's chronicles, Espaing or Espan du Leu (a fief situated at Oraas, Basses-Pyrénées, arr. Orthez, cant. Sauveterre) riding along with the wandering chronicler on the road of Lourdes, positively states that origin: « Messire Garcis du Chastel, un moult sage homme et vaillant chevalier de ce pays-ici et bon François. » See Luce's Froissart, vol. vi, p. xxiii.

Garcie du Chastel, according to Lobineau, (*Hist. de Bret.*, t. i, p. 383,) was afterwards one of the 200 lances under Olivier de Clisson, and in 1379 promised his service to the Duke of Brittany. He seems to be included as one of those who had broken the treaty with the King of France, in Edward's charter, *de frangentibus pacis puniendis*, (Rymer's *Fœdera*, t. iii, p. 808,) where he is called *Gassiot du Castel*.

2265. Gérard, or Gaillart, de la Motte. He appears as one of the 200 lances under Olivier de Clisson, unless by the person there mentioned is intended Robert de la Motte, afterwards named as one of the league for the defence of Brittany. (Lobineau, *Hist. de Bret.*, t. i, p. 421.)

2266. Aymery de Rochechouart, sire de Mortemart, son of

Aymery de Rochechouart, taken prisoner at Crécy; he was made seneschal of Limousin in 1384, was appointed captain general of Poitou and Saintonge in 1392, and died in 1397.

2267. Called by Froissart and Barnes *Sir Robert de Cheney*.

2269. Called by the same writers *Sir Richard Curton or Courton*.

2270. Sir William de Felton, brother of Sir Thomas; he fell in a skirmish with the French and Spaniards shortly before the battle of Nájera (see line 2754); he was then seneschal of Poitou.

2271. Barnes, Johnes and Buchon are at variance as to the identity of William le Botiller; the first calls him William Butler of Oversley, in Warwickshire; and that this knight is intended appears from an entry in the French Rolls, 29 Edw. III., membr. 9, where in 1355, letters of protection are granted to Willelmus the Botiller (1º with Walterus Manny, Thomas Chute; 2º Nicholaus Burnet, Robertus Marny, « alii milites et chivalers, ») on the point of going abroad. Cf. Carte, *Catalogue des Rolles François*, p. 57; and Kervyn's Froissart, t. xx, p. 365.

In the same record (39 Edw. III., membr. 10) we find at the date of 1365 : « Willielmus Percehay, Johannes Aunsel, ac Thomas filius et heres Henrici Peverell, in partes transmarinas profecturi, habent literas de generali atornatu. » (*Cat. des R. Fr.*, p. 92.)

2275. In the safe-conduct for the parties forming the retinue of the Duke of Lancaster, Robert Hauley is styled *chivaler*. (Rymer's *Fœdera*, vol. iii, p. 812.) At the battle of Nájera the count de Denia, a Spanish nobleman, became the prisoner of Hauley and Shakell, and his son was delivered into their hands as a hostage. He was afterwards claimed by the Duke of Lancaster, and upon their refusing to give him up they were committed to the Tower, and afterwards, 11th August 1378, murdered in the Sanctuary at Westminster. See Collins's History of John of Gaunt, at the end of that of the Black Prince, Lond. 1740, 8vo., p. 37. Hauley was buried in Westminster Abbey; the inscription on his tomb may be seen in Weever's *Ancient funeral monuments*, p. 484.

2282. Stephen de Cosington we find first mentioned in the retinue of Henry, Earl of Derby, afterwards Duke of Lancaster, in the expedition of 1345. In 1349, he was appointed with Richard

Talbot and John de Carleton to renew the oath of fealty in the towns of Flanders. In 1351, he was again appointed with Sir Frank van Hale, knight of the Garter, to treat with Louis, count of Flanders. In 1355, letters of protection were granted him, then in the retinue of the Prince of Wales. Letters of safe-conduct are again addressed to him, *in partes transmarinas profecturus*, dated the 16th April, 1364, and again on his going into Gascony, the 26th of June, in the same year. He appears to have been at Crécy, Poitiers and Nájera.

2319. Louis d'Harcourt, vicomte de Châtellerault, son of Jean d'Harcourt, who was killed at Crécy. He was governor and lieutenant general in Normandy in 1360, and died in August 1388.

2321. Sir Thomas and Sir William de Felton were at this time seneschals of Aquitaine and Poitou. The names of the seneschals following are taken from Chandos's list at the end of the poem; they were John Harpesden of Saintonge [1], Sir Richard Baskerville of Agenais [2], more correctly Baldwin de Treville, as appears from writs issued to him as seneschal of Poitou in 1366, Thomas Walkfare of Périgord and Quercy, and John Roche of Bigorre. See above, l. 2270.

2322. He is again mentioned by Froissart as serving under the Earls of Cambridge and Pembroke, at la Roche-sur-Yon, etc.

2324. « Jean Helye et Aymenou. » John and Elias were afterwards with Sir John Chandos at Montauban and elsewhere. See above note on line 1320.

2327. Roger, grand-son of Roger, second lord de la Warre, was at the night attack on Calais, at Romorantin and Poitiers, where, for being instrumental in taking the French King, the crampet or chape of a sword was added as a badge to his armorial bearings. He was summoned to Parliament 14th August. 36 Edw. III. and 1st June, 37 Edw. III. He died in 1370.

2329. « Sir Robert Knolles, says Weever, was but of mean paren-

---

[1] Sir John Harpeden calls himself « seneschal de Xaintonge, » châtelain and captain of Fontenay-le-Comte, in a deed dated Niort November 17, 1369. (B. Fillon, *Jean Chandos, connetable d'Aquitaine*, Fontenay, 1856, p. 30, 31.) On another side, Baldwin de Freville is mentioned as seneschal of Poitou in a bond subscribed at Burgos by D. Pedro, 12 May 1367; the result of which is that in 1369 the aforesaid Baldwin had not been long seneschal of Saintonge. See Luce's Froissart, t. vii, p. LXXVI, note 1.

[2] Sir Thomas Molineux occurs as seneschal of Agenois a few years after this.

tage, but by his valour advanced from a common soldier in the French wars under Edward III. to a great commander. » Froissart speaks of him in 1357, as at the head of a band of free companies in Normandy, conquering every town and castle before him. In the following year Henr. de Knyghton tells us that « dictus Robertus Cnollis ad xij. leugas ab Avinonia venit, et tantam virtutem secum duxit quod Papa et cardinales non audebant extra palatium moram facere, et quasi deludentes intra se dicebant :

« Roberte Cnollys, per te fit Francus mollis ;
Ipsius tollis praedas, dans vulnera collis. »

De Eventibus Angliae, lib. iv, ap. Twysden, *Hist. Angl. Script.* X, col. 2620, l. 56.

He was also one of the combatants at the battle of the Trente. After having uttered an idle history concerning what was called *Knolles's mitres*, Weever adds that « to make himself well beloved of his country, he built a good fair bridge at Rochester over the Medway, with a chapel and chauntry at the east end thereof. He built much at the Grayfriars, London, and an hospital at Rome for English travellers and pilgrims. He deceased at his manor of Scone Thorpe in Norfolk, and was buried by the lady Constance, his wife, in the church of Grayfriars, London, 15th August, 1407. » (*Funeral Monum.*, p. 436.)

Sir Robert Knolles was created a knight of the Garter by Richard II. and a great landed proprietor in Brittany by Duke John de Montfort in 1365 ; but already he kept a large estate, as we may judge by letters of conduct granted to his wife, on her way home with a retinue of 10 squires, 20 archers and a multitude of servants. (*Rot. Franc.*, 34 Edw. III., membr. 13 ; ap. Rymer, vol. iii, p. 480. Cf. Lobineau, *Histoire de Bretagne*, t. i, from p. 343 to 433 *passim*.)

2333. John, second Lord Bourchier, son of Robert Lord Bourchier, who was one of the distinguished heroes of Crécy. He went with the Black Prince into Gascony in 1355 ; was at the battle of Auray in 1364, and employed in France in 1369, 1375, 1377. In 1384, he was appointed governor in chief of Flanders, elected into the Garter on the death of Sir Robert Newman in 1392, and he died on the 21st of May 1400.

2363. L. Cl. Brugelles has published the last will of Jean I., comte d'Armagnac, in 1373, (*Chroniques ecclesiastiques du diocèse d'Auch*, etc., Toulouse, 1746, 4to., preuves of the 3d. part, p. 83, 84.). See, on the same, above l. 1919, and farther on, l. 3371.

2369. Sir Perdiccas d'Albret is mentioned as one of the leaders of the free companies, who left Enrique the bastard upon the Prince's determination to help Don Pedro. After the siege of Bourdeille and the illness of the Prince, we find that he had deserted the interests of England for France, and was at Cahors at the head of 300 companions. He was however again brought over to the Prince's party by the agency of Sir Robert Knolles, with whom he had before served. On the death of Sir Thomas de Felton, he was invested with the barony of Caumont in Gascony; all which estate he bequeathed to his nephew on condition that he remained loyal to the English. See Luce's Froissart, t. vi, p. LXXXI, t. vii, p. LXVIII, note 4, and LXXV, note; B. Fillon, *Jean Chandos*, etc., p. 30-34.

Bertrucat d'Albret was not put in his place by Anselme in his pedigree of the Albret family, but mentioned by him under the name of *Bernical*, or *Berneguet*, as having given in 1365 a receipt of 300 gold francs to Jean, duke of Berry, for the sale of the castle of Belloc. See *Procès-verbal de délivrance à Jean Chandos, commissaire du roi d'Angleterre, des places françaises abandonnées par le traité de Brétigny*, etc. par A. Bardonnet. Niort, 1867, gr. 8vo. (Extrait des *Mémoires de la Société de Statistique, Sciences et Arts du département des Deux-Sèvres*), p. 84.

2371, 2374. The bastard of Breteuil and Naudon de Bageran are mentioned by Froissart as in this year (1366) in conjunction with Sir Perdiccas d'Albret, having defeated the viscount of Narbonne and the seneschal of Toulouse at Montauban, and taken many prisoners, whom the Pope ordered them to dismiss without ransom. (Kervyn's Froissart, t. vii, p. 130, 132, 133, 137-139.)

2375. The name of *Lamit* is included in M. Luce's list, as follows: « Desous le pennon Saint Jorge et le baniere de monsigneur Jean Chandos, estoient les Compagnes, où bien avoit douze cens pennonchiaus. Là y avoit des bons chevaliers et escuiers, durs, hardis et appers, telz que monsigneur Perducas de Labreth, monsigneur Robert Seni [1], monsigneur Robert Briket, monsigneur Garsis dou Chastiel,

---

[1] Perhaps the same as Robert de Cheney; however we would propose to read *Sevi*, for *Sen* in or *Seguin*. As to *Beguey*, we have seen that it was the patronymic name of a powerful family of Bordeaux. On the eighth of February 1348, Edward III. gave to Peter Beguey of the Rousselle, Bordeaux, the castle and castellany of Soubize, with its belongings, during

monsigneur Gaillart Vighier, Jehan Cressuelle, Naudon de Bagherant, Aymeniou d'Ortige, Perrot de Savoie, le bourch Camus, le bourch de Lespare, le bourch de Bretuel, Espiot et Lamit et plusieur autre. » (*Chroniques de Jean Froissart*, t. vii, p. 39.) — Farther on we meet again « Lamit de Maleterre, Breton. » (*Ibid.* p. 304. Cf. p. 2, 65, l. 19, 222, 244, 263, 287, 354, 410.)

2433. Compare the letter as given by Froissart. It agrees nearly word for word with the text.

2459. Sir Thomas Ufford, son of Robert, first earl of Suffolk; succeeded to the stall in St. George's Chapel on the death of the earl of March, one of the founders of the Order in 1359-1360. G. Fr. Beltz imagines that he fell in the skirmish before the battle of Nájera, under Sir Thomas de Felton. (*Hist. of the Garter*, p. 128.) His son, William de Ufford, was, in 1376, with William de Montagu, earl of Say, appointed admiral of England (*Rot. Franc.*, 50 Edw. III., membr. 14 ; ap. Rymer, t. iii, p. 1057.)

2464. Sir Simon Burley was first in active service at the sea-fight with the Spaniards off Winchelsea. In 1369, he was taken prisoner in Poitou, and released in the following year, when he was with the Prince at the sacking of Limoges. On the accession of Richard II., he had the custody of Windsor Castle given him. In 1381, having concluded the treaty of alliance with Winceslaus at Nuremberg, he was rewarded with the Garter; in 1383, he was appointed warden of the Cinque Ports, In 1387 was impeached at the instigation of the duke of Gloucester, and in the following year, on the 15th of May, was beheaded on Tower Hill [1].

---

his life time, on condition that the aforesaid Peter would provide for their defence ; moreover the King authorized him to take every year 500 gold florins *de scuto* out of the wordly goods of the rebels being on the borders, that is to say in the territorial circle of the said castle and castellany. See Bertrandy, *Étude sur les Chroniques de Froissart*, p. 50, note.

[1] The following curious entry is from the Issue Roll, 16 Ric. II. 7th of March :

« To the venerable father John, bishop of Salisbury. In money paid to him in discharge of 20 marks which the lord the King commanded to be paid him of his gift for the price of a bed of green tarteryn, embroidered with ships and birds, consisting of a covering, a tester, and a half coverlet, with three curtains, valued at the same sum, which bed belonged to Sir Simon de Burley, knight, deceased, forfeited to the King by reason of a judgment pronounced against the said Simon ; L13. 6s. 8d. (Devon, *Issues of the Exchequer*, p. 230.) .

2478. On the taking of the King of Navarre, compare Froissart, Kervyn's edit., t. vii, p. 163, 164.

2505. Barnes calls this pass *the pass of Echarri Aranaz*, Froissart has *Sarris* and below *Espuke* (Guipuzcoa). By *Sarris* may be intended either *Sarries* in the valley of Salazar, or *Echarri*, another valley of Navarre.

2512. Salvatierra, a town of the province of Alava, which must not be confounded with Salvatierra de Aragon, a strong place seized upon by the King of Navarre in 1364, nor with Salvatierra, partido de Cinco Villas, diocese of Pampeluna. See Yanguas y Miranda, *Diccionario de Antigüedades del Reino de Navarra*, t. iii, p. 100.

2605. Sir Thomas Holland, eldest son of Thomas, first earl of Kent. He joined the army of the Prince in Aquitaine, in his sixteenth year. In 1375, he was in the expedition under the earl of Cambridge and duke of Brittany, and upon his return with the army into England, was admitted into the order of the Garter. He was first summoned to Parliament as Earl of Kent the 16th of July, 1381, having in the previous year been constituted marshal of England. He died the 25th of April 1397.

2607. Hugh, son of Sir Hugh Courtenay, one of the founders of the order of the Garter; he married Maud, sister of Sir Thomas Holland, above mentioned. In 1370, he was summoned to Parliament amongst the barons of the realm, and died in February 1374.

2608. Sir Philip and Sir Peter Courtenay were the sons of Hugh, second earl of Devon, and brother to Sir Hugh Courtenay above mentioned. They together attacked the Spanish fleet in 1378, when Sir Philip was severely wounded and his brother taken prisoner, but liberated in the following year. Sir Peter afterwards became in 1388 principal chamberlain and knight of the Garter, in 1390 constable of Windsor Castle; he died the 2nd of February 1405. See Ezra Cleveland's *Genealogical History of the noble and illustrious Family of Courtenay*. Exoniæ, 1735, folio, p. 197; and Beltz, p. 328.

2609. Called by Johnes and Barnes *Sir John Covet*, but *John Trivet* in the affair of Montauban. In Rymer's *Fœdera*, 47 Edw. III., we find a grant of certain lands formerly held by the sire d'Albret made to Nicholas Bond, for good service rendered the Prince of Wales (*Rot. Vasc.*, 47 Edw. III., m. 8; ap. Rymer, vol. iii, p. 994, 995.)

Of the family of the above name, who has produced a dominican friar, Nicholas Triveth, author of a Latin chronicle of the Plantagenets from 1135 to 1307, we know only his father, Sir Thomas Triveth, one of the King's justices, and another of the same name mentioned under the year 1384, in Rymer's *Foedera*, 7 Ric. II.

2611. He is named as one of the captains of the free companies. See Collins, *Life of the Prince of Wales*, p. 187.

2613. Walter de Urswick, constable of Richmond Castle, we find appointed to choose a hundred archers, for the use of John, Duke of Lancaster, in 1366, and in the same year he has protection to pass over into Aquitaine. (Rymer's *Fœdera*, vol. iii, p. 812.) In the following year is a grant of £40. a-year made to him by the Duke of Lancaster to enable him the better to maintain his rank of knight, which he had received at the Duke's hands on the day of the battle of Nájera (*Ibid.*, p. 825); in 1369, he is again appointed to choose archers for the service of the Duke of Lancaster, and in the same year has protection to pass with him, *ad partes transmarinas*. (*Ibid.*, p. 799, 864, 871.)

2614. This individual is called *Demery*, *Danmore* and *Danvers*; but the easiest solution to the difficulty appears to be found in the protection afforded to Thomas Daventre and others in conjunction with Walter Urswyck, for free passage to Aquitaine, in the company of the Duke of Lancaster, 1366. (Rymer's *Fœdera*, vol. iii, p. 326, 812.) He is again mentioned with John de Grendon, Urswyck and others, in the retinue of the same duke, in 1369. (*Ibid.*, p. 871.)

2648. Don Tello de Castilla, brother to Enrique. He died at Medellin in Estramadura in 1370, not without suspicion of poison.

2724. It is difficult to identify Sir Richard Taunton, and Degory Says, the former being called by Barnes and Johnes *Causton*, the latter *Dangouses*, and the Earl of Angus; but it is scarcely possible to have been Umfraville, at that time Earl of Angus. The nearest name to that in the text seems to be *De Grey*, born by Henry de Grey, *chivaler*, who crossed in the retinue of the Duke of Lancaster, in 1366. (Rymer, vol. iii, p. 812.)

2725. Ralph de Hastings. Froissart and Barnes have *Hugh*; but

that the text is right is probable from entries taken from the Gascon and French Rolls, published in Rymer's *Fœdera*, where in 1366 and 1369 are notices of letters of safe-conduct, addressed to « Radulphus de Hastynges » in the retinue of the Duke of Lancaster. In 1373, we find him also appointed as a mediator in the quarrel between Henry, lord Percy, and Douglas. In 1 and 4 Ric. II. he was sheriff of Yorkshire. According to Dugdale, he was the son of Sir Ralph de Hastings and Margaret de Herle, and died in 1397. See the *Baronage of England*, t. i, p. 579, col. 2. In the *Fœdera*, vol. iii, p. 862, 888, there are two entries relating to a John of Hastings; and in *The Siege of Carlaverock in the xxviii. Edward I. A. D.* MCCC., the arms of Hastings, or, a maunch gules, an ornament very common at the time. (Edit. Sir N. Harris Nicolas, London, 1828, 4to., p. 38-39, 42-43, 56-57, etc.)

2727. Gaillard Vigier. (Froissart, ed. Kervyn, t. ix, p. 497.) He is named as one of the captains of the free companions. In the Gascon Rolls, 5 Ric. II. is an entry *de accusatione versus Galiardum Beguer faciendis, audiendis et terminandis*. See above, p. 190, l. 2799, and p. 361, note to l. 2375.

Before being a family name, *Vigier, Beguer*, was a title of office. See *Administration municipale et institutions judiciaires de Bordeaux pendant le moyen-âge*, par M. Rabanis, in the *Revue historique de droit français et étranger*, etc. 7e année, 6e livraison, novembre-décembre, 1861, p. 461-523.

2930. Lobineau has *Naddres*, or *Nevaret*; but it seems clear from the mention of the river and an evident distinction between the two places, that Nájera is here intended.

2975. The letter is to be found also in Froissart's chronicle. It differs essentially in point of fact and style from the authentic letter dated from Navarrete in Castile, April 1st, 1367, and addressed by the Prince of Wales to D. Enrique, count of Trastamare. The document has been published by Rymer both in Castilian and Latin. (*Fœdera*, ed 1830, vol. iii, pars II, p. 823, 824.) The reply of D. Enrique, who entitles himself King of Castile and Leon, is dated Nájera April 2, and has reached us under its double shape, Castilian and Latin. (*Ibid.*, p. 824, 825. Cf. Ayala, *Crónica del rey D. Pedro*, 1367, cap. XI, p. 555, 556.)

3090. Don Sancho de Castilla, brother of Enrique and Don Tello.

He was created by Enrique, count of Albuquerque, and married in 1373 Beatrix, daughter of Pedro, King of Portugal, by Inez de Castro. In the following year he was murdered in the streets of Burgos in endeavouring to stop an affray between his followers and those of Gonzales de Mendoza. (H. A. Dillon, *The History of the reign of Peter the Cruel*, etc. London, 1788, 8vo., vol. ii, p. 152.)

3091. The count de Dene or Denia, marquis of Villena, of the house of Aragon, was taken prisoner at Nájera by Hawley and Shakel, of whom we have before spoken. He obtained his own liberty by leaving with his captors his son as a hostage; who, the ransom agreed upon not having been paid, remained in their custody until, on their refusal to give him up, at the command of the duke, the two esquires were murdered at Westminster.

In the French and Gascon Rolls are several entries respecting the count of Denia and the detention of his son Alfonso. See Rymer's *Fœdera*, third edition, t. iii, pars 4, p. 91, col. 1. (*Super financia comitis de Denia sæpememorata, de represaliis*, 23-25 Oct. 1393.)

3093. Pierre de Villaines, knight, surnamed *le Bègue*, who derived his title from his fief of Villaines (départ. of Seine-et-Oise, arrond. of Pontoise, canton of Ecouen), mentioned as early as May 1360 in the capacity of seneschal of Carcassone and Béziers (Arch. Nat., JJ 91, n° 302) seems to have kept the post as late as the end of 1362. Appointed chamberlain to the dauphin, duke of Normandy, he made war in the first month of 1363 in the neighbourhood of Falaise, where he was made prisoner. (*Ibid.*, JJ. 92, n° 208.) There undoubtedly he became acquainted with du Guesclin, who took him to Spain, where he fought at Nájera, was taken prisoner and exchanged with marshal d'Audinghen, for Sir Hugh Hastings and other knights. In the year following the battle he was rewarded for his services with a grant of the county of Ribadeo in Galicia. According to Froissart, he was the captor of Don Pedro, when attempting to escape from the castle of Montiel in 1368.

By the by, the last editor of Froissart's chronicles remarks that the gallant general of the French forces had taken along with him some of the chieftains and a certain number of soldiers of the garrisons of the towns he had passed on his way to Spain. It was thus that the captain of Lyons, Jean de Saint-Martin, knight, was killed at Nájera.

(*Ibid.*, JJ. 100, n° 135 ; JJ. 99, n° 494), with « Garcilaso de la Vega, Suer Perez de Quiñones, Sancho Sanchez de Rojas, Juan Rodriguez Sarmiento, Juan de Mendoza, Ferrand Sanchez de Angulo é otros fasta quatrocientes omes de armas. » (*Crónica del rey Don Pedro*, t. i, p. 557, 1367, cap. XIX.)

3095. From many entries in the Issue Rolls of 44 and 46 Edw. III., it would appear that this knight was taken prisoner at Nájera, and confined in the Tower, where he was allowed by the King two shillings a-day for his support. In the 47 Edward III. is also an entry of *L*14. for divers clothes, the gift of the King to John de Nevell, against the feast of the Nativity, « to wit, for eleven yards of black cloth, *L*2. 9*s*. 9*d*., and for making up the same, *L*6. 8*d*. ; also for the fur of one gown, one surtout and a coat, *L*11. 3*s*. 10*d*. (Devon, *Issue Rolls of Thomas de Brantingham*, p. 214 ; *Issues of the Exchequer*, p. 193, 196.)

3126. Gomez Carillo de Quintana, whose death after the battle is described below, l. 4156.

3127. The prior of San Juan is not mentioned either by Froissart or Ferreras, as having been in the action.

3130. In Ferreras he is spoken of as having been left at Toledo by Enrique with six hundred horse, and is styled Don Garcia Alvarez, grand master of Santiago. Dillon, vol. ii, p. 51, calls him *Sanchez Moscoso*, and says that he was put to death after the battle with Gomez Carillo.

3133. According to Ferreras, vol. iv, p. 392, Don Martin Lopez de Cordova, where he is mentioned as having been left by Don Pedro in command of the city of Cordova ; if so, it would appear that he must have changed his party immediately after the battle.

3180. Froissart's narration of the same ceremony occurs, book 1st, § 578 ; t. vii, p. 34, 282 : « Là aporta messires Jehans Chandos sa baniere entre ses mains, que encores n'avoit nulle part boutée hors, au Prince et li dist ensi : « Monseigneur, vechi ma baniere : je vous le baille par tel maniere qu'il le vous plaise à desveloper et que aujourd'ui je le puisse lever ; car, Dieu merci, j'ai bien de quoi, terre et hyretage pour tenir estat, ainsi qu'il apartient à ce. » Adonc prisent li princes et li rois dans Pietre, qui là estoit, la baniere entre leurs mains, et developerent, qui estoit d'argent à un peu aguisiet de gueules, et li

rendirent par le hanste en disant ensi : « Tenés, messire Jehan, vesi votre baniere : Diex vous en laist vostre preu faire. » Lors se partist messire Jehans Chandos, et raporta sa baniere entre ses gens, et la mist en mi yaus, et si dist : « Signeur, veci ma baniere et la vostre ; or le gardés ensi que la nostre. » Adonc se prisent li compagnon, qui en furent tous resjoy, et disent que, s'il plaisoit à Dieu et à mousigneur Saint George, il le garderoient bien et s'en acquitteroient à leur pooir. Si demora la baniere ens ès mains d'un bon escuier englés que en appeloit *Guillaume Aleri*, qui le porta ce jour, et qui bien et loyaument s'en acquitta en tous estas. »

M. Luce remarks in a note of his edition of Froissart's chronicle, t. vii, p. xiv, that John Chandos possessed the landed rank of a baronet, at least since Edward III. had given him in 1360 the splendid estate of Saint-Sauveur-le-Vicomte; but such grant having taken place a short while after the conclusion of the treaty of Brétigny, the new viscount had not had an occasion to raise or otherwise to display, his banner on a battle field.

On Chandos at his estate see again Luce's Froissart, t. vii, p. xxviii, note 1, 69 and 104.

3225. In the Gascon Rolls, 38 Edw. III. (Rymer, vol. iii, p. 727) are letters of protection addressed to Hugh Curson, going into Gascony, in the retinue of the Prince of Wales. Twenty years later, occurs in the same Rolls, June 1358, a *dom. de Curton* going to Germany.

— In 43 Edw. III. (Rymer, p. 871), are similar letters addressed to Thomas de Eiton[1], probably intended in the text, going *ad partes transmarinas* in the retinue of the Duke of Lancaster. Of Prior I find no mention elsewhere, unless Thomas Prior, *armiger*, having letters of protection, going into Picardy. (*Rot. Fr.* 402.)

3226. Froissart speaks of Sir William de Farrington as narrowly escaping before Soubise, afterwards governor of Saintes, and then as one of those joining Sir Thomas de Felton and the Gascon Lords, going to assist Thouars. In 50 Edw. III. we find William de Faryndon, knight, appointed with John de Cornwaille and John de Fastolfe to

---

[1] There is a book, which we could not find in Paris, the *Scalacronica*, by Sir Thomas Gray of Heton, Knight, edited for the Maitland Club by the Rev. Joseph Stevenson (Edinburgh, 1836, 4to.) : is the author the same as the traveller mentioned above?

keep the truce with France, renewed in that year, 1376. (Rymer's *Fœdera*, Record edit, vol. iii, part. ii, p. 1066.) In 1402, he had custody of the castle of Fronsac on the Dordogne, near Libourne (*Rot. Vasc.*, 4 Henry V. membr. 9), in 1412 was constable of the castle of Bordeaux, and in such capacity obtained letters of protection. (*Ibid.*, 4 Hen. IV., membr. 9, 3; 11, Hen. IV. membr. 15. — *Rot. Fr.* 4 and 5 Hen. IV., membr. 15.)

3227. Aimery de Rochechouart, viscount of that ilk, as they say in Scotland, was son of Louis, son of Jean, 1st of the name killed at the battle of Poitiers, and of Jeanne de Sully, dame de Corbeffy, brother of John de Rochechouart, archbishop of Bourges (Anselme, *Hist. génèal.* etc., t. iv, p. 653. — *Gallia christiana*, t. i, p. 580. — *Histoire de la maison de Rochechouart*, par le général comte de Rochechouart. Paris, 1859, 4to., t. i, p. 134-148; t. ii, p. 308-316.) By a deed dated Paris, June 1369, Charles V granted to his beloved and feal cousin Louis, viscount of Rochechouart, 2000 pounds of rent settled on the castle and manor of Rochefort-sur-Charente, diocese of Maillezais, or, in case of need, on the island of Oléron, in the same diocese. (Arch. Nat., JJ 100, n° 137.)

3248. He is mentioned by Froissart as serving under the banners of the Duke of Lancaster and Chandos, as Sir John d'Ypre. (Kervyn's ed., t. xxiii, p. 306-309.)

3302. « Martin Ferrans, qui moult estoit, entre les Espagnolz, renommés d'outrage et de hardement. » (Ed. Luce, t. vii.)

3311. M. Siméon Luce thinks that Froissart borrowed the account of this fight from Chandos Herald's narration. See vol. vii, p. xv, 38, 285.

3353. Sir Thomas Percy, afterwards Earl of Worcester, younger brother to the first earl, Henry, of Northumberland, and second son of Henry Lord Percy. The first mention of him in the English records is that he was of the council of the Black Prince, at Bordeaux, in 1369. He was with the Earl of Pembroke in Anjou, attended Chandos on his last sally from Poitiers, whom he succeeded in 1370 as seneschal of Poitou, having previously held the seneschalship of la Rochelle. He was afterwards at Limoges, Montpaon, and was taken with the captal de Buch before Soubise. In 1376, he was invested with the order of the Garter; and was afterwards engaged on active service until 1389. He

was in 1392 and 1395 nominated ambassador to France to treat with the French King, and in 1397 was created Earl of Worcester. On the usurpation of Henry IV. he was continued in his situation as admiral of the fleet and steward of the household; in 1403, he rose up in arms against the King, and, having been taken prisoner at the battle of Shrewsbury, he was beheaded on the 23d of July in that year. Cf. Luce, t. vii, p. LXXX, note 3.

3355. Sir Walter Hewett in 1362 was captain of the castle of Colet in Brittany, (Rymer, vol. iii, p. 642,) in the same year he was appointed keeper « omnium forestarum et aquarum de Poyters et Poyctou. » (Ibid., p. 650.) In 1364, he had safe-conduct for himself with forty lances and one hundred bows, into Brittany. (Ibid., p. 731.) In 1364, with Sir Richard Burley and Sir Robert Knolles, he had the command of the van at the battle of Auray. He is afterwards mentioned by Froissart as leader of one of the free Companies, who joined the Prince in his expedition into Spain; in 1368, he was governor of the Islands of Guernsey, Serk and Alderney, and of Jersey with the same islands in 1371. He was killed in a skirmish near Soissons in the autumn of 1373, whilst accompanying the expedition of the Duke of Lancaster.

3373. Berart d'Albret having declined to go with his father to the help of the King of France and having seized the castle of Gironde and Vayres, was completely disinherited of all his family property in 1319, 1333. (Archives historiques de la Gironde, t. vi, p. 367, 368, n° CLXX.) His son, bearer of the same name, a judge in the jurisdiction of Aquitaine, being prisoner, first of William de Beauchamp, afterwards of Thomas de Felton, obtained in 1374 a safe-conduct to travel in the English possessions on the continent. (Rot. Franc., 48 Edw. III., membr. 7; ap. Rymer, vol. iii, p. 971, 973, 1017. Cf. Rot. Vascon., 47 Edw. III. membr. 8-4.)

3445. John, son of Robert, Lord Ferrers, grand-son of Robert Earl of Derby, accompanied the expedition into Gascony, in 33 Edw. III. He married Elizabeth, widow of Fulke le Strange, and left by her Robert, his son and heir, at the time of father's death seven years of age. In some editions of Froissart, he is called *Raoul de Ferrieres*, who was captain of Calais in 1358, and in 1370 appointed to command

the fleet on the passage of Sir Robert Knolles and others. (*Rot. Fr.* 32 Edw. III., membr. 14 ; Rymer, vol. iii, p. 389, etc.)

M. Kervyn de Lettenhove has printed a certificate on behalf of another Ferrers, Aymon or Edmund, as being in his retinue « ès parties de Gascoigne en le service nostre seigneur le roy au temps où mondit seigneur le roy arriva à Hogges. » (Froissart, t. xxi, p. 192.)

3485. Froissart's expression (Luce's edit., t. vii, p. 411) is « estoient bouté en une forte maison ouvrée et machonnée de pierre. »

3504. In the Bodleian Library (Digby Ms. 166) is a poem of 560 rhythmical elegiac verses upon Prince Edward's Expedition into Spain, and the battle of Nájera, written by W. Burgensis, or Walter de Burgo, monk of Revesby. Analyzed by O. Coxe, that piece of poetry has been published in full by Thomas Wright in his *Political Poems and Songs relating to English History*, etc., vol. i, p. 94-122.

3528. This line has no precise meaning ; it is a common-place topic. A young maid says to Fergus, whom she does not know :

<blockquote>
Par cele foi ke moi devés,
Sire, jà n'ert à vous celés.
</blockquote>

Li Romans des aventures Fregus, p. 207.

3578. Gomez Carillo and Sancho Sanchez Moscoso, great comendador de Santiago, delivered to D. Pedro, were at once beheaded before the tent and by the order of the King of Castile, on April 5, 1365. (*Crónica de D. Pedro primero*, t. i, cap. xix, A. D. 1367.)

3688. We must confess that our translation of *Haumonsque*, the name of a place taken by the Black Prince, is merely conjectural ; but, as people say in Spain, *un clavo saca al otro :* this renowned warrior directs, concerning his monuments in his will, « qe entour laditte tombe soient dusze escuchons de laton, chacun de la largesse d'un pié, dont les syx seront de noz armez entiers, et les autres six des plumes d'ostruce *houmont*, » etc. Must that word be translated by *above* (Fr. *amont*), or is there an allusion to a fact quite unknown ? It is no less remarkable that the motto on the shields of *laton*, or copper gilt, on the tomb of the Black Prince in Canterbury Cathedral, is not *houmont*, but *Ich dien* [1]. Cf. J. R. Planché, *Observations on the Mottoes*,

---

[1] *A Collection of all the Wills... of the Kings and Queens of England, Princes and Princesses of Wales*, etc. London, 1780, 4to., p. 67. — The will is found at p. 66 and finishes on p. 77. The Prince directs also that on his tomb he shall be placed « tout armez de fier de guerre. »

« Houmont » *and* « Ich Dien, » *of Edward the Black Prince.* (*Archæologia*, etc., vol. xxxii, p. 69-71 and 332-334 ; *Thomas Willemont's Heraldic Notices of Canterbury Cathedral*, etc., 4to. ; Sir Samuel Rush Meyrick's *Critical Inquiry into Antient Armour*, etc. London, 1824 and 1844, fol. and 4to.)

3719. The knights that acted as the Prince's ambassadors on this occasion were Sir Nele Loranch, al. Lornich, one of the founders of the order of the Garter, Sir Richard de Pontchardon and Sir Thomas Banastre, afterwards knight of the Garter. See Froissart, p. 19, 104, and Rymer, t. iii, p. 812.

« Monsieur Neel de Loreyng, chivalier » (*Rot. Franc.*, 21 Edw. III. membr. 14), al. Sir Nigel Loring, left a daughter Isabella, who married Robert, third baron Harington of Aldingham, co. Lancaster, whose monument is to be seen in Porlock church, Somerset. The tomb, illustrated by Mrs. Maria Halliday of Glenthorne (Torquay, 1882, 4to.), has been fancifully awarded to Sir N. Loring himself, although he was No. 20 of the knights of the Garter, a founder knight, who died in 1385 or 1386, and was buried at Dunstable.

3729. This imputation of disloyalty could only be a blot on one's character in the age of chivalry. Notwithstanding Chaucer gives D. Pedro the greatest commendations.

DE PETRO, REGE ISPANNIE.

O noble, o worthy Petro, glorie of Spayne,
Whom Fortune heeld so hy in magestee,
Wel oughten men thy pitous deeth complayne !
Out of thy lond thy brother made thee flee ;
And after, at a sege, by subtiltee,
Thou were bitrayed, and lad un-to his tente,
Wher as he with his owen hond slow thee,
Succeding in thy regne and in thy rente.

The feeld of snow, with thegle of blak ther inne,
Caught with the lymrod, coloured as the glede,
He brew this cursednes and al this sinne.
The wikked nest was werker of this nede ;
Nought Charles Olyver, that ay took hede
Of trewthe and honour, but of Armorike
Genylon Olyver, corrupt for mede,
Broughte this worthy king in swich a brike.

The Monkes Tale, l. 3564-3580.

This passage, which casts a foul and unjust aspersion upon the character of both Bertrand du Guesclin and Olivier de Mauni, had long been a puzzle; it was first cleared up by Mr. Furnivall in *Notes and Queries*, 4th series, vol. viii, p. 449, and more completely by Mr. Skeat, who has identified *wicked nest* with old French *Mau ni*. (See Chaucer of the Clarendon Press Series, 2nd edition. Oxford, 1877, post 8vo., p. 187.)

We will not expatiate any more on the Spanish Nero, but only state that there exists a chronological index of documents and works containing all the different appreciations of him : *Indice cronológico de algunos Documentos y obras que contienen juicios del rey Don Pedro (de Castilla, el Cruel). Por D. Aureliano Fernandez-Guerra y Orbe. (Discursos leidos ante la Real Acad. de la Hist. en la... recepcion de D. Francisco Javier de Salas.* Madrid, Fortanet, 1868, 4to., p. 179-200.)

3735. The invaders who had, on the faith of a popular fiction [1], followed the Black Prince over the Pyrenees, were awfully disappointed. Knyghton says that the mortality among the English was so great, that scarcely a fifth part of them escaped ; Walsingham, that very many were attacked with dysentery and other sicknesses of which they died, and adds, that a report prevailed that the Prince was poisoned, so that from that time he never again enjoyed good health.

3845. Chandos Herald passes over in silence a fact, which must be mentioned here as it has been noticed by Froissart, t. vii, p. 59, and other chroniclers, one of whom speaks from hearsay. No doubt the bad faith of D. Pedro had determined the Black Prince to leave Spain ; but, tried by that sunny climate, he had another reason to oblige him to recross the Pyrenees : he was labouring under an incurable disease, and the remainder of his followers were in no better condition. « Edwardus Princeps, per idem tempus, ut dicebatur, intoxicatus fuit ; a quo quidem tempore usque ad finem vitæ nunquam gavisus est corporis sanitate. Sed et plures, strenui et valentes, post victoriam Hispanicam, fluxu ventris et aliis infirmitatibus perierunt ibidem, » etc. (Thomæ Walsingham, *Hist. Angl.* London, 1863, 8vo., p. 305,

---

[1] Far in see, bi west Spaynge,   Ther nis lond under hevenriche
    Is a lond ihote *Cokaygne*;   Of wel of godnis hit iliche.
                               Warton's *Hist. of English Poetry*, vol. i, p. 9.

306.) — « Post hæc periit populus Anglicanus in Hispania de fluxu ventris et aliis infirmitatibus, quod vix quintus homo redierit in Angliam. » Henr. Knyghton, ap. Twysden, *Hist. Anglic. Script.* X, col. 2629.)

One might suppose that those disorders arose from the use of the fiery Spanish wines; but it must be noticed that in Spain, already so long under the musulman sway, and where the immoderate use of the grape was unknown, the vine was scarcely even cultivated in the north, wine being prohibited in certain places, notably in Pampeluna since 1365.(Yanguas, *Diccionario de antigüedades del reino de Navarra*, t. ii, p. 677, note 1.) Down to modern times, wines were imported from Gascony. See our *Histoire du commerce et de la navigation à Bordeaux principalement sous l'administration anglaise.*

3870. Cécile, daughter of Centulle IV, comte d'Astarac, dead in 1406, had for second husband Jean Jourdain, comte de l'Isle, from whom she was separated in 1392. Jean de l'Isle is not mentioned by Froissart as one of the disaffected noblemen; but his namesake was mayor of Bordeaux in 1342, and three years afterwards commanded Gascons of the French side.

3871. Pierre Raymond, comte de Cominges, seigneur de Ferrières, son of Pierre Raymond and Françoise de Fezensac. His will is dated 19th October, 1375. (Anselme, *Hist. généal.*, etc., t. ii, p. 265.) His daughter Marguerite married in 1378 Jean, comte d'Armagnac.

3871. Arnaud, sire d'Albret, great chamberlain of France, had just married Margaret de Bourbon, sister to the Queen of France. (Anselme, t. i, p. 300.)

3900. The names of the bearers of this summons to the Prince were Bernard Palot, juge criminel de Toulouse, and Jean de Chaponval. According to Froissart, they were imprisoned at Agen, but not murdered, as has been falsely stated by several historians [1].

3955. John Hastings, second earl of Pembroke, only son of Lawrence, first earl; on the death of the Earl of Warwick in 1369

---

[1] See L. Lacabane's biography of King Charles V, in the third volume of the *Dictionnaire de la conversation et de la lecture.* Paris, 1834, 8vo., p. 153. — The King's letters published there at length are so much the more valuable, that they show the falsity of those which are given by Froissart.

he was admitted into the order of the Garter, when he accompanied the Earl of Cambridge into Aquitaine. He was present at the taking of Bourdeille and la Roche-sur-Yon, and the sacking of Limoges. In 1372, he was taken prisoner by the Spaniards at la Rochelle, and remained in chains at Saint-André nearly three years, whence he was liberated at a ransom of 120,000 francs; but he died on reaching Arras in April, 1375, being then only 28 years of age. He has been often confounded with his father on account of the received date of the latter's demise being also 1375.

3970. Barnes (p. 170) has shown that this is an error, originating from the fact of James Audley, the son, having died in Gascony at this time, and that Sir James Audley, the father, did not die until April 1st, 1386. Cf. Ashmole, p. 706. Beltz has fallen into the same error, and made de Granson his successor in the stall at St. George's.

3976. The interesting account of the death of Chandos is given by Froissart, t. vii, p. LXXXVII, p. 206 and 394. Cf. Delisle's *Histoire du château et des sires de Saint-Sauveur-le-Vicomte*, p. 157 and sqq.

3998. According to Froissart, D. Enrique harangued his troops in that terms : « Bonnes gens, vous m'avés fait roy et couronné roy. Aidiés-moy à deffendre et garder l'iretage dont vous m'avés ahireté. »

4024. Buchon has printed an act passed upon the occasion of this appeal of the comte d'Armagnac, and the conditions agreed on between the parties. (Edit. of the *Panthéon littéraire*, t. i, p. 558, col. 2, note 1. Cf. Luce, t. vii, p. xxxi, note 2.)

4034. Louis, duc d'Anjou, and Jean, duc de Berry, the second and third sons of Jean le Bon, and brother of Charles V. Kings of France. It appears from letters to Philip and the duke himself in the French Rolls, 1364, that the duke of Anjou had broken his parole whilst an hostage in England for his father, and had returned to France. (Rymer, vol. iii, p. 756.)

4035. Louis, son of Pierre, duc de Bourbon, and Isabelle de Valois, was eight years in England, as one of the hostages for John, King of France. To perfect the payment of his ransom, by a deed dated Paris 16th December 1368, he gave in pawn to Jean Donat, citizen and spicer in London, at the rate of 5200 golden crowns, « sa cotte

d'armes rousée, ordonnée à vesteure de homme, semée et ouvrée de plusieurs et divers ouvraiges de grosses perles et rubis baillais et saphirs. » (Archives Nationales, P. 1358, 998, etc.) He was in 1380 one of the princes of the blood appointed to govern the kingdom during the minority of Charles the Sixth. He afterwards commanded in Flanders in 1382 and in Africa, 1390. He died at Montluçon, in August, 1410.

4062. The bishop of Limoges, Jean de Cros, had been the personal friend of the Black Prince, and had held at the font his eldest son Edward. At this critical juncture of affairs in Aquitaine he had been trusted with the governorship of Limoges, which city he had delivered up to the Duke of Berry. At the taking of the city, the Bishop's life was spared through the interest made for him by the Duke of Lancaster and the Pope, Urban the fifth. He died in 1383. See *Gallia christiana*, t. ii, col. 533. Cf. Luce's Froissart, t. vii, p. cxv, 243, § 663 sqq., p. 423, etc.

4067. Roger de Beaufort, messire Jean de Villemur and messire Hugues de la Roche, the nephew of the first, saved their lives by engaging hand to hand with the Duke of Lancaster, the Earls of Cambridge and Pembroke, to whom after a severe fight they surrendered. In Lobineau's *Hist. de Bret.*, t. i, p. 395, we find Beaufort in 1370 with his nephew joining du Guesclin with five knights and eighty-five esquires. In 1375, in the treaty of Bruges, Roger de Beaufort and Jean de la Roche, his nephew, are allowed, as prisoners, liberty for four months to go where they please, except into Guienne. (Rymer's *Fœdera*, vol. iii, p. 1034.) Jean de Villemur is mentioned by Froissart as having been in the Duke of Anjou's campaign in 1374, and elsewhere.

4086. Edward of Angoulême, born in 1365. He was buried in the church of the Augustine Friars, in London. See Weever, p. 419.

4100. When the Earl of Pembroke with his forces arrived off la Rochelle, he found the harbour preoccupied by a Spanish fleet, his superiors in every respect. The engagement however lasted for two days, when the English were entirely defeated and the Earl taken.

4124. Le Grand d'Aussy has given an extract detailing the particulars of a siege from the Roman de Claris, in his *Fabliaux*, vol. iii,

p. 73, ed. 1829. See also t. iv, p. 33. The Romance of Claris is likewise quoted by Roquefort, *Etat de la poésie françoise*, p. 121.

4132. In Chandos Herald's opinion such was the ensemble of the accomplishments of a true knight, and the Black Prince was one of the heroes of chivalry. No doubt he was obedient to the law of personal honour, and very different from D. Pedro, his confederate, he had nothing of the self confidence and caprice, of the violent and ungovernable temper, of the lustfulness and lavishness, of the cruel impiety of the Spanish despot. The fundamental idea of chivalry—on its good side, that of knightly obligation, as well as on its bad side, that of brutal and contemptuous disregard of all other obligations—finds expression in Edward the Black Prince, for the hollowness and falsehood of the law of chivalry as displayed by many knights at Crécy and Poitiers, were exhibited at Limoges. During the siege he spent his days in playing at dice with his chamberlains so eagerly as to pledge his coral beads to clear up a gambling debt. He was not, however, stranger to feeling when his purse was not empty. Being on the point of returning to his dominions, he bestowed a charity of 60 sous on behalf of a poor little boy who had been found alone in a lodging where the Prince had rested during his journey. Who knows whether the heart of the iron warrior was not affected at the remembrance of the child whom the unfortunate bishop of Limoges, Jean de Cros, had brought to be baptised in the capacity of godfather [1]. See above, p. 375, note to l. 4062.

4200. In a transcript of a chronicle of the time of Edward the Third, printed in the *Archæologia*, vol. xxii, p. 227, is « A chapter of the Princes Death, » in which occurs the following passage : « O holy Trinite, blessed be thou for evermore, whose name upon earthe I have alwaies worshipped, whose honor I have studied to enlarge, in whose faith, although otherwise a wicked man and a synner, I have alwaies lyved. I hartely pray the that as I have magnified this thy feast upon earthe, and for thy honor have called the people together to celebrate the same feast with me, deliver thou me from this deathe, and vouchsafe to call me to that most delectable feast that is kept this day with the in heaven; whose prayers as we

---

[1] Luce's Froissart, t. vii, p. cxi, note 3.

may thynke were heard of the Lord God, for the very same day about three of the cloke he departed this life. »

4224. This knight is mentioned in an officer's accompt for a tournament at Canterbury A. D. 1349 : « Et ad faciendum diversos apparatus pro corpore Regis et suorum pro hastiludio Cantuariensi, an. Reg. xxii. ubi Rex dedit octo hernesia de syndone ynde facta, et vapulata de armis domini Stephani de Cosyngton, militis, dominis principibus comiti Lancastriæ, comiti Suffolciæ, Johanni de Gray, Johanni de Beauchamp, Roberto Maule, Johanni Chandos et domino Rogero de Beauchamp. Et ad faciendum unum harnesium de bokeram albo pro Rege, extencellato cum argento, viz. tunicam et scutum operatum cum dictamine Regis :

« Hay hay, the whyte swan !
By Godes soule I am thy man. »

« ... Et ad faciendum unum dublettum pro Rege de tela linea habente, circa manicas et fimbriam, unam borduram de panno longo viridi operatam cum nebulis et vineis de auro, et cum dictamine Regis : *It is as it is.* » (Comp. J. Cooke, provisoris magn. garderob. ab ann. 21 Edw. III. ad ann. 23, membr. xi.)

Sir Stephen de Cosyngton is mentioned in many entries of the French Rolls of the Record office, from 1345 to 1356. See Rymer, vol. iii, p. 40, 181, 224, 326 ; and above, p. 154, I, 2281.

4230. Baldwin de Freville occurs in the Gascon Rolls, 39 Edw. III. (1365) as accompanying the Prince in the expedition of that year. He witnessed, as seneschal of Saintonge, the charter of Don Pedro, binding himself to repay the Prince the money paid on his behalf to the King of Navarre ; in 1367, he was seneschal of Poitou. He was with the expedition under Sir R. Knolles, in the attack on Cahors and Domme, and with the Prince in his assault on Limoges. Cf. Rymer's *Fœdera*, vol. iii, p. 825, A. D. 1367 ; and Luce's Froissart, t. vii, p. xix, note 4.

In a book which is not worth quoting, instead of *Freville*, we read *Treville* as the name of the Prince's high officer. *Tréville* is the title of a powerful family of the Pays Basque[1], and one may conjecture that *Baskerville* was derived from it by a process easy

[1] « Pierre de Tardetz, sr de Troisville, et Fortmon Daguerre, son lacay, » are mentioned in a register of the Parlement de Bordeaux, B. 24, 30th September 1542.

to fancy. The termination *ville* being exclusively norman, the name might strictly be considered as imported from that province; but we do not know any place of that name there, except Bacqueville, département de la Seine-Inférieure, arrond. de Dieppe. In Rymer's *Fœdera*, t. iii, p. 842, occurs the name of Sir Richard de Baskerville. Cf. Fuller's *History of the Worthies of England*, etc. London, 1811, 4to., vol. i, p. 458, 464.

4239. Thomas, lord Roos, of Hamelake,. was one of those who, after the joust held by the Prince in honour of his son's birth in 1364, prepared to accompany the King of Cyprus in his crusade for the recovery of Jerusalem. Dugdale shows that from the Gascon and other Rolls he served in Gascony in 33 Edw. III., and in the 43, 44 and 45, and that he was on board the fleet destined for the relief of Thouars. In the letter of protection granted him to go in the company of the Duke of Lancaster, 1369, he is styled, *Thomas de Roos de Hamelak, chivaler*. (Rymer, vol. iii, p. 871. Cf. p. 848.)

4242. From the Gascon Rolls it appears that in 1356 and 1368 this knight had letters of safe-conduct to go abroad. In 1377 he was captain of Brest castle, in 1379 was commissioned to treat with the Duke of Brittany, with Portugal in the following year, and again in 1385. In 1389 he was appointed to inspect fortresses in Calais and Poitou, and in 1389 to treat with the duke of Bavaria. He is mentioned as one of the executors of the will of the Princess of Wales, in 1385. Ses Collins, p. 308.

4243. Thomas de Wetenhale, knight, kindred of the illustrious Hugh de Calverly, had, in 1364, letters of protection to pass in the retinue of the Prince of Wales into Gascony. (*Rot. Vasc.*, 38 Edw. III., membr. 3; ap. Rymer, t. iii, p. 731[1].) Cf. Luce's Froissart, t. vii, p. XLI, note 2; LV, note 3; and LXIII, note 2.

4247. It would seem from two entries in the French Rolls 1357 and 1359, respecting Tristan de Magnelay, his prisoner, that Sir Thomas de Walkfare was present at Poitiers. He had letters of protection in the February of that year, *ad partes transmarinas profecturus*.

---

[1] In the same convoy we note *Willielmus de Packington, persona ecclesiæ de Burton Noverey*, ready for sailing and to stay with the Black Prince (*Rot. Vasc.* 38 Edw. III., membr. 1 (A. D. 1334), John Basset, *chivaler*, and many others mentioned in Rymer's *Fœdera*, vol. iii, p. 719, 736, 747, 753, 760, 763, 765.

(*Rot. Vasc.*, 34 Edw. III., membr. 4 ; Rymer, vol. iii, p. 763.) Buchon has noticed that Thomas de Walkfare was hanged at Toulouse in September, 1370, by order of the duke of Anjou [2].

4253. Sir William le Moine, seneschal of Agenais, is mentioned by Froissart as having been commissioned to seize the messenger of the French King who had brought the summons to the Black Prince for his appearing at Paris. In the French Rolls, 33 Edw. III., part 1, membr. 3, are letters of protection addressed to him. (Rymer, vol. iii, p. 443.)

4258. Richard Walkfare, *chivaler*, had letters of protection to proceed abroad in 1356 and again into Gascony in the retinue of the Prince of Wales in 1365. (Rymer, vol. iii, p. 40 and 763.)

4260. John de Roche, knight, had letters of safe-conduct in 1365 to pass in the Prince's retinue into Gascony, governed in the mean time by another knight the soudan de Préchac, sire de Didone, being formerly at war with the soudan de Latrau, his neighbour. (*Rot. Vasc.*, ann. 28 Edw. III., membr. 15. — Carta Johann. reg. Franc. ann. 1350 ; Reg. 80 Chartoph. reg. ch. 69. — *Rot. Franc.* 31 Edw. III. membr. 14 et 13 dorso. Cf. Rymer's *Fœdera*, vol. iii, p. 350, 765. Later he was appointed seneschal of Bigorre : *De comitatu Bigorræ, per Principem Walliæ, dominum de Biscaya, et de castro de Ordialibus, capitali de Bogio concesso*. (Rot. Vascon., 43 Edw. III., membr. 8 ; ap. Rymer, vol. iii, p. 874.)

4262. A sire de Poiane of Poitou is mentioned by Froissart in Sir John Chandos's, and afterwards in Sir J. Audley's company at Bruges, as in the Prince's company in the attack on la Roche-sur-Yon, in his attack upon Limoges. (Kervyn's ed., t. v, p. 283.) In the Gascon Rolls, 46 Edw. III. is a writ *pro Michaele de Poyane habendo hæreditates domini de Lebret*. Cf. Rymer, record edition, t. iii, p. 651, 657, 674.

---

[2] He appears to have been occasionally confounded with Sir Thomas Wake, who Johnes says was the seneschal of Rouergue, and defeated by the comte de Cominges and others at Montauban. In Buchon, however, the name is printed *Wakefair*; whilst Collins again has called him *Wake*, and given his family history from Dugdale. (*Baronage of England*, vol. i, p. 539-542.) In support of this opinion we have entries in the French Rolls of a Thomas Wake de Bliseworth, having letters of protection in 1358 and again in the retinue of Edmund, earl of March, in 1374. (Rymer, vol. iii, p. 1014, col. 2.)

Line ult. The following is the metrical translation of the epitaph as given by Weever:

> Whoso thou be that passeth by
> Where these corps interred lie,
> Understand what I shall say,
> As at this time speak I may:
> Such as thou art sometime was I,
> Such as I am, such shalt thou be.
> I little thought on the houre of death,
> So long as I enjoyed breath,
> Great riches here I did possess,
> Whereof I made great nobleness;
> I had gold, silver, wardrobes, and
> Great treasures, horses, houses, lands.
> But now a catife poor am I.
> Deep in the ground, to here I lie;
> My beauty great is all quite gone,
> My flesh is wasted to the bone,
> My house is narrow, now and throng,
> Nothing but truth comes from my tongue;
> And, if ye should see me this day,
> I do not think but ye would say
> That I had never been a man,
> So much altred now I am.
> For God sake pray to the Heavenly King,
> That he my soul to Heaven would bring.
> All they that pray and make accord
> For me unto my God and Lord
> God place them id his Paradise,
> Wherein no wretched catiffe lies.

APPENDIX

In the XIVth century three languages were in use in England :

> Latyn als, I trowe, canne nane
> Bot thase that it of scole han tane.
> Some canne Frankes and Latin
> That hanes used courte and dwelled theryn,
> And som canne Latyn a party
> That canne Frankes bot febely,
> And some understandes in Inglys
> That canne nother Latyn ne Frankys,
> Bot lere and lewed alde and younge,
> Als understandes Inglysche tounge :
> Thare fore I halde it maste syker thon
> To schew that langage that ilk a man konne,
> And for all lewed men namely
> Thet can no maner of clergy,
> To kenne thanne what ware maste nede,
> For clerkes canne bathe se and rede, etc.
>
> Hampole's *Speculum*, or *Mirrour of Life*, ap. Warton's *Hist. of Engl. Poetry*, vol. iii, p. 9, note *g*.

It would be bold to assert that the English aristocracy of the XIVth century, Edward III., as well as the Black Prince, used indifferently the French and English languages, chiefly the latter, when they had to address unlettered people [1], as did in the 1337 « uns clers d'Engleterre, licensiiés en drois et en lois, et moult bien pourveus de trois langages, de latin, de françois et dou

langage englès. » He spoke softly, « à la fin que il fust mieuls entendus de toutez gens ¹, » etc.

Walter de Mauni was not, as it appears, such a scholar. In 1347, presenting the citizens of Calais to his liege, he spoke English ². As to the Black Prince, he had, in his principality, to understand, more or less, the Gascon language. At all events, he had a secretary and treasurer, William Packington, who, being quite master of the French idiom, compiled a fine history in it ³.

The history of the use and decay of the French language in England from the twelfth century would require a volume ⁴. We will content ourselves to illustrate them, by offering some examples.

The Romance of Blonde of Oxford and Jehan of Dammartin by a celebrated lawyer of the XIIIth century, exhibits a young Frenchman in search of fortune and who finds a situation in the house of the Earl of Oxford in the capacity of a carving esquire to his daughter. The adventurer teaches her the French language, which she knew imperfectly ⁵, likely « After the scole of Stratford atte Bowe ⁶. »

> Et en milleur françois le mist
> Qu'ele n'estoit quant à li vint ⁷.

---

¹ *Chroniques de Froissart*, t. i, 2d part, p. 360.

² *Ibid.*, t. iv, p. 291.

³ *Scriptorum illustrium Majoris Brytanniæ... Catalogus*, etc. Basileæ, 1559, fol., p. 490, n° LXVIII.

⁴ Till we have a more elaborate one, we must refer to J.-B. Thommerel's *Recherches sur la fusion du franco-normand et de l'anglo-saxon*. Paris et Londres, 1841, 8vo.

⁵ *The Romance of Blonde d'Oxford and Jehan of Dammartin* by Philippe de Reimes (Philippe de Beaumanoir), edited by M. le Roux de Lincy. Printed for the Camden Society, 1858, sm. 4to., p. 404. Cf. l. 395, 1634, 2463.

⁶ *The Canterbury Tales*, the Prologue, l. 125. « Of whyche speche, Chaucer says elsewhere, the Frenchmen have as good a fantasye as we have in hearing of Frenchmennes Englyshe. »

⁷ L. 130.

The Earl of Oxford understood French well, having been in France to learn it; but such was not the case with the Earl of Gloucester, Blonde's suiter. Meeting Jehan of Dammartin, his rival, he wished to speak French to him;

> Mais sa langue torne en Englois [1] :...
> « Amis, bien fustes-vous vené.
> Coment fu vostre non pelé ?...
> Et où volé-vous aler tôt ?
> Cil varlet fou-il vostre gent,
> Qui fu munté seul' cheval gent ? »

Afterwards the earl speaking again to the same Jehan, says:

> « Disa-vos çou que vous vola [3]...
> Et où vola-vous dont tourner ?
> Duisse veoir qu'il fu jà nuit,
> Viene-vous haubergier maishuit,
> Où vous me conta vo besoing,
> Où nul tourner vous je ne doing [4], etc.

In a fabliau of the same age, an Englishman attempts to speak as they did in France;

> Mais onc tant ne s'i sot garder
> Que n'l entrelardast l'anglois :
> Ainsi farsisoit le fransois [5].

The story is silly enough, and offers us no other interest than strokes of mock French like this:

> « Sire, fait-il, par saint Tomas,
> Se tu avez 'nul anel cras,
> Mi chatera moult volentiers,
> Et paie-vos bones deniers
> Et bones maailles frelins,
> Et paie-vos bons estellins. »

---

[1] L. 2624. — [2] L. 2627. — [3] L. 2767. — [4] L. 2804.
[5] *Des deux Englois et de l'Agnel.* Ms. of Nat. Libr. n° 1830 or 1239, fol. 47 v°. — Robert, *Fabliaux*, Paris, 1834, 8vo., p. 11. — *Histoire littéraire de la France*, t. xxiii, p. 106, 107.

The previous quotations from poems composed in France by Frenchmen who no doubt had never crossed the British Channel, cannot be called upon as vouchers for the spread or decay of the French language at the court of King Henry III.; but we have a mystery [1] and a ballad of the times [2], which may be offered as specimens of the vulgar Norman-French delivered by the gleemen in the public thoroughfares.

In a song, written about the year 1264, when the King of France made an unsuccessful attempt to interfere between Henry III. and his barons, the English King and his court are the object of very coarse satire, which consists in making them talk broken and corrupt French,

---

[1] *La Résurrection du Sauveur*, fragment de mystère, publié par Ach. Jubinal, etc. Paris, 1839, 4to., p. 10-20. Beginning :

> En ceste matere recitom
> La seinte Resurecion.
> Primerement appareillons
> Tus les lius e les mansions :
> Le crucifix premierement,
> E puis après le monument,
> Une jaiole i deit aver
> Pur les prisons enprisoner, etc.

Such miracle-plays, in which the people at this time still delighted, generally took place in churchyards, but were forbidden by some abbots, for instance at St. Edmund's, where Samson, one of them, entertained minstrels or harpers at his palace, though unwillingly. See *Chronica Johannis de Brakelonda*, etc., ed. Joh. Gage Rokewode. Londini, 1840, 4to., p. 31, 69, 139. Cf. Fitz-Stephen, Excerpta e Vit. S. Thomæ, ad calcem Stowe's *Survey of London*, p. 480, edit. 1689.

[2] *Hugues de Lincoln, Recueil de Ballades anglo-normande et écossaises*, etc. Paris, 1834, 8vo.

> Or oez un bel chançon
> Des Jues de Nichole, qui par traïson
> Firent la cruel occision
> De un enfant que *Huchon* out non.
>
> En Nicholo, la riche cité,
> Droit en Dernestal l'enfant fut né
> De Peitevin le Ju fut emblé
> A la gule de aust, en un vespré, etc

and use equivocal expressions. It ends by the King declaring that he will place his son Edward on the throne of France, which is highly approved by Roger Bigot :

> « Je crai que vous verra là-endret grosse fest
> Quant d'Adouart arra corroné France test.
> Il l'a bien asservi, ma fil, il n'est pas best ;
> Il foui buon chivaler, hardouin et honest. »
>
> — « Sir rais, ce dit Rogier, por Dieu, à mai entent,
> Tu m'as percé la cul [1] ; tel la pitié ma prent.
> Or doint Godelamit [2] par son culmandement
> Que tu fais cestui chos bien gloriousement ! »

Here is now a small work expressly compiled to be instrumental for the teaching of the French language. It is the treatise of Walter of Biblesworth (alias *G. de Bithesicey*), which must have enjoyed a certain popularity, if we may judge by the number of manuscripts still extant both at the British Museum and Cambridge. Composed for a noble lady Dionysia de Monchensy, who lived, according to Thomas Wright [3], at the end of the XIIIth century and at the beginning of the XIVth, this opuscule offers abundant proofs of the state of decay in which the French language spoken in England had already fallen [4], and shows that the matter had attracted the attention of authority [5].

Still it was made use of by authors of a certain credit. We might mention more than one ; but it will be quite

---

[1] The earl, in his broken French, used this expression instead of *le cœur*.

[2] A corruption of *God-Almighty*.

[3] Thomas Wright, *Essays on archæological Subjects*, etc., vol. ii, London, 1861, 8vo., p. 248.

[4] See his *Volume of Vocabularies*, etc. (London,) 1857, sm. 4to., p. 142-174. Cf. *Essays on archæological Subjects*, etc., vol. ii, p. 39, 40.

[5] By a statute of a parliament held at London, it was ordered that the people of all rank should put out their children to the practice of the French language, in order the men might be able to get information and be less outlandish in their wars. (Froissart's chronicles, t. i, p. 402.) The congress at Lolinghem in 1393 showed the necessity of this statute.

sufficient for us to quote a historian of the last of the Plantagenets [1].

About the same time, perhaps a little later, we find several manuscripts of a short treatise on French spelling, written in Latin, which is probably the first attempt to reduce to rules the French orthography. It is not the small number of the manuscripts that have preserved to us this little treatise, which leads us to believe that it had obtained a certain success; it is rather because in one of those volumes it is accompanied with a commentary in French.

Here comes in, in order of time, the opuscule published by M. Paul Meyer [2]. It has not a didactical character like the treatise of Walter of Biblesworth and the *Orthographia Gallica*; it was not compiled to teach the value, the gender, and the spelling of the words: its object was to provide French conversational exercises for English readers. It is probably the oldest book of French dialogues written for foreigners. Later, at the beginning of the XVIth century, Giles du Guez, of whom we will speak hereafter, added also dialogues to his little grammar; but those conversations, written for a princess, have something ceremonious and stiff, far removed from the colloquial language. The unknown author of the *Manière de langage*, etc., gives occasionally a series of words arranged according to subjects; but he only inserts in his work such words as he thinks would be required for conversation.

[1] *The Chronicle of Pierre de Langtoft in French verse*, edited by Thomas Wright. London, 1866-68, 8vo. Cf. *Histoire littéraire de la France*, t. xxv, p. 337-348.

[2] *Manière de langage qui enseigne à parler et à écrire le françois*, etc. (*Revue critique d'histoire et de littérature*, n°˚ complémentaires de 1870, p. 374-376.) Compare that opuscule with another of the utmost rarity: *Here is a boke to lerne to speke French. Vecy ung bone liure a apprendre a parler fraunchoys*, etc. Per me Ricardum Pinson, (London, no date,) 4to., bl. lett.

He had travelled in France (as he says in his last chapter), and it is obvious to the eye that he exerted himself to reproduce faithfully the style of the conversation in the various classes of society. The diversity of expressions in reality equivalent, but different as to the form, which he took the trouble of collecting, separating them by the words *vel sic*, is already a proof of the attention he bestowed upon his labour. But otherwise there is no doubt those samples of conversation, probably reflecting personal recollections, had been written *con amore*, since one may see with what enthusiasm our author speaks at the beginning of his opuscule of the pre-excellence of the French idiom, the « doulz françois, qu'est la plus bele e la plus gracious langage e plus noble parler (après latin d'escole) qui soit au monde, e de tous gens mieulx prisée et amée que nul autre ; car Dieulx le fist si doulce et amiable, principalment à l'oneur e loenge de luy-mesmes. Et pour ce il peut bien comparer au parler des angels du ciel, pour la grant doulceur e biaultée d'icel. »

It will thus be understood that at the end of the XIVth century the anglo-norman language was in a very unsettled condition, and that in the hand of writers of different classes, rank or county, it assumed every variety of character. One of the last has left us a long work [1], to

---

[1] *Scalacronica*, by Sir Thomas Gray de Heton, knight. Edinburgh, printed for the Maitland Club, 1836, 4to., p. 1. Cf. Introduction, p. xxxvi, and Appendix, p. 259 : « Notable thinges translatid in to Englisch by John Leylande oute of a booke, caullid *Scalacronica*, the which a certein Inglisch man... did translate owte of Frenche ryme yn to Frenche prose. » The original text begins thus :
« Qe eit delite ou voet savoer coment le isle del Graunt-Bretaigne (jadys Albeon, Tere de geaunz, or Engleter) fust primerment enhabité, et de quel gent, et de lour naissaunce, et de la processe du ligne de rois qe y ount esté, et de lour conversacioun, solunc ceo quy cest cronicle emparlas, et de la maner avoit trové en escript en divers livers en latin et en romaunce, pust-il conoistre en party

be compared, as to gibberish, with numerous letters and documents of the time, namely a history of the foundation of Wigmore priory, Herefordshire [1], which, after all, may be a forgery.

At the beginning of his translation, Sir Thomas Gray informs us in what circumstances he was when he made it.

We have seen what state of decay the French language had reached in England. There was, however, at least, one English poet who wrote tolerably good verses at the end of the XIVth century : witness a poem *On the Dignity or Excellence of Marriage, cinkante Balades*, and some shorter pieces in praise and commemoration of King Henry IV., like in the following epilogue and colophon which close the ballads :

> O gentile Engleterre, à toi j'escrits
> Pour remembrer ta joie q'est novele,
> Qe te survient du noble roi Henris,
> Par qui Dieus ad redrescé la querele.
> A Dieu pur ceo prient et cil et cele
> Q'il de sa grace au fort roi coroné
> Doignt pees, honour, joie et prosperité.

par cest estoir suaunt la processe de eaux. Et sy ne voet pas au plain nomer se un noune, qe cest cronicle translata de ryme en prose, mais prisoner estoit pris de guer al hour q'il comensa cest tretice. »

[1] See the *Monasticon Anglicanum*, vol. vi, part i, London, 1830, fol., p. 344-348. It begins thus : « En le temps del roy Estevene, fitz al counte de Bloys, qui regna en Engleterre per force après le roy Henry fitz à William Bastard, estoit un très-noble bachiler en Engleterre, prouz, vaillant et hardy, mounsieur Hugh de Mortimer à nome, noble de nature, de sanc, de beale estature, vaillant en armes, très-noble en parler, perfond de cousail et très-riche de teriens facultés, et le plus glorious chevaler renomé et doté devant toutz que adonque furent en Engleterre vivantz ; de quy mist neissuns en escrit toutz les pruesces lesquels il fist chevalerousement en Engleterre, en Gwales et per ailors, si amounteroit-il à un graunt volume. Et outre ceo fut-il le plus franc et liberal de toutz ceux qui onc conus seyent en son temps nule part. Le noble counte de Hereford Roger, riche et vaillant et de grant retenaunce de gentz, et feers et orgoilous, tant fort demena sovent, que à force ly covint en refut demorer en ses chastels demeyne pur doute de ly. Ensement le roy Henry proschen après le roy Estevene sovent... od tout son host travailla, come est pleinement desouz escrit. »

Towards the end of another of his poems, Gower introduces an apology for any inaccuracies, which, as an Englishman, he may have committed in the French idiom :

> A l'université de tout le monde
> Johan Gower ceste balade envoie ;
> Et si jeo n'ai de françois la faconde,
> Pardonetz-moi qe jeo de ceo forsvoie.
> Jeo sui Englois : si quier par tiele voie
> Estre excusé ; mais quoi que nuls en die,
> L'amour parfit en Dieu se justifie [1].

After having read those lines, how can one agree with the historian of English Poetry [2] when he asserts that Edward III. greatly contributed to establish the national dialect, by abolishing the use of the Norman tongue and substituting the natural language of the country ?

We had an occasion to mention Gower's disciple, the celebrated Geoffrey Chaucer. What he says of his Prioress [3], leaving apart his translation of the Roman de la Rose, shows that he was a refined master of the French language. A ballad directed to him by Eustache Deschamps is also an unexceptionable testimonial of his knowledge in this respect [4]; but what a pity he did not entirely follow Gower's example ! France would have had a poet more.

For the XVth century, we have a long specimen of the

---

[1] Want of space prevents us from entering into details concerning the Norman element in the spoken and written English of the XIIth, XIIIth and XIVth centuries ; we will content ourselves with referring to the able work published under this title for the Philological Society by Joseph Payne.

[2] See sect. xii, vol. ii, p. 178, 179.

[3] Vid. supra, p. 382. — The instructions from Michael, abbot of St. Albans, in 1338, to the nuns of Sopwell, are in the French language; they are to be found in the *Monasticon Anglicanum*, vol. iii, p. 365, 366.

[4] E.-G. Sandras, *Etude sur Chaucer*, etc. Paris, 1859, 8vo., p. 28, 161, 202. Cf. Delécluse's paper in the *Revue française*, April, 1838.

French as spoken by the English [1]; but we suspect it is simple caricature, like *la Chartre de la pais aux Engiois* [2].

> Aiquet bin futy-vous venu!
> Je croy bin vous futy haraut;
> Vous porté de l'arm qui fut beau :
> Ce fut, je croy, l'arm de mon mer.

Later occurs this dialogue between the king and the *connestable* of England. This officer begins thus :

> Milort, bigot! flodin tast ly
> Gost art tel meust als mat gout det
> Ast gode chine foule det.
> L'Armenac a la Franchequin
> Hourson quenanc a gent Helquin [3]
> Galst stot forque tostat dog la.

The king answers :

> Bigot! j'entendy bin cela.
> Contably, nous faut pas la mer.
> — Vin çà, haraut. Landy mon mer
> Qui fout qu'à ly j'ala bin tot;
> Dyt-moy, jous empri, tot de mot
> Je faity army tout mon gent [4].

Specimens of Englishmen's attempts to give genuine pronunciation are copiously supplied by Palsgrave's l'*Esclarcissement de la langue françoyse*, etc. [5]; but it would be also advisable to glance at John Hart's phonetic rendering of the French Pater Noster and of the French

---

[1] *Le Mystère de saint Louis, roi de France*, etc., imprimé par le Roxburghe Club, Westminster, 1871, 4to., p. 55, col. 2.

[2] *Histoire litteraire de la France*, t. xxxiii, p. 452, 453.

[3] Helquin, *Hell King?* As to *Hourson*, we would not go so far as the « Aula quatuor filiorum Edmundi, » called, *Fourson Edmund Hall*, in the *Reliquiæ Hearnianæ*, etc., collected by Philip Bliss. Oxford, 1857, 8vo., p. 754.

[4] *Le Mystère de saint Louis*, p. 56, col. 1.

[5] We do not mention Giles du Guaz's *An Introductorie for to lerne to rede, to pronounce and to speke trewly*, etc. London, 1532, 8vo. because the compiler was a Frenchman. His book, reprinted by François Génin at the end of his edition of Palsgrave (Paris, 1852, 4to.), is described in the *Bibliotheca Grenvilliana*, vol. i, p. 200.

pronunciation of the Latin Lord's Prayer in the last chapter of his *Orthographie* [1], to which may be added Howel's tract, *de Pronunciatione linguæ Latinæ*, quoted by Francis Douce, *Illustrations of Shakspeare*, p. 140; and the first French and English dictionary published in England [2].

On the other hand the Frenchmen of former days did not seem to care for English at all : those transcriptions of semi-saxon in *Roman de Rou*, vol. ii, p. 184, l. 12437-76, and the examples of French and English puns in Thomas Wright's *Political Songs of England* [3] are not worth much.

The English tourists being rather scanty in France [4], the frolicksome Gauls had few occasions to chaff at their pronunciation of the French language; but there was on view a standing body of Scottish Archer Guards, and they were constantly exposed to jokes. A *balade de deux Escossois* and a Christmas carol in the same gibberish, have been preserved and are like that which was ascribed to the English. The ballad begins thus :

> Hac, ma mignon ! que dit y capitain !
> Homs vous tantost où plaira moy que l'ail ?
> A Naple, à Naple ? c'est-y nouvel certain ?
> A Naple, saie sus mon, c'est ches qu'il vail.

[1] London, by W. Seres, 1569, 16mo.

[2] *A Dictionarie French and English* by Claudius Holyband. London, 1595, 4to.

[3] London, 1839, 4to., p. 49. (Issued by the Camden Society and different from another collection published by the same under the direction of the Master of the Rolls under the title of *Political Poems and Songs relating to English History, composed during the Period from the Accession of Edward III.*, etc. London, 1859-1861, two vols. 8vo.) Cf. Alexander J. Ellis's *Early English Pronunciation*, p. 462 and 531.

[4] For their use there was also published a small hand-book under the title of *Book for travellers*. Westmestre by London, fol. French and English vocabulary.

Mont à cheval continent eu batail.
Qui faict cela? le roi dit par vostre am
Donny dedans luy-mesmes d'estoc, de tail
Moy conseil point entry hors de ream [1].

Those who had not the means and the luck of going to France for the purpose of enlisting into the Scottish Archer Guard, had the opportunity of acquiring the language at home. In the " Statuta et leges ludi literarii Grammaticorum Aberdonensium, " it was enacted that the boys should not speak in the vernacular, but in Latin, Greek, Hebrew, French or Gaelic. In fact, the French language was taught in the chief schools of Scotland, notably at St. Andrews, in 1566, " with the reading and right pronunciation of the tongue [2]. "

What was the result of those regulations? we are afraid nothing but the rise of a provincial stray dialect, which is almost obsolete.

---

[1] *Les Ecossais en France, les Français en Ecosse*, Londres, 1862, 8vo., vol. ii, p. 5-8. — It is no use noting that those lines, as to the date, speak for themselves.

[2] *A critical Inquiry into the Scottish Language, with the view of illustrating the Rise and Progress of Civilisation in Scotland.* London and Edinburgh, 1882, 4to.

In the English schools, the teachers did not require so much, as we may judge from one of them, John Baret, the compiler of *An Alvearie, or quadruple Dictionarie, English, Latine, Greeke, and French*. London, 1580, fol. A former edition, containing only three languages, appeared in London, 1573, fol.

www.ingramcontent.com/pod-product-compliance
Lightning Source LLC
Chambersburg PA
CBHW071902230426
43671CB00010B/1449